Syndicated Loans

Palgrave Macmillan Studies in Banking and Financial Institutions

Series Editor: **Professor Philip Molyneux**

The Palgrave Macmillan Studies in Banking and Financial Institutions is international in orientation and includes studies of banking within particular countries or regions, and studies of particular themes such as Corporate Banking, Risk Management, Mergers and Acquisitions, etc. The books will be focused upon research and practice, and include up-to-date and innovative studies on contemporary topics in banking that will have global impact and influence.

Titles include:

Yener Altunbaş, Blaise Gadanecz and Alper Kara
SYNDICATED LOANS
A Hybrid of Relationship Lending and Publicly Traded Debt

Santiago Carbó, Edward P.M.Gardener and Philip Molyneux
FINANCIAL EXCLUSION

Franco Fiordelisi and Philip Molyneux
SHAREHOLDER VALUE IN BANKING

Munawar Iqbal and Philip Molyneux
THIRTY YEARS OF ISLAMIC BANKING
History, Performance and Prospects

Philip Molyneux and Munawar Iqbal
BANKING AND FINANCIAL SYSTEMS IN THE ARAB WORLD

Palgrave Macmillan Studies in Banking and Financial Institutions
Series Standing Order ISBN 1–4039–4872–0

You can receive future titles in this series as they are published by placing a standing order. Please contact your bookseller or, in case of difficulty, write to us at the address below with your name and address, the titles of the series and the ISBN quoted above.

Customer Services Department, Macmillan Distribution Ltd, Houndmills, Basingstoke, Hampshire RG21 6XS, England

Syndicated Loans

A Hybrid of Relationship Lending and Publicly Traded Debt

Yener Altunbaş
University of Wales, Bangor

Blaise Gadanecz
Bank for International Settlements

and

Alper Kara
University of Leicester

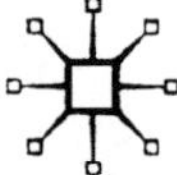

First published 2006 by
PALGRAVE MACMILLAN
Houndmills, Basingstoke, Hampshire RG21 6XS and
175 Fifth Avenue, New York, N.Y. 10010
Companies and representatives throughout the world

PALGRAVE MACMILLAN is the global academic imprint of the Palgrave Macmillan division of St. Martin's Press, LLC and of Palgrave Macmillan Ltd. Macmillan® is a registered trademark in the United States, United Kingdom and other countries. Palgrave is a registered trademark in the European Union and other countries.

ISBN-13: 978–1–4039–9671–8
ISBN-10: 1–4039–9671–7

This book is printed on paper suitable for recycling and made from fully managed and sustained forest sources.

A catalogue record for this book is available from the British Library.

Library of Congress Cataloging-in-Publication Data
Altunbaş, Yener.
Syndicated loans : a hybrid of relationship lending and publicly traded debt / by Yener Altunbaş, Blaise Gadanecz, and Alper Kara.
p. cm. – (Palgrave Macmillan studies in banking and financial institutions)
Includes bibliographical references and index.
ISBN 1–4039–9671–7 (cloth)
1. Syndicated loans. 2. Syndicates (Finance). 3. Bank loans. I. Gadanecz, Blaise. II. Kara, Alper, 1977–. III. Title. IV. Series.
HG1641.A417 2006
332.7—dc22 2005045623

10 9 8 7 6 5 4 3 2 1
15 14 13 12 11 10 09 08 07 06

Printed and bound in Great Britain by
Antony Rowe Ltd, Chippenham and Eastbourne

Contents

List of Figures and Tables

Figures

Tables

Preface

The topic of syndicated lending has attracted the attention of practitioners, policy-makers and, more recently, academic researchers. The international market for syndicated credits – loans where several banks form a group to lend to a borrower – emerged as a sovereign business in the 1970s and subsequently became a source of funding widely relied upon by corporate borrowers, currently representing no less than one third of funds raised on international financial markets, including securities and equity issuance. On the eve of the sovereign default by Mexico in 1982, most of developing countries' debt already consisted of syndicated loans, which then shaped policy to work out the crisis. The default threatened large Western financial institutions and indeed parts of their countries' financial systems. The eventual restructuring of Mexican debt into Brady bonds, whereby creditors saw their loans exchanged for securities guaranteed by the US government, created a precedent in the way it changed the structure of financial markets.

The approach of this book is pragmatic. We have attempted to write in a manner that will be useful for students and academics as well as practitioners. Since the field of syndicated lending is interdisciplinary, theoretical material relating to financial and development economics is presented along with practical elements of corporate finance. Thus, the first chapters provide an overview of global market for syndicated loans and discuss its development during the past decades. The focus is then placed on the analytical investigation of the determinants in the demand and supply in syndicated lending, with special attention paid to borrowers from emerging and industrialized countries for the demand side, and, for the supply side, banks' balance sheets and income structures, strategies and information sets. The differences between syndicated lending and disintermediated securities financing are highlighted. Information asymmetry issues are explored between borrowers and lenders, as well as lenders of various seniorities. A special chapter is devoted to the role of syndicated lending in distressed economies. To all intents and purposes, while the text summarizes a great amount of parctitioners' material by describing the workings of the market, it also attempts to synthesize some of the more important and relevant academic research studies in this field, highlighting some relevant policy issues along the way.

The authors are very grateful to Claudio Borio, Shanti Chakravarty, John Goddard, Ashoka Mody, Philip Molyneux, Victor Murinde, Güldal Seçener, Kostas Tsatsaronis, Baptiste Venet, Jon Williams as well as participants of seminars held at the University of Wales and at the Bank for International Settlements (BIS), for very helpful comments and suggestions on the research papers that provided the original material for the various chapters of this text. Thanks are also due to Rebecca Pash, Jacky Kippenberger (Palgrave) and Keith Povey, for editing of the manuscript. Finally, thanks to our families and loved ones for their patience and support during the project.

The views expressed in this book are the authors' own and do not necessarily reflect those of the Bank for International Settlements, the University of Wales or the University of Leicester. All remaining errors are our sole responsibility.

The authors and publishers are grateful to the BIS, Taylor & Francis and Dealogic for permission to materials and data used in this work. Every effort has been made to contact all copyright-holders, but, if any have been inadvertently omitted the publishers will be pleased to make the necessary arrangement at the earliest opportunity.

List of Abbreviations

m	million 1,000,000
bn	billion, one thousand million
trn	trillion, one thousand billion
BIS	Bank for International Settlements
bp	basis point
CDO	collateralized debt obligation
CIS	Commonwealth of Independent States
CPI	Consumer Price Index
EMBI	Emerging Market Bond Index
EMU	European Monetary Union
EURIBOR	Euro (or European) Interbank Offered Rate
FDIC	Federal Deposit and Insurance Corporation (US)
FYR	Former Republic of Yugoslavia
GAAP	Generally Accepted Accounting Principles (US)
GDP	Gross Domestic Product
GRA	General Resources Account (IMF)
HLT	highly leveraged transaction
IADB	Inter-American Development Bank
IFC	International Finance Corporation
IMF	International Monetary Fund
LBO	Leveraged Buyout
LDC	less developed country
LIBOR	London Inter-Bank Offered Rate
LMA	Loan Market Association
LOLR	lender of last resort
M & As	mergers and acquisitions
MBO	Management Buyout
NIF	note issuance facilities
OLS	ordinary least squares
OPEC	Organization of Petroleum Exporting Countries
PPP	purchasing power parity
REIT	Real Estate Investment Trust
ROA	return on assets

SAP	structural adjustment programme (IMF)
SAR	Special Administrative Region
SPV	special-purpose vehicle
TI	Transparency International
WTP	willingness-to-pay

About the Authors

Yener Altunbaş is a senior lecturer at the University of Wales, Bangor. He holds a BSc (Economics) degree from the University of Hacettepe, Ankara, and a PhD from the University of Wales, Bangor. He worked first as an analyst with Ziraat, as an economist in Etibank Banking, Inc. in Turkey and then as a research officer within the Institute of European Finance in the UK. He was employed as a research fellow with the Business School at South Bank University, London, and as a Research Associate at the Centre of Business Research in Cambridge University. Author of a number of articles on the structure and efficiency of banking markets, his main fields of research interest include the study of European banks, efficiency, stock market analysis, electoral studies, regional economics and urban economics. Some of his recent research is also concerned with marine biology.

Blaise Gadanecz is currently working as an economist at the Bank for International Settlements in Basel, Switzerland. He holds a postgraduate degree in Banking, Finance and Insurance from Université Paris-Dauphine, as well as an MA in Banking and Finance and a PhD in Economics from the University of Wales, Bangor. Prior to joining the Monetary and Economic Department of the BIS in 1999, he worked in various capacities at the Bank of England and at the French Treasury. At the BIS he has been involved in the analysis of international banking and derivatives markets, financial institutions and infrastructure. His research interests and publication record cover a range of banking topics; most recently the focus has been on the term structure of credit spreads in project finance, the micro-structure of international syndicated loan and bond underwriting markets, and the effects of government safety nets on international bank lending.

Alper Kara is currently working as a teaching fellow at the University of Leicester and undertaking PhD research with a scholarship awarded by University of Wales, Bangor. He holds a BSc (Economics) degree from Orta Doğu Teknik Universitesi, Ankara, and an MBA in Banking and Finance from the University of Wales, Bangor. Before moving to academia, he was employed by Dışbank of Turkey (acquired by Fortis in July 2005). He started his career as a management trainee in 1999, working afterwards in the treasury department, undertaking responsibilities on foreign exchange and treasury marketing unit desks as an assistant manager and later on the fixed income trading desk as a manager. At present he is conducting research in the areas of syndicated loan markets, bank lending, corporate finance and emerging market financing.

1
Introduction

With $2.4 trn of facilities signed in 2004, the global market for syndicated loans represented no less than one-third of funds raised worldwide on financial markets. *Syndicated lending* – where several banks form a group to lend to the same borrower – is deemed to have generated more underwriting revenue in recent years than either the equity or the bond market. On the eve of the sovereign default by Mexico in 1982, most of the developing countries' debt already consisted of syndicated loans. The default threatened large Western financial institutions and indeed parts of their countries' financial systems. The eventual restructuring of Mexican debt into Brady bonds, whereby creditors saw their loans exchanged for securities guaranteed by the US government, created a precedent in the way that it changed the structure of financial markets.

The aim of this book, intended for both academics and practitioners, is to provide a comprehensive overview of the development of the international market for syndicated loans and to investigate the determinants of risk-taking on this market segment. Particular attention is paid to the characteristics of both lenders and borrowers, controlling for microeconomic and macroeconomic effects. Loan demand and supply are analysed separately and the book comprises eight main chapters, each looking at one particular area. An overview of the development of the international market for syndicated credits during the past four decades is first provided, bringing together practitioners' and academics' views on this form of financing. Previously little-explored research questions are then dealt with: what influences the pricing of emerging country loans, particularly in times of crisis, what determines banks' participation choices and supply, how do emerging country loans compare with industrialized country loans and bonds. The structure of the book is outlined in greater detail below.

Chapters 2 and 3 provide an overview of the global market for syndicated loans and discuss its development since the 1960s. The emergence of the Eurodollar market in the 1960s, the balance of payments problems of non-oil exporting emerging countries in the 1970s, the Latin American financial crises and the US merger wave of the 1980s, and finally the competitive financial environment, together with the advent of the secondary loan market during the 1990s are reviewed. These have been the most influential financial developments that have shaped the syndicated loan markets in the last few decades.

Chapter 4 explores the relationship between developing country economic structure and the pricing of syndicated credits to borrowers in emerging markets. It also introduces a standard analytical framework for analysing the pricing of syndicated credits. It is reasonable to begin any study of the syndicated loan market with developing country borrowers, as lending to sovereign developing countries was how syndicated loans came into existence in the first place in the 1970s and 1980s, providing an indispensable source of financing for these countries by recycling the OPEC countries' oil wealth. As a consequence, some developing countries became excessively dependent on aid or foreign bank lending, which left them unable to escape the poverty trap by their own means. Economic problems in developing countries have often triggered major international financial crises since the 1970s. The Mexican crisis of 1982 was among the first crises to have a major impact on the functioning of international capital markets, with the development of Brady bonds.

More recently, the financial crises in South-East Asia (1997) and Russia (1998) also had a major impact on international lenders' behaviour. Sovereign borrowers' macroeconomic conditions (such as solvency, liquidity, debt repudiation and rescheduling history, economic investment and output) can thus be thought as influencing the financing conditions obtained by them. Yet, in addition to macroeconomic considerations, banks also take into account microeconomic factors – such as the borrower business sector, loan purpose, maturity or guarantees – to determine the terms of their lending. Indeed, many banks these days, at least the larger ones, run sector as well as country desks and use their research as information inputs for their loan decisions. Information asymmetry theory suggests that financial contracts should be formulated in such a way as to address the problems of *adverse selection* (supply of credit such that the less risky projects drop out of the market) and *moral hazard* (risk of non-repayment by the borrower, who has been prompted by a higher interest rate to choose a riskier project). The microeconomic characteristics of each loan contract are related to the equilibrium rate of interest in the theoretical and empirical literature.

Overall, the determinants of bank lending to developing countries have been examined in the existing academic literature within a risk–return framework, but the conclusions of earlier articles have often been only partial or contradictory.[1] Chapter 4 brings together the macroeconomic and microeconomic determinants and gauges their relative importance. Evidence supporting the dominance of macroeconomic effects over microeconomic factors is provided. It is also shown that banks might have been exploiting their market power during the 1990s by charging higher prices to emerging country borrowers that were most dependent on the international market for syndicated credits for their external financing.

In Chapters 5 and 6, the supply-side determinants of syndicated lending are analysed, a task not yet sufficiently performed at an international level in a formal academic framework. In Chapter 5, the objective is to investigate the relationships between the structure and pricing of syndicated loans and lender characteristics, using international data and distinguishing between banks with different seniorities present in the syndicates. First, the effects of bank capital constraints on syndicated loan pricing are examined. Attention is then turned to agency issues in the syndication of loans, such as whether senior banks sell 'lemons' to junior banks and how senior banks' reputations are related to the proportions of loans sold to junior banks. The effect on loan specifications of lender location relative to that of the borrower is also controlled for. Evidence is presented of some senior banks potentially offloading riskier credits to uninformed junior participants. This tends to happen particularly when the senior banks are poorly capitalized or have insufficient liquidity positions.

Chapter 6 sheds further light on the supply-side determinants of syndicated loan markets, by presenting evidence on the rationale behind the decision of banks to participate in loan syndications. First, the advantageous features of loan syndications that attract banks towards this market are discussed. The chapter then investigates the impact of banks' structural characteristics on the decision of participating in loan syndications. The results reveal that poorly performing banks – which have lower capital adequacy ratios, lower net interest margins and lower returns on equity and higher cost to income ratios – tend to be more involved in loan syndications on average.

In today's globalized financial environment, emerging and industrialized country borrowers compete for funds: for instance, developing country bonds and loans compete for investors with US junk bonds. This increases the potential of investor sentiment affecting developing country borrowers to impact industrialized country borrowers and vice versa. Thus, *contagion* – reflected, for instance, by higher spreads or flight to quality – can happen between these market segments during times of crisis or financial turbulence. After the Mexican sovereign default of 1982, the appearance of Brady bonds had implications for world financial markets as a whole. Likewise, commentators have argued that the Asian financial crisis for a while threatened the entire world economy (*The Economist*, 6 July 2002). While most of the earlier loan and bond pricing literature has focused on developing countries or on industrialized countries separately, Chapter 7 makes a first attempt at comparing pricing mechanisms and market structure for industrialized and developing country loans and bonds, combining these two branches of the academic literature. While the international market for syndicated credits was, at its inception in the 1970s, driven by the financing needs of developing countries, the situation has since then reversed and industrialized country borrowers now raise far more funds on the syndicated loan market than developing countries. Indeed, the US today drives the world market for syndicated loans.

There are a number of theoretical, practical and empirical justifications for comparing the characteristics of loan and bond instruments. The theoretical ones can be found in the information asymmetry literature, which extensively compares the characteristics of bonds and loans from a monitoring, incentives and debt seniority perspective.[2] Practitioners of financial markets actively compare the characteristics of bonds and loans when resorting to securitization[3] of loans, issuance of backstop or liquidity credit facilities to refinance maturing bonds,[4] or to arbitrage between highly leveraged transaction loans, high-yield bonds and credit default swaps. Following the logic of the 'pecking-order theory' of finance, companies use internal money (retained profits) in the first instance to finance their development and when they subsequently seek external funds, they graduate from bank finance to bond finance as information about their creditworthiness becomes more complete (e.g. Myers and Majluf, 1984). While this may be so for industrialized country borrowers, however, there could be more risk in bonds than in bank loans in the case of developing country borrowers.

After a review of the loan and bond pricing literature, Chapter 7 re-estimates refined versions of the developing country loan pricing model elaborated earlier in the book, for developed and industrialized country loans and bonds. It compares the riskiness of developing and industrialized country bonds and loans with reference to the 'pecking-order theory', and explores how negative market sentiment – reflected by peaks in issuance spreads – may have spilled over from one market segment to the other. It draws inferences about the relative influences of market structure, perceived risk concentration and bank market power on pricing on each market segment.

Chapter 8 examines the effect of the International Monetary Fund's (IMF) imprimatur on the cost of borrowing in the international capital markets between 1993 and 2001. It appears that the IMF-assisted countries paid higher spreads over LIBOR for short term loans and had obtained fewer long-term loan contracts compared to their non-IMF peers for the financing of similar purpose projects. This might indicate a lack of confidence on the part of creditors that IMF prescriptions would have the desired effect in the long run on the economies of client nations. The pricing of loans for projects in these countries is also inversely related to the level of short-term debt, signalling that creditors perhaps expect a bailout if a financial crisis occurs in the assisted nations.

Chapter 9 contains an extensive set of facts and figures on the trends that have prevailed on the international market for syndicated loans between 1993 and 2004, while Chapter 10 draws some brief conclusions.

2
A Global Overview of the Syndicated Loans Market*

Introduction

Syndicated loans are credits granted by a group of banks to a borrower. They are hybrid instruments combining features of relationship lending and publicly traded debt. They allow the sharing of credit risk between various financial institutions without the disclosure and marketing burden that bond issuers face. Syndicated credits are a very significant source of international financing, with signings of international syndicated loan facilities accounting for no less than a third of all international financing, including bond, commercial paper and equity issues (Figure 2.1). This chapter describes the functioning of this increasingly global market, focusing on participants, pricing mechanisms, primary origination and secondary trading.

A hybrid between relationship lending and disintermediated debt

In a syndicated loan, two or more banks agree jointly to make a loan to a borrower. Every syndicate member has a separate claim on the debtor, although there is a single loan agreement contract. The creditors can be divided into two groups. The first group consists of senior syndicate members and is led by one or several lenders, typically acting as mandated arrangers, arrangers, lead managers or agents.[1] These senior banks

* An earlier version of this chapter was published in the December 2004 issue of the BIS *Quarterly Review*, under the title 'The syndicated loan market: structure, development and implications'. It is available from the BIS website at http://www.bis.org/publ/qtrpdf/r_qt0412g.pdf.

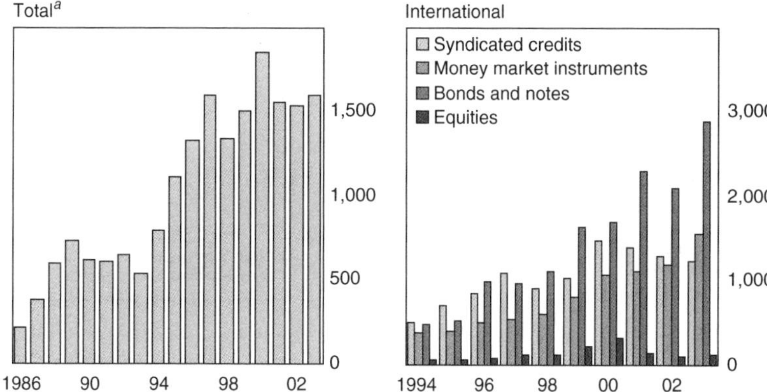

Figure 2.1 Syndicated lending,1986–2003, gross signings, $US bn
Note: [a] Of international and domestic syndicated credit facilities.
Sources: Dealogic; *Euromoney*; BIS.

are appointed by the borrower to bring together the syndicate of banks prepared to lend money at the terms specified by the loan. The syndicate is formed around the arrangers – often the borrower's relationship banks – who retain a portion of the loan and look for junior participants. The junior banks, typically bearing manager or participant titles, form the second group of creditors. Their number and identity may vary according to the size, complexity and pricing of the loan as well as the willingness of the borrower to increase the range of its banking relationships. Thus, syndicated credits lie somewhere between relationship loans and disintermediated debt (Dennis and Mullineaux, 2000). Figure 2.2 shows, in decreasing order of seniority, the banks that participated in a simple syndicate structure to grant a loan to Starwood Hotels & Resorts Worldwide, Inc. in 2001.

Senior banks may have several reasons for arranging a syndication. It can be a means of avoiding excessive single-name exposure, in compliance with regulatory limits on risk concentration, while maintaining a relationship with the borrower. Or it can be a means to earn fees, which helps diversify banks' income. In essence, arranging a syndicated loan allows banks to meet borrowers' demand for loan commitments without having to bear the market and credit risk alone.

For junior banks, participating in a syndicated loan may be advantageous for several reasons. These banks may be motivated by a lack of origination capability in certain types of transactions, geographical areas or

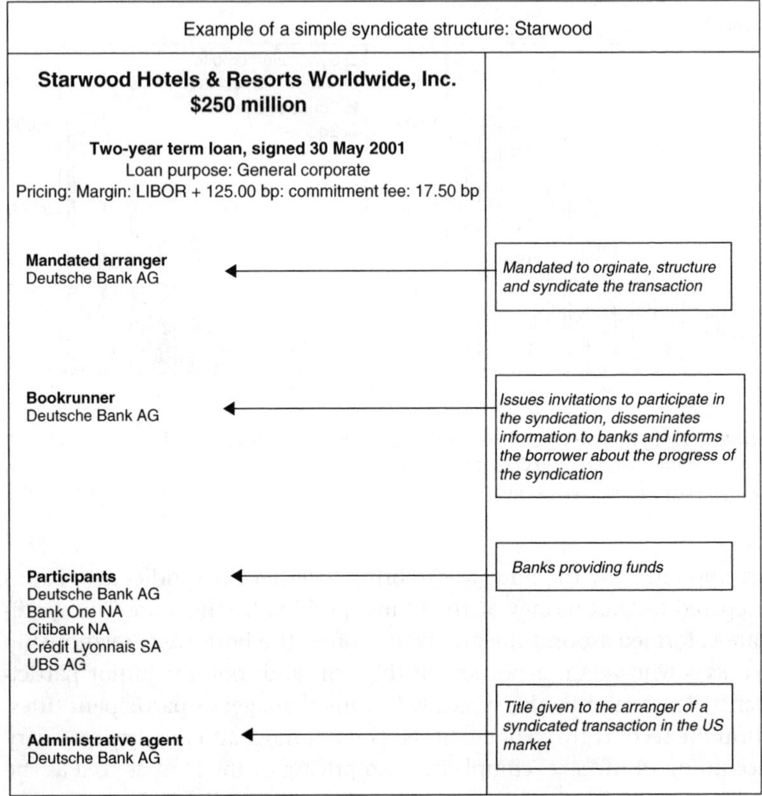

Figure 2.2 Example of a simple syndicate structure: Starwood
Source: Dealogic.

industrial sectors – or, indeed, a desire to cut down on origination costs. While junior participating banks typically earn just a margin and no fees, they may also hope that in return for their involvement, the client will reward them later with more profitable business, such as treasury management, corporate finance or advisory work (Allen, 1990).[2]

Pricing structure: spreads and fees

As well as earning a spread over a floating rate benchmark (typically LIBOR) on the portion of the loan that is drawn, banks in the syndicate receive various fees (Allen, 1990, Table 2.1). The arranger[3] and other members of the lead management team generally earn some form of upfront fee in exchange for putting the deal together. This is often called a

Table 2.1 Structure of fees in a syndicated loan

Fee	Type	Remarks
Arrangement fee	Front-end	Also called *praecipium*; received and retained by the lead arrangers in return for putting together the deal
Legal fee	Front-end	Remuneration of the legal adviser
Underwriting fee	Front-end	Price of the commitment to obtain financing during the first level of syndication
Participation fee	Front-end	Received by the senior participants
Facility fee	Per annum	Payable to banks in return for providing the facility, whether it is used or not
Commitment fee	Per annum, charged on undrawn part	Paid as long as the facility is not used, to compensate the lender for tying up the capital corresponding to the commitment
Utilization fee	Per annum, charged on drawn part	Boosts lender's yield; enables the borrower to announce a lower spread to the market than what is actually being paid, as the utilization fee does not always need to be publicized
Agency fee	Per annum	Remuneration of the agent bank's services
Conduit fee	Front-end	Remuneration of the *conduit bank*[a]
Prepayment fee	One-off if prepayment	Penalty for prepayment

Note: [a] The institution through which payments are channelled with a view to avoiding payment of withholding tax. One important consideration for borrowers consenting to their loans being traded on the secondary market is avoiding withholding tax in the country where the acquirer of the loan is domiciled

Source: Compiled by authors.

praecipium or *arrangement fee*. The underwriters similarly earn an *underwriting fee* for guaranteeing the availability of funds. Other participants (at least those on the 'manager' and 'co-manager' level) may expect to receive a *participation fee* for agreeing to join the facility, with the actual size of the fee generally varying with the size of the commitment. The most junior syndicate members typically only earn the spread over the reference yield.

Once the credit is established, and as long as it is not drawn, the syndicate members often receive an annual commitment or facility fee proportional to their commitment (largely to compensate for the cost of regulatory capital that needs to be set aside against the commitment). As soon as the facility is drawn, the borrower may have to pay a per annum *utilisation fee* on the drawn portion. The agent bank typically earns an *agency fee*, usually payable annually, to cover the costs of administering the loan. Loans sometimes incorporate a *penalty clause*, whereby the borrower agrees to pay a *prepayment fee* or otherwise compensate the lenders in the event that it reimburses any drawn amounts prior to the specified term. Figure 2.2 provides an example of a simple fee structure under which Starwood Hotels & Resorts Worldwide, Inc. has had to pay a commitment fee in addition to the margin.

At an aggregate level, the relative size of spreads and fees differs systematically in conjunction with a number of factors. Fees are more significant for EURIBOR-based than for LIBOR-based loans. Moreover, for industrialized market borrowers, the share of fees in the total loan cost is higher than for emerging market ones. Arguably this could be related to the sectoral composition of borrowers in these segments. Non-sovereign entities, more prevalent in industrialized countries, may have a keener interest, for tax or market disclosure reasons, in incurring a larger part of the total loan cost in the form of fees rather than spreads. However, the total cost (spreads, front-end and annual fees)[4] of loans granted to emerging market borrowers is higher than that of facilities extended to industrialized countries (Figures 2.3, 2.4). There is also more variance in commitment fees on emerging market facilities. In sum, lenders seem to demand additional compensation for the higher and more variable credit risk in emerging markets, in the form of both spreads and fees.

Spreads and fees are not the only compensation that lenders can demand in return for assuming risk. Guarantees, collateral and loan covenants offer the possibility of explicitly linking pricing to corporate events (rating changes, debt servicing). Collateralization and guarantees are more often used for emerging market borrowers (Table 2.2), while covenants are much more widely used for borrowers in industrialized countries (possibly because such terms are easier to enforce there).

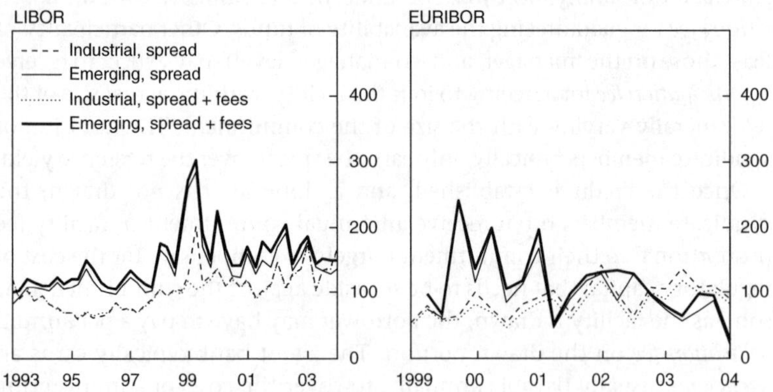

Figure 2.3 Spreads and fees, basis points, 1993–2004[a]

Note: [a] Quarterly averages weighted by facility amounts. Front-end fees have been annualized over the lifetime of each facility and added to annual fees.

Source: Dealogic.

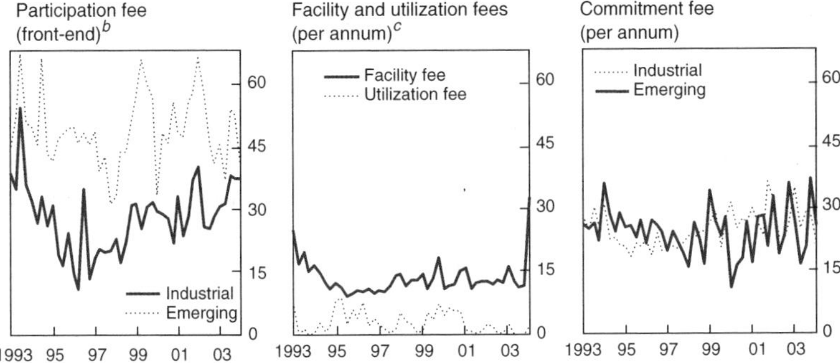

Figure 2.4 Breakdown of fees, basis points, 1993–2003[a]

Notes [a] Quarterly averages weighted by facility amounts.
[b] Not annualized.
[c] Industrialized country borrowers only.

Source: Dealogic.

Table 2.2 Non-price components in the remuneration of risk, share of syndicated loans with covenants, collateral and guarantees, by nationality of borrower, 1993–2004, per cent

	Covenants		Collateral		Guarantees	
	Emerging	Industrialized	Emerging	Industrialized	Emerging	Industrialized
1993–6	0	16	40	15	31	7
1997–2000	2	24	49	16	22	4
2001–4[a]	3	19	37	13	21	4

Note: [a] First quarter only for 2004.

Source: Dealogic.

Primary and secondary markets: sharing versus transferring risk

While commercial banks dominate the primary market, at both the senior arranger and at the junior funds provider levels, other institutions have made inroads over time. Globally, there are virtually no non-commercial banks or non-banks among the top 200 institutions that have around 90 per cent market share. However, investment banks have benefited from the revival of syndicated lending in the 1990s. They have taken advantage of their expertise as bond underwriters and of the increasing integration of bank lending and disintermediated debt markets[5] to arrange loan syndications. Besides the greater involvement of investment banks, there is also growing participation by multilateral agencies such as the International Finance Corporation (IFC) or the Inter-American Development Bank (IADB).[6]

Syndicated credits are increasingly traded on secondary markets. The standardization of documentation for loan trading, initiated by professional bodies such as the Loan Market Association (LMA, in Europe) and the Asia Pacific Loan Market Association, has contributed to improved liquidity on these markets. A measure of the tradability of loans on the secondary market is the prevalence of transferability clauses, which allow the transfer of the claim to another creditor.[7] The US market has generated the highest share of transferable loans (25 per cent of total loans between 1993 and 2003), followed by the European marketplace (10 per cent). The secondary market is commonly perceived to consist of three segments: par/near par, leveraged (or high-yield) and distressed. Most of the liquidity can be found in the distressed segment. Loans to large corporate borrowers also tend to be actively traded.

Participants in the secondary market can be divided into three categories: market-makers, active traders and occasional sellers/investors. The *market-makers* (or two-way traders) are typically larger commercial and investment banks, committing capital to create liquidity and taking outright positions. Institutions actively engaged in primary loan origination have an advantage in trading on the secondary market, not least because of their acquired skill in accessing and understanding loan documentation. *Active traders* are mainly investment and commercial banks, specialist distressed debt traders and so-called 'vulture funds' (institutional investors actively focused on distressed debt). Non-financial corporations and other institutional investors such as insurance companies also trade, but to a lesser extent. As a growing number of financial institutions establish loan portfolio management departments, there appears to be increasing attention paid to relative value trades. Discrepancies in yield/return between loans and other instruments such as credit derivatives, equities and bonds are arbitraged away (Coffey, 2000; Pennacchi, 2003). Lastly, *occasional sellers/investors* are present on the market either as sellers of loans to manage capacity on their balance sheet or as investors which take and hold positions. Sellers of risk can remove loans from their balance sheets in order to meet regulatory constraints, hedge risk, or manage their exposure and liquidity.[8] US banks, whose outstanding syndicated loan commitments are regularly monitored by the Federal Reserve Board (Fed), appear to have been relatively successful in transferring some of their syndicated credits, including up to one-quarter of their problem loans, to non-bank investors (Table 2.3). Buyers of loans on the

Table 2.3 US syndicated credits, 2000–2003[a]

	Share of total credits[b]				Percentage classified[c]			
	US banks	Foreign banking organizations	Non-banks	*Memo: Total credits ($ bn)*	US banks	Foreign banking organizations	Non-banks	Total credits
2000	48	45	7	*1,951*	2.8	2.6	10.2	3.2
2001	46	46	8	*2,050*	5.1	4.7	14.6	5.7
2002	45	45	10	*1,871*	6.4	7.3	23.0	8.4
2003	45	44	11	*1,644*	5.8	9.0	24.4	9.3

Notes: [a] Includes both outstanding loans and undrawn commitments.
[b] Dollar volume of credits held by each group of institutions as a percentage of the total dollar volume of credits.
[c] Dollar volume of credits classified 'substandard', 'doubtful' or 'loss' by examiners as a percentage of the total dollar volume of credits.

Source: Board of Governors of the Federal Reserve System.

secondary market can acquire exposure to sectors or countries, especially when they do not have the critical size to do so on the primary market.[9]

While growing, secondary trading volumes remain relatively modest compared to the total volume of syndicated credits arranged on the primary market. The biggest secondary market for loan trading is the US, where the volume of such trading amounted to $145 bn in 2003. This is equivalent to 19 per cent of new originations on the primary market that year and to 9 per cent of outstanding syndicated loan commitments. In Europe, trading amounted to $46 bn in 2003 (or 11 per cent of primary market volume), soaring by more than 50 per cent compared to the previous year (Figure 2.5). Admittedly, this to some extent reflects higher levels of corporate distress in Europe. But as the investment grade segment matures, it is also indicative of sustained investor appetite and of the market's improved ability to absorb a larger share of below par loans (BIS, 2004).

Distressed loans continued to represent a sizeable fraction of total secondary trading in the US, and gained in importance in Europe. In the Asia-Pacific region, secondary volumes are still a tiny fraction of those in the US and Europe, with only six or seven banks running dedicated desks in Hong Kong SAR, and no non-bank participants. In 1998, the Asian secondary market was exceptionally active. That year, large blocks of loan portfolios changed hands as Japanese banks restructured their distressed loan portfolios.[10] Trading was more subdued in subsequent years,[11] although banks' interest appears to have recently been rekindled

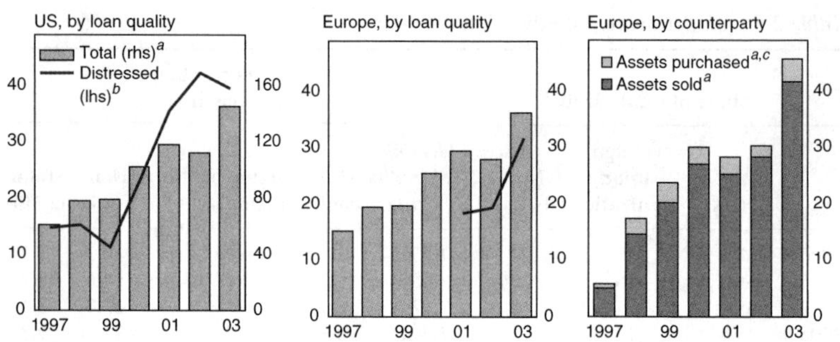

Figure 2.5 US and European secondary markets for syndicated credits, 1997–2003

Notes: [a] In billions of US dollars.

[b] As a percentage of total loan trading. For Europe, distressed and leveraged.

[c] From non-LMA members.

Sources: Loan Market Association; Loan Pricing Corporation, www.loanpricing.com.

by the secondary prices of loans, which have decreased less than those of collateralized debt obligations and bonds.[12]

Conclusion

This chapter has presented the workings of the primary and secondary market for syndicated loans, focusing on pricing, structure and participants. The historical development of the market is discussed in greater detail in Chapter 3. The syndicated loan market has advantages for junior and senior lenders. It provides an opportunity to senior banks to earn fees from their expertise in risk origination and manage their balance sheet exposures. It allows junior lenders to acquire new exposures without incurring screening costs in countries or sectors where they may not have the required expertise or established presence. Primary loan syndications and the associated secondary market therefore allow a more efficient geographical and institutional sharing of risk origination and risk-taking.

3
Historical Analysis, 1970–2004

Introduction

Today's syndicated loan market is a crucial element of the global financial system. According to Thomson Financial, $2.4 trn worth of syndicated loans were granted worldwide in 2004, amounting to no less than one-third of total international financing including bond and equity issuance. From modest volumes ($7 bn) in 1972, lending on this market has developed in a spectacular way during the past three decades (Figure 3.1). This chapter draws a historical perspective of the global financial developments that have shaped the syndicated loan markets since the early 1970s. In this context, the emergence of the Eurodollar market in the 1960s, the balance of payments problems of non-oil exporting emerging countries in the 1970s, the Latin American financial crises and the US merger wave of the 1980s, and finally the competitive financial environment and the emergence of the secondary loan market during the 1990s, are found to be most influential economic events in advancement of syndicated loan markets.

Emergence of the syndicated loan market

Syndicated lending has its roots in the early 1960s. Growing internationalization in banking and the relaxation of exchange controls by Western European countries gave rise to dynamic growth in financial activity and increasingly free movement of capital in.

Eurodollar and Eurobond markets of the 1960s

The advent of the Eurodollar market – dollar-denominated financial intermediation outside the US – in Europe was a primary cause for internationalization. The Eurodollar market grew as banks in Europe began

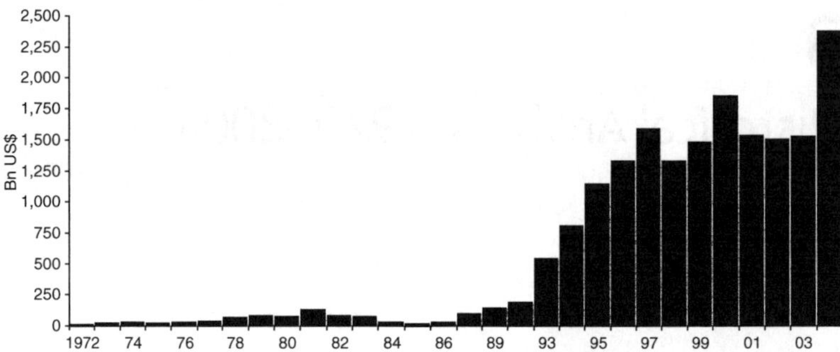

Figure 3.1 Announcements of international syndicated credit facilities, 1972–2004

Sources: IMF, *World Economic Outlook* and *International Financial Statistics* databases; BIS, *Bank of England Quarterly Reviews*.

offering dollar loans, free of US regulatory control, at or below the rates prevailing in the US market. The Eurodollar market was attractive given that banks operating there were liberated from requirements to hold non-interest-bearing reserve balances. In addition, restrictions capping interest rates that could be served on deposits did not apply in the Eurodollar market, which prompted banks to look for new innovative financial products to sell to investors, while satisfying borrowers seeking to raise cheaper funds.

One of the notable inventions of the era was the establishment of the Eurobond markets which allowed international companies to issue dollar-denominated bonds that would be bought by European and overseas branches of US banks. Typically a Eurobond was underwritten by a syndicate of international banks and denominated in an international currency, issued outside the borrower's home country, paying a long-term fixed or floating interest rate. The abundance of cheaper funds in the Eurodollar market through Eurobonds eventually generated demand for loan markets structured in the same way. Roberts (2001) argues that the syndication issuance techniques used on Eurobond markets were emulated in loan markets when the scale of credits required by clients became too large for individual banks in the late 1960s. The banks began to 'syndicate' such loans among groups of banks put together for the purpose. Thus, the basic techniques of syndication were initially developed in the international arena, where innovation has traditionally proceeded at a faster pace than in the more regulated national domestic markets (Armstrong, 2003).

The oil shocks of the 1970s

The price of oil, affected by oil embargo of 1973 and the Iranian revolution in 1979, is the foremost phenomenon that drove the world economy in the 1970s. The price of a barrel of imported crude oil was $1.8 at the beginning of the 1970s and by the end of the decade it had soared to around $39 (Figure 3.2).

The first shock came along with the start of the oil embargo in October 1973 announced by the Arab members of OPEC, which froze petroleum shipments to nations that had supported Israel in its conflict with Egypt. When the embargo ended in March 1974 the price of crude oil was $12.73 per barrel more than three times its level of $4.06 at the beginning of the embargo. The second shock came in the wake of Iranian revolution. The regime change was accompanied by a drop in the supply of Iranian oil, which became unreliable, driving up prices. A series of political events ending in 1980 with Saddam Hussein's Iraqi invasion of Iran, meant that oil production in Iran and Iraq virtually stopped, leading to the record high oil price of $39 per barrel in January 1981.

The rising oil price, pushing commodity prices higher, generated inflationary pressures around the world which lead to imbalances in the balance of payments of the developing world (Figure 3.3). Non-fuel-exporting developing nations faced serious balance of payments problems in the 1970s and 1980s, while fuel exporters enjoyed high current account surpluses.

Activity in the Eurodollar market got a spectacular impetus from the need to recycle the excess funds – dollar-denominated bank deposits – of oil-exporting countries after 1973. Measured by the US dollar value of non-bank liabilities of the Eurobanks active on the Eurodollar market, thus excluding the interbank segment, the net size of the Eurodollar market was $925 bn in 1982, compared to $42 bn in 1970 (Figure 3.4).

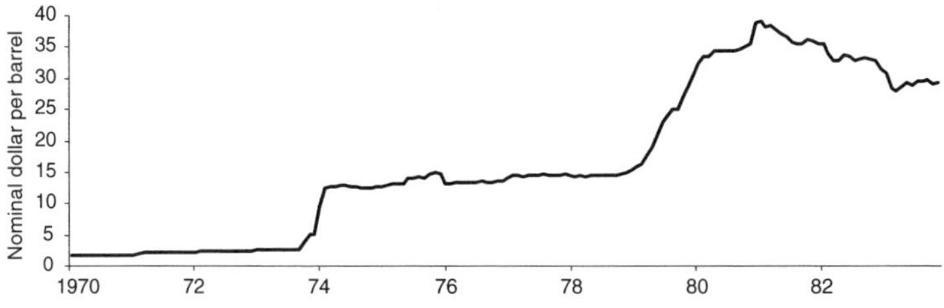

Figure 3.2 Trends in oil prices, 1970–83

Source: Energy Information Registration, http://www.eia.doe.gov/emeu/cabs/chron.html.

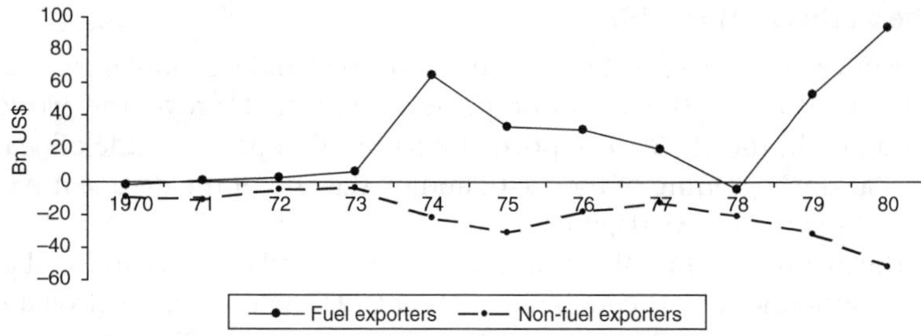

Figure 3.3 Current account balances, 1970–80

Sources: IMF, *World Economic Outlook* and *International Financial Statistics* databases.

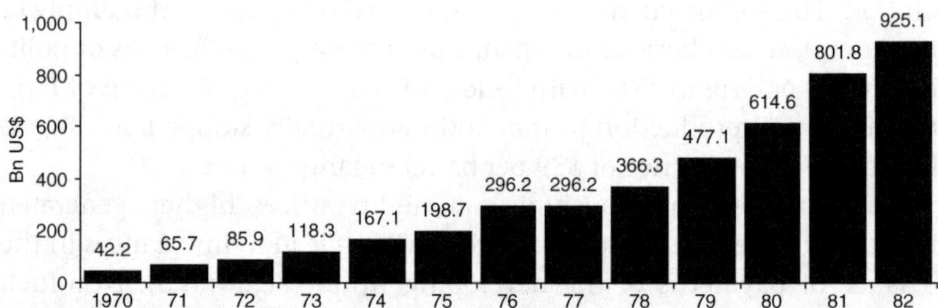

Figure 3.4 The growth of Eurodollar markets, 1970–82

Source: The Congress of the US Congressional Budget Office Staff Working Paper (August 1985), p. 10.

The surpluses of oil exporters had to be recycled to oil-importing countries in one way or another. Following widespread defaults on international bonds issued by the developing countries in the 1930s, lending to the developing countries before 1974 was generally restricted to government-to-government loans or loans from international organizations such as the World Bank and the IMF (Dooley, 1994). However, in recycling the oil-exporting countries' funds, governments – particularly the US government – were not keen on taking the responsibility with the traditional pattern of bridging through international organizations. Instead, international commercial banks, predominantly US-based, played an important role in re-channelling medium- and long-term credit to residents of developing countries, which essentially saw the funds as a way to promote exports and to mitigate the in balance of payments problems.

The rationales for lending to emerging markets

There were three main rationales behind this changing intermediation pattern of sovereign lending:

The search for new profit sources by international banks

According to the Federal Deposit and Insurance Corporation (FDIC, 1997) the primary motivation of US banks turning to overseas markets during this period was the search for new markets and profit opportunities in response to losing their share of households' savings to other types of intermediaries and to the capital markets. Lending opportunities in their own markets, especially in Western Europe, were being squeezed. Moreover, restrictions on capital movements, on domestic branching and on interest rates, together with tax laws and reserve requirements, forced the US banks to diversify their lending by turning to the Eurodollar in the late 1960s. Economies of scale were also a factor. It was much easier and potentially more profitable to make a single $100 m loan to the Mexican government as opposed to hundreds of separate loans to American developers, businesses, or homeowners (Ewert, 1988). Still another cause of this lending appetite was that bankers believed that governments, guaranteeing the loans, would never go to bankrupt since they had the power to impose tax increases. Weintraup (1984) notes that if commercial banks had not taken the opportunity and loaned the funds to other entities instead of non-oil-exporting developing countries, those to whom the funds were transferred to would have done the recycling instead. The new business of *intermediation* seemed a profitable business for US-led multinational banks.

Pressure by industrialized countries' governments to recycle 'petrodollars'

Dooley (1994) argues that lending to sovereign developing countries by financial intermediaries in this period took place with the approval, encouragement and implicit support of the governments of the industrial countries. Official support for aggressive foreign lending – in some instances, with a view to destabilizing the borrower nations in the long run – may have contributed to a climate in which US bankers exercised less caution than they otherwise would have done (O'Driscoll and Short, 1984).

Moral hazard issues

Banks were seen as willing to undertake this lending, at relatively low interest rate spreads, because of the belief that, if losses on such lending were to occur, they would receive assistance from the official sector (IMF, 2000). From this perspective, banks had strong incentives to expand their lending to developing countries, even to the point where debt-servicing problems could cause widespread solvency problems for banks (Rhodes, 1989).

Loan syndications as a widely used financing tool

In the 1970s, medium-term loans from large syndicates of commercial banks to developing country governments and public sector organizations were the dominant form of international capital flows (Lipworth and Nystedt, 2001). The typical developing country syndicated loan was a medium-to long-term credit priced with a floating-rate contract. The spread was charged over LIBOR, and the loans were re-priced approximately every six months. The technique of syndicating or packaging loans made it possible for US banks to participate aggressively in floating foreign loans of unprecedented magnitude (O'Driscoll and Short, 1984). Syndicated loans displaced traditional bilateral loans and club deals, to the extent that they allowed smaller, primarily domestic banks in many countries to lend directly to emerging market borrowers without having to establish a local presence in those regions. Furthermore, the banks were offered diversification, and were able to earn high yields and get fee income. The periodically adjustable loan rates appealed to the lenders, who saw them as a protection against inflation (which was rampant in the 1970s, due to rising oil and commodity prices) depleting their loan assets.

The growth of syndicated loan markets in the 1970s and the 1980s is presented in Figure 3.5. In 1972, signings of new facilities totalled only

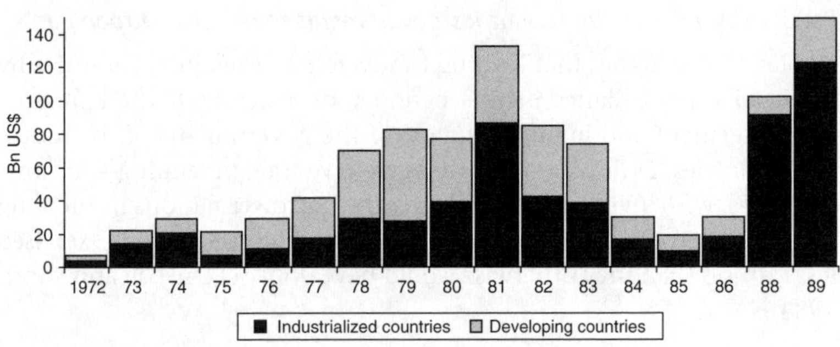

Figure 3.5 Announcements of international syndicated credit facilities by borrower nationality, 1972–89

Sources: IMF, *World Economic Outlook* and *International Financial Statistics* databases; BIS, *Bank of England Quarterly Reviews*.

Table 3.1 Average financial ratios for 8 money-centre banks,[a] 1977–1989, %

Year	LDC loans to total assets	LDC loans to total loans	LDC loans to capital	LDC loans to capital and reserves	Net income to capital	Provisions to total loans
1977	9.4	16.9	227.9	205.8	10.9	0.47
1978	9.1	16.5	232.0	207.6	12.4	0.40
1979	9.7	17.9	256.3	228.1	13.5	0.30
1980	9.7	17.3	251.7	224.3	13.8	0.32
1981	10.3	17.2	263.9	232.6	12.9	0.34
1982	10.0	16.4	247.1	217.3	12.4	0.48
1983	10.3	16.5	230.1	201.6	11.8	0.57
1984	10.4	16.3	219.5	190.2	10.6	0.72
1985	9.5	15.6	200.5	168.0	9.0	1.19
1986	9.0	15.0	179.2	145.7	8.8	1.32
1987	8.9	15.6	211.3	125.3	−22.2	3.86
1988	8.5	14.8	167.2	107.3	21.3	0.68
1989	7.5	12.7	164.7	93.2	−9.9	2.77

Note: [a] BankAmerica, Bankers Trust New York, Chase Manhattan, Chemical New York, Citicorp, First Chicago, Manufacturers Hanover and J.P.Morgan & Co.

Source: Adapted from FDIC (1997), p. 196.

$7 bn. However, a decade later, in 1981, they had reached $133 bn, 19 times the lever of 1972. Until 1974 industrialized country borrowers were the main customers of the market, accounting for around two-thirds of loans. Between 1975 and 1980, non-oil-exporting developing countries became the major borrowers. Their share peaked at 67 per cent of total syndicated lending (equivalent to $55 bn).

The eight large US money-centre banks thus accumulated significant exposure to developing countries, up to two-thirds of it to Latin American countries. In 1979, the portion of less developed country (LDC) loans in loan portfolios of these banks peaked at 18 per cent, 2.5 times the capital employed (Table 3.1).

Largely as a result of borrowing extensively from credit markets, the total outstanding external debt of Latin America grew sharply, reaching $327 bn in 1982 on the edge of the financial crisis, up from $29 bn in 1970 (Table 3.2). Brazil was the largest debtor, accounting for an average of 28 per cent of all Latin American exposures, followed by Mexico, Argentina and Venezuela, 26 per cent, 13 per cent and 10 per cent, respectively.

The emerging market crises of the 1980s

The problems created by the initial world energy crisis in 1973–4 were serious enough, but the second oil shock in 1979 and 1980 further

Table 3.2 Latin American external borrowing,[a] 1970–92, bn US$

Year	Argentina	Brazil	Mexico	Venezuela	Latin America
1970	5.2	5.1	6.0	1.0	28.6
1971	5.6	6.6	6.4	1.3	30.0
1972	6.0	10.2	7.0	1.7	36.4
1973	6.4	12.9	9.0	1.9	43.0
1974	6.8	19.4	11.9	1.8	56.3
1975	6.9	23.7	15.6	1.5	66.7
1976	8.3	29.0	20.5	3.3	83.0
1977	11.4	41.4	31.2	10.7	128.1
1978	13.3	53.6	35.7	16.6	158.5
1979	21.0	60.4	42.8	23.9	192.7
1980	27.2	70.6	57.5	29.5	238.4
1981	35.7	80.4	78.3	32.1	291.1
1982	43.6	91.9	86.1	32.0	326.9
1983	45.9	97.5	93.1	37.4	353.0
1984	48.9	104.3	94.8	36.8	369.9
1985	50.9	104.6	96.9	35.2	381.0
1986	52.4	112.0	100.9	34.6	400.0
1987	58.4	123.9	109.3	35.2	435.4
1988	58.9	114.6	101.6	34.7	417.5
1989	65.3	111.4	93.8	32.4	451.0

Note: [a] Amounts are flow figures.
Source: Adapted from Goldberg and Grosse (1996), p. 287.

exacerbated the problems and ultimately created a condition in which very hard choices became inevitable (Jordan, 1984). What scared the creditors at the end of the 1970s and the first two years of the 1980s took place on 20 August 1982, when Mexico's Finance Minister announced that his country was no longer able to service its external obligations worth $80 bn. The situation had worsened by October 1983 when 27 other emerging countries rescheduled their debt obligations to foreign creditors worth $239 bn.

What went wrong?

The record high interest rates of the early 1980s (see Figure 3.6), caused by the Federal Reserve's efforts to curb the oil-based inflation of the 1970s, brought on a global recession and triggered the crisis (FDIC, 1998). As mentioned above, because syndicated loans raised by emerging market borrowers were mostly priced over LIBOR, the impact of high interest rates on debt-service costs was enormous. It is estimated that for

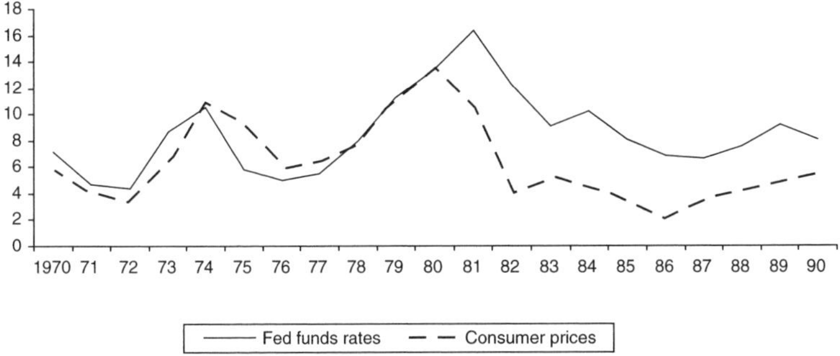

Figure 3.6 US Fed funds rates and consumer prices, 1970–90, per cent
Sources: IMF, *World Economic Outlook* and *International Financial Statistics* databases.

every percentage-point increase in LIBOR, debt-service costs for all developing nations rose by $2 bn. Even so, the price of credit (interest rates) increased less than the average price level, resulting in negative real interest rates – and, not surprisingly, further stimulating the demand for borrowing (Burnham, 1984). Meanwhile, the value of the dollar – the currency of denomination of most LDC debt – increased by 11 per cent in 1981 and 17 per cent in 1982 against the currencies of the debtor countries. This led to even higher debt-service costs. Besides, a global slowdown in the world economy, accompanied by a decrease in commodity prices, left LDC exports stagnant, thereby further undermining these countries' debt-service capacity. Investors, fearing a possible devaluation as a result of overvalued national currencies, moved their funds to safer havens: *capital flight* began.

Although the crisis was initially seen as a liquidity problem, it reflected more fundamental *solvency* issues. Many researchers have criticized the way the funds were used by sovereign borrowers. Initially, a large portion of the loans extended had been used to support domestic consumption, directly or indirectly. Ewert (1988) claims that the loans were used to expand state ownership and support state-owned businesses. Banks had been financing the construction of state-owned or subsidized steel mills, automobile factories and other projects, where there was no reason to believe the country had a natural comparative advantage (Jordan, 1984). Moreover, long-term social development plans, such as improving education services, were not income-generating investments to pay the debt in the short-term.

The Brady Plan

Lending came to an abrupt halt in 1982, after Mexico suspended interest payments on its sovereign debt, soon followed by other countries including Argentina, Brazil, the Philippines and Venezuela. Lending volumes reached their lowest point at $9 bn in 1985. In 1987, Citicorp wrote down 100 per cent of its emerging market loans and several large US banks followed suit. That move catalysed the negotiation of a plan, initiated by former US Treasury Secretary Nicholas Brady, which resulted in creditors exchanging their emerging country syndicated loans for *Brady bonds*, eponymous debt securities that could be traded on secondary markets and whose interest payments and collateral benefited from varying degrees of collateralization on US Treasuries. It is estimated that under the Brady Plan agreements between 1989 and 1994, the forgiveness of existing debts by private lenders amounted to approximately 32 per cent of the $191 bn in outstanding loans, or approximately $61 bn for the 18 nations that negotiated Brady Plan reductions (FDIC, 1998).

Funding takeovers in US market

Coinciding with the international emerging market crises, a major trend change in US corporate governance had a major impact on syndicated loan markets after 1985. In the 1980s, the explosive growth of corporate takeovers became a prominent feature of the US business world. The boom, taking place between 1984 and 1989, was identified as the fourth merger wave in US history and was characterized primarily by restructuring assets and recapitalization of firms. Over 1,000 acquisitions were registered in 1988, a record level of deals worth over $200 bn.

Leveraged buyouts of the 1980s

The most common technique for acquisitions in the 1980s was leveraged buyouts (LBOs), where the acquirers financed their acquisition by issuing *debt*, rather than stock or cash on hand. The value of such transactions peaked at $185 bn in 1998 (Figure 3.7) when 400 deals were recorded.

The financing needs emanating from LBO activity catalysed the junk-bond market and also gave an impetus to the syndicated loan market. The widespread use of leverage entailed net equity repurchases of more than $500 bn between 1984 and 1990 (Holmstrom and Kaplan, 2001). Mitchell and Mulherin (1996) note further that nearly half of all major US corporations received a takeover offer in the 1980s.

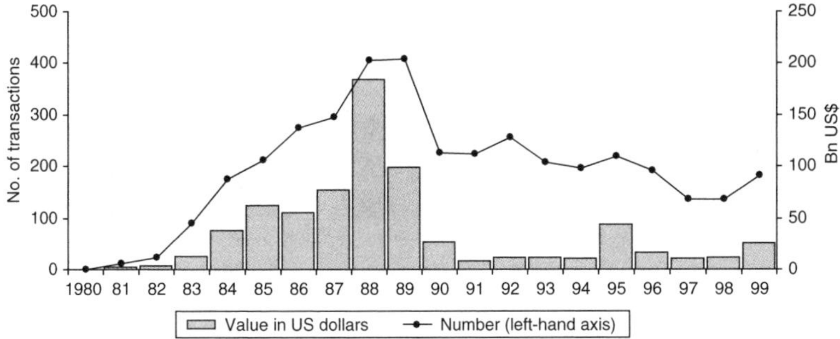

Figure 3.7 Total volume and number of leveraged buyouts in the US, 1980–99
Source: Thomson Financial Securities database.

LBO transactions generally required large borrowings and were often considered too risky for a single bank to underwrite and carry on its balance sheet. The need for a more efficient and liquid loan market arose to manage these exposures more efficiently. To handle this activity, a new type of loan syndication process was pioneered by the major New York money-centre banks, which established loan distribution operations to arrange, underwrite and distribute pieces of large corporate loans to syndicates of banks (Barnish, Miller and Rushmore 1997), limiting their risk as well as diversifying their portfolios. According to Borio (1990), one incentive for banks to underwrite LBO loans was a significant erosion of their traditional lending business as creditworthy corporate borrowers bypassed banks and raised capital directly from the capital market using debentures and commercial paper. In 1986, US banks' LBO loan exposure accounted for 73 per cent of the banks' merger-related loans, and for 13 per cent of all commercial and industrial loans outstanding (Figure 3.8).

As banks were engaging in LBO financing and recovering slowly from emerging market loan losses, the volume of total syndicated loan transactions increased sharply, totalling \$150 bn in 1989 – 7.5 times the volume of 1985, when activity had bottomed out. Borrowers from industrialized countries obtained 82 per cent of funds (Figure 3.5). A series of high-profile trading scandals towards the end of the 1980s instigated a regulatory backlash against the perceived greed and recklessness of dealmakers (Oram, 2003). New regulations set by the US authorities on disclosure rules, shareholder equity and the negotiating powers of target companies resulted in a slowdown in takeover activities.

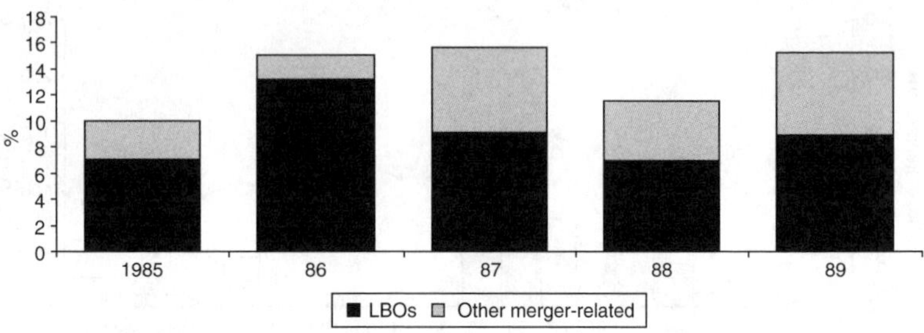

Figure 3.8 Merger-related loan exposure of 60 large US banks as a percentage of total commercial and Industrial loans outstanding, 1985–89

Source: Borio (1990).

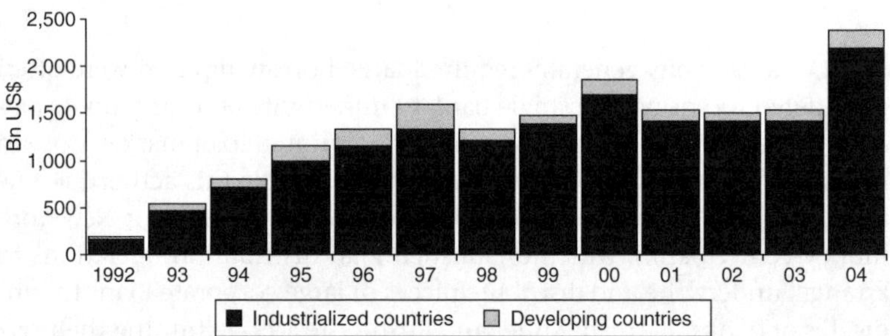

Figure 3.9 Announcements of international syndicated credit facilities, 1992–2003

Sources: IMF, *World Economic Outlook* and *International Financial Statistics* databases; BIS, *Bank of England Quarterly Reviews*.

The expansion of the 1990s

The market for syndicated loans expanded rapidly in the 1990s and was tapped by emerging market and industrialized-country borrowers alike (Figure 3.9). Total loan syndication volume represented $1.5 trn in 2000, more than seven times the level of $194 bn in 1992. Unlike in the 1970s, the share of developing country borrowers did not exceed 15 per cent during the 1990s. The increasing trend and popularity of loan syndications has been driven by several developments on both the supply and demand side of the market.

Supply-side issues that contributed to the growth of the market

First, the lending practices of commercial banks were more conservative in 1990s when compared to earlier periods. The losses suffered during the emerging market crises of the 1980s and in the economic recession of 1990–91 caused banks to adopt a more sophisticated approach towards assessing the *riskiness of loans* – some of these techniques had been developed on the bond market. Banks also started to make wider use of covenants, triggers which linked pricing explicitly to corporate events such as changes in ratings and debt servicing (Gadanecz, 2004). Previously, one or more banks would originate a loan, underwrite it and, often, hold it to maturity. There was little data on the performance of loans, so pricing often bore little relation to risk. Since the beginning of the 1990s, banks originating loans were typically part of a syndicate (traditional single-bank lending was genuinely dying out) and sold on a loan to other investors, such as pension funds.

Secondly, competition in financial markets caused non-commercial bank financial institutions to take an interest in the syndicated loan market, in an attempt to boost their fee income. Investment banks, which had developed an expertise in securities underwriting, established loan underwriting departments after the mid-1990s. In 1998, the underwriting of syndicated loans generated revenues of around $6 bn, compared with $4.6 bn for equities and $3.2 bn for corporate bonds (Madan, Sobhani and Horowitz, 1999). The intertwined – if not exactly merged – nature of bank and institutional debt markets reinforced this trend. For instance, it is very common nowadays for a medium-term syndicated loan provided by a syndicate to be re-financed by a bond at, or very much before, the loan's stated maturity. Another frequent hybrid format is the US commercial paper programme backed by a syndicated letter of credit. These packages have contributed to blurring the lines between investment and commercial banking. It has become usual to see bank loan syndicates led by major investment banks include commercial banks.

The convenience for borrowers

In the 1990s, corporate institutions in the developed countries became eager to restructure their existing lines of credit into more flexible financing arrangements, such as multiple-option facilities. Second-tier corporate borrowers that did not possess a sufficiently high credit rating to obtain access to the Eurobond market and use interest rate swaps at favourable rates were also tapping the syndicated credits market.

But the pre-eminence of syndicated loans came when their convenience for supporting corporate acquisitions was recognized. In the 1990s, prime borrowers became cognizant of the rapidly developing 'new-style' syndication market, which seemed to offer the possibility of raising

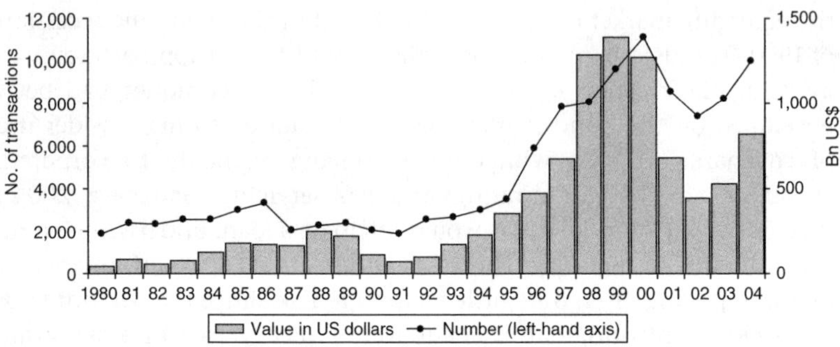

Figure 3.10 Total volume and number of merger and acquisition (M&A) activity of US and US cross-border transactions, 1980–2004[a]

Note: [a] Value is the base equity price offered.

Source: www.mergerstat.com.

larger amounts at attractive terms in a tight time frame (Armstrong, 2003). This feature of loan syndications made them a powerful financial tool for strategic corporate transactions such as mergers and acquisitions.

As shown in Figure 3.10, the total volume of M&As grew considerably in the 1990s, peaking at almost $1.4 trn, with a total number of 9,628 transactions in that year. Telecommunications, entertainment and financial services firms were intensively consolidating to meet the new market and technological challenges of the 1990s. Moreover, while the fourth merger wave of the 1980s was largely confined to the US, large-scale M&As finally made their way to Europe in the mid-1990s (Gaughan, 2000), increasing the overall regional demand for syndicated loans.

Development of secondary market trading

The third important driving force behind the strength of the syndicated loan market in the 1990s was the development of *secondary trading*. The biggest market for secondary loan market trading of loans is the US, where during the 1990s the volume of secondary market trading rose quickly, reaching almost $150 in 2003 (see Figure 3.11). This is equivalent to 19 per cent of new originations on the primary market in that year and to 9 per cent of outstanding syndicated loan commitments (Gadanecz, 2004). In Europe, trading amounted to $46 bn in 2003 (or 11 per cent of primary market volume), soaring by more than 50 per cent compared to the previous year. Distressed loans continued to represent a sizeable fraction of total secondary trading in the US, and gained

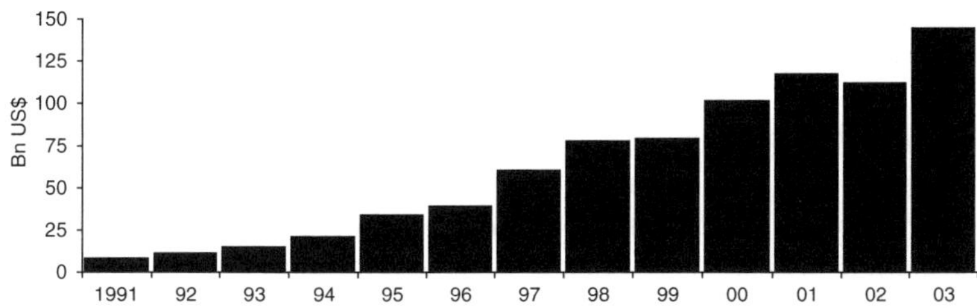

Figure 3.11 Secondary market trading in syndicated loans, 1991–2003
Source: Loan Pricing Corporation, www.loanpricing.com.

importance in Europe. Admittedly, this to some extent reflected higher levels of corporate distress in Europe. But as the investment grade segment matured, it was also indicative of sustained investor appetite and of the market's improved ability to absorb a larger share of below-par loans (BIS, 2004b).

One significant force behind the development of a secondary market for syndicated loans has been the rising number of bank loans rated by independent rating agencies. Secondary market activity combined with independently rated syndicated loans has led to more recognition of these assets by institutional investors as an alternative investment to bonds and debentures. Apparently, the economic recession in the US in the early 1990s forced banks to reduce their loan portfolios by selling them off partially with high returns in the secondary market, attracting large institutional investors, such as pension and mutual funds, insurance companies – and, in the case of distressed debt, so-called 'vulture funds', institutional investors that specialize in this asset class.

A liquid secondary market shifted the attention of firms from the old bilateral credit agreements to contemporary loan syndications which allowed firms to facilitate portfolio adjustments after the primary process of a syndicated loan. Furthermore, secondary markets catalysed the development of new products in derivative markets that allowed counterparties to buy protection against credit risk while keeping the loans on the balance sheet (and therefore maintain their relationship with the borrowers).

The exponential growth in secondary market trading resulted in a need for standardization of settlement, operational procedures and practices in the market. The standardization of documentation for loan trading, initiated by professional bodies such as the Loan Syndications and Trading Association in the US, the LMA (in Europe) and the Asia-Pacific Loan Market Association, has contributed to improved liquidity on these markets.

Emerging market financing trends in the 1990s

Following a spate of privatizations in emerging markets, utilities, banks and transportation and mining companies – often with large asset bases, substantial capital needs and good debt-service capacity – started to displace sovereign borrowers in these regions (Robinson, 1996). They turned the focus on capital investment to the private sector, from the previous balance of payments lending to the public sector or sovereign states. They were also able to obtain longer-term loans, thus ending the dominance of self-liquidating short-term finance geared to emerging markets. Even though the syndicated loan market showed exceptional growth in the 1990s, the share of emerging market borrowers in this type of funding shrank from the beginning of the decade, from 11 per cent in 1992 to 6 per cent in 2003 (Figure 3.12). Conversely, industrialized countries increased their share of syndicated loans significantly, from 86 per cent to 92 per cent in the same period.

As a major source of finance for emerging market corporate and sovereign borrowers, syndicated loans represented 67 per cent of all emerging market financing in 1991, twice the amount of total bond and equity financing (Figure 3.13), although they subsequently lost ground to equities and bonds.

The Asian crises in 1997 significantly affected financing flows to emerging markets, which dropped from a total of $274 bn in 1997 to $149 bn in 1998. The beginning of Asian financial crisis, corresponding to the devaluation of Thailand's Baht on 2 July 1997 and followed by depreciations of several other countries' currencies, further deteriorated the condition of the Japanese banking system, which had already been grappling with non-performing loans throughout the 1990s. Forty per cent of total Japanese exports were directed to Asian countries and Japanese banks had large loan exposures to Asian borrowers (Figure 3.14).

As a consequence, late in 1997 and early in 1998 Japanese banks restructured their loan portfolios, putting large quantities of syndicated loans up for sale in the secondary markets. Representing 10–15 per cent of the total syndicated loan market, this withdrawal of Japanese banks curbed the activity in the market. Although the global syndicated loan market recovered quickly and outperformed its 1997 level in 2000 and afterward, the volume of syndicated loan issues to emerging countries has not reached its pre-Asian crises levels. Following the Russian crises in 1998 and the South American crises in 2001, emerging markets were deprived of such funds.

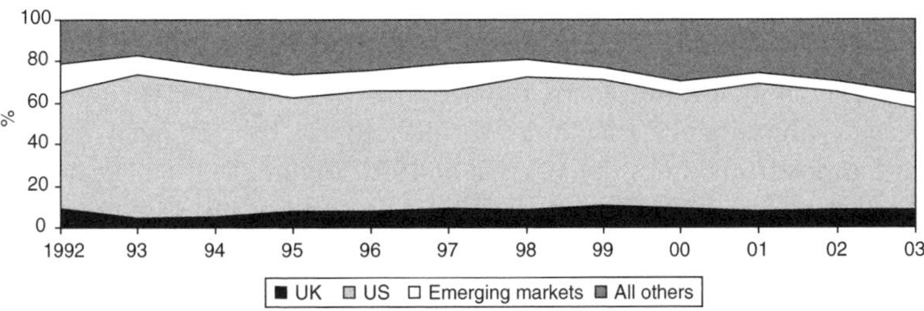

Figure 3.12 Syndicated loan announcements, by selected borrowers, 1992–2003

Sources: BIS, *International Banking Statistics*.

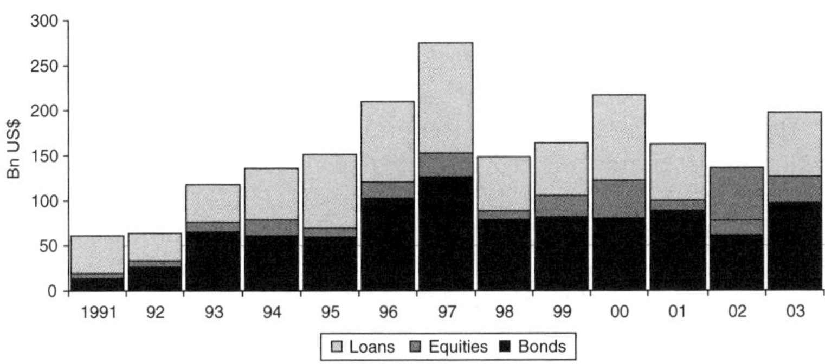

Figure 3.13 Emerging market financing, 1991–2003

Sources: IMF, *International Financial Stability Reports*.

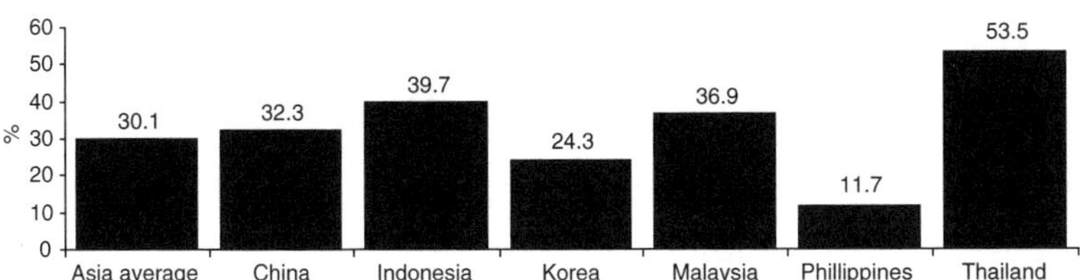

Figure 3.14 Debt owed to Japanese banks as of December 1996 by Asian borrowers, per cent of total

Source: Kaminsky and Reinhart (1999), p. 21.

2000 and onwards

Signings of syndicated loans totalled $2.26 trn in 2004, their highest yearly volume since they were introduced on the financial markets and almost four times the volume of 1993 (Figure 3.1). The year 2004 marked a watershed in Europe, when the largest borrowers in the syndicated loan markets were all European telecommunications firms. France Télécom signed a deal worth €30 bn, to fund a takeover and its strategic expansion involved purchase of a third-generation mobile phone licence (Table 3.3). Generally this funding was in the format of *bridge loans*, a temporary or supplementary means of funding before or while tapping securities markets.

Since 2000, M&A- and LBO-related financing has accounted for the lion's share of all syndicated loan financing (19 per cent). The energy sector, mainly oil and gas companies and electricity utilities, have been the largest active borrowers, constituting 25 per cent of the total volume of issues.

The signs of a deteriorating performance of the US economy were reflected on the syndicated loan market. US signings were sluggish between 2001 and 2003 (Figure 3.1); however, in 2004 they staged a revival with a record high volume of $1.8 trn. Meanwhile, trading on the secondary market has continuously increased since 2000, with US turnover reaching $140 bn in 2003, and European activity also being strong, at $45 bn.

Table 3.3 Selected telecommunication sector syndicated loan announcements, 2000

Company acquiring	$bn equivalent
France Télécom	30
AT&T	25
British Telecom	16
Vodafone Airtouch	15
KPN	13
Telecom Italia	13
Netherlands KPN	13
Pacific Century CyberWorks	9
Telefónica de España	8

Source: BIS (various years).

Conclusion

Since its birth in the 1970s, the market for international syndicated loans has become one of the key sources of international financing, representing no less than one-third of global debt and equity issuance in 2004. The advent of the Eurodollar market in Europe in the late 1960s contributed to the birth of the international market for syndicated loans. The fact that banks could operate free of US regulations gave rise to an abundance of cheaper funds which further generated demand for bond and loan syndications by large corporate borrowers. With the two oil crises of the 1970s, the customer base of syndicated lending switched to sovereign emerging market borrowers. During the 1970s syndicated loans became the key instrument for international commercial banks to channel the surplus of oil-exporting countries to the emerging markets. Lending came to an abrupt halt when the banks suffered large losses from defaulted loans during the Latin American financial crises of the mid-1980s. Chapters 4 and 8 provide an empirical analysis of the role of syndicated loans in developing and distressed countries, respectively. However, the market survived by becoming an ideal financing tool for the LBOs of the US merger wave of the late 1980s. Experts had predicted that the process of financial disintermediation, combined with the development of the interest rate and currency swap markets, would render syndicated lending obsolete. However, its flexibility and relative cheapness (in terms of issuance costs related to marketing and disclosure) in comparison to bond and commercial paper markets ensured its survival in the international financial community in the 1980s. A comparative empirical analysis of pricing and structure issues on the loan and bond markets is provided in Chapter 7. During the 1990s and later in the 2000s, increasing competition in the financial sector by non-bank financial institutions, conservative lending practices by banks, the development of secondary loan markets and ongoing M&A activity have sustained a demand for syndicated loans.

4
Borrower-Country Economic Structure and the Pricing of Syndicated Loans

Introduction*

The determinants of bank lending to developing countries have been investigated in the existing academic literature within the risk–return framework, but the conclusions of earlier research have often been only partial or even contradictory. The analysis of a large sample of individual syndicated credit facilities allows the application of the risk–return framework to study the determinants of syndicated lending to developing countries in a more systematic manner. That is the approach taken in this chapter.

One stream of academic literature, which started to appear in the late 1970s and early 1980s with the Latin American financial crisis, examines the effects of sovereign borrowers' macroeconomic characteristics, such as solvency and liquidity on the financing conditions obtained by them. More recent studies on secondary bond spreads consider the determinants of spreads, including local and global factors (Mauro, Sussman and Yafeh, 2002; Forbes and Rigobon, 2002). Other research on market discipline analyses the interest rates charged to different banks according to bank characteristics and macroeconomic variables (Martinez Peria and Schmukler, 2001).

More recent studies explore the microeconomic determinants of loan pricing (Kleimeier and Megginson, 2000; Eichengreen and Mody, 2000),

* Previous versions of this chapter have been published in the BIS Working Paper series, No. 132, and in the *Journal of Development Studies* 40(5) June 2004, pp. 143–73(31). For more information, visit www.bis.org and http://www.tandf.co.uk.

such as the borrower's business sector, loan purpose, maturity and size and risk mitigants.[1]

This chapter aims to bring together these two streams of literature and, relying on a developing country data sample that is more comprehensive in terms of information content and also covers the Asian and Russian financial crises, makes a number of important contributions:

- Most previous authors have used spreads over a *benchmark interest rate* (e.g. LIBOR) to study syndicated loan pricing. However, this does not represent the true economic cost of loans, as additional pricing factors (such as fees) are typically charged in loan syndications. The empirical analysis looks at the determinants of the full economic cost of loans, distinguishing between spreads and fees.
- Contrary to the existing literature, which considers the effects of explicit guarantees, a distinction is made here between the notion of *explicit guarantees* and *implicit guarantees* as determinants of loan pricing. Explicit guarantees are formal commitments by third parties while implicit ones can arise from ownership of the borrower by a parent company. Different effects are found on loan pricing.
- The relative influence of the *microeconomic* and *macroeconomic determinants* of loan pricing is analysed. Most of the existing literature focuses on these two groups of factors separately. In accordance with previous authors, individual characteristics of borrowers and loans are generally found to influence the pricing of credits in the expected way (i.e. riskier loans or borrowers correspond to higher pricing). However, this effect is in several instances weaker when macroeconomic conditions prevailing in the countries of the borrowers are also controlled for. Microeconomic factors viewed favourably on their own by lenders, such as implicit financial safety nets for financial sector borrowers, or loan transferability, lose their significance or can even penalise borrowers when the possibility of macroeconomic distress arises.
- The implications for syndicated loan pricing of a variety of *market structure indicators* for this loan market are also evaluated to answer questions that the existing literature does not examine when supply-side effects are not integrated with the demand side. Are loans granted by smaller syndicates to developing country borrowers cheaper than those granted by larger ones, and are borrowers who have used the market more extensively able to obtain cheaper rates than others? Does a transferable loan (this characteristic is a proxy for the liquidity of the secondary loan market) command a price discount? It is found that countries most heavily dependent on syndicated loans as a means of

external financing are charged higher prices for additional credit facilities, as a result of banks charging more for a higher perceived concentration of risk, or potentially exploiting their market power.

Emerging markets: past perspective

Grinols and Bhagwati (1976) report that some developing countries are excessively dependent on foreign funds or aid, which leaves them unable to escape the 'poverty trap' by their own means. Balassa (1986) notes differences in the response of inward- and outward-oriented countries (i.e. countries relying or not relying on international trade for their economic growth) to external economic shocks, partly because the former depend excessively on foreign funds and do not have the right policies to make use of them, which eventually results in lower economic growth rates and reduces their creditworthiness. Economic problems in developing countries have often triggered major international financial crises since the 1970s. The Mexican crisis of 1982 was among the first to have a major impact on the functioning of international capital markets, with the development of Brady bonds (Rhodes, 1996, p. 10). More recently, the financial crises in South-East Asia (1997) and Russia (1998) also had a major impact on international lenders' behaviour (see, for instance, IMF, 1998). Several more recent papers discuss bank lending to emerging markets (Goldberg, Dages and Kinney, 2000; Van Rijckeghem and Weder, 2001; Goldberg, 2001) and crises (Kaminsky and Reinhart, 1999). The sustained availability of foreign credit to developing countries is viewed as one means for deepening capital markets in these countries and potentially reducing the severity of crises when they occur (Goldberg, 2001).

Syndicated loans have always been an important source of international financing for developing countries and indeed were in the limelight during the Mexican debt moratorium of August 1982, since most Latin American debt then consisted of syndicated credits. The international market for syndicated credits saw its first large wave of development in the 1970s with lending to developing country borrowers, followed by a dominance of bond markets over loans in the 1980s, until syndicated credits again became an indispensable source of finance in the 1990s, largely complementary to securities.

Syndicated lending has been as significant as bond financing since the first half of the 1990s (Table 4.1). While international developing country bond issues rose from negligible levels at the beginning of the 1990s to more than $120 bn in 1997, before falling back to $82 bn in 2000 after the Asian crisis, loan commitments have kept pace, reaching levels comparable to bond issues. Signings of international developing

Table 4.1 Various sources of international financing for developing countries, 1992–2001, $bn

Gross announcements	**1992**	**1993**	**1994**	**1995**	**1996**	**1997**	**1998**	**1999**	**2000**	**2001**
International syndicated credit facilities	26.5	26.2	46.6	76.6	89.3	140.1	75.8	56.7	95.7	71.1
International bonds	20.6	47.1	38.1	36.9	103.3	120.9	77.3	76.6	81.6	105.6
International equities	6.7	7.7	17.3	8.9	15.1	26.0	10.1	22.7	44.0	11.6

Sources: Dealogic; BIS.

Table 4.2 Announcements of international syndicated credit facilities, by regions, 1980–2001, $bn

	1980	**1982**	**1984**	**1985**	**1986**	**1988**	**1989**	**1992**	**1994**	**1996**	**1998**	**2000**	**2001**
Industrialised countries	39.9	41.0	16.1	9.5	18.1	91.1	122.6	159.9	441.6	729.6	821.0	1,332.2	1,280.1
Developing countries	41.9	45.8	13.5	9.3	10.4	10.5	26.2	26.5	46.6	89.3	75.8	95.7	71.1
Other[a]	1.0	1.4	0.5	0.2	1.1	0.2	0.2	7.8	13.7	20.3	8.5	37.8	37.7
Total	**82.8**	**88.2**	**30.1**	**19.0**	**29.6**	**101.8**	**149.0**	**194.0**	**501.9**	**839.3**	**905.3**	**1,465.4**	**1,388.8**

Note: [a] Including offshore centres and international organizations.

Sources: Allen (1990); BIS; Dealogic.

country loan facilities actually exceeded bond issuance in several years, and totalled $71 bn in 2001. Robinson (1996) notes that 'the rapidity with which [the Latin American syndicated loans] market has recovered from the problems [of the Mexican crisis], its growing size and increasing breadth of participation indicate that this market has staying power'.

As Table 4.2 shows, in times of financial crisis in developing countries, syndicated lending generally tended to fall quite rapidly (refer to the statistics for 1985 and 1998) and took some time to pick up again. This form of lending thus seems very much market-oriented and determined by lenders' short-term considerations, based on macroeconomic conditions in the borrowers' countries. This provides an important justification for the inclusion of macroeconomic variables in the analysis of the determinants of syndicated lending to emerging markets, for which the data used are now presented.

Data and methodology

A sample of 10,304 syndicated credit facilities granted to developing country borrowers from 1993 to 2001 is used. These data were extracted from the database of Dealogic Loanware, a primary market information provider on individual syndicated credit facilities, in particular the characteristics of the loans (amount, maturity, currency, pricing) and the borrowers (name, nationality, business sector). A large part (80 per cent) of the facilities were contracted in US dollars.

Macroeconomic data are also used for the analysis, corresponding to the characteristics of the borrowers' countries. The data sources for these variables were the BIS–IMF–OECD–World Bank Joint Statistics on external debt, the IMF's *International Financial Statistics* and *World Economic Outlook* databases, as well as the International Institute of Finance's developing country database. The macroeconomic variables were linked with the microeconomic information contained in the loans database on the country and the date. For instance, for a loan granted to an Argentine borrower in 1995,[2] the real gross domestic product (GDP) growth variable represents Argentina's real economic growth for 1995.

Loan pricing

In the sample of 10,304 syndicated loan contracts, the spread charged to the borrower (over LIBOR, EURIBOR or another pricing reference) is available for 6,831 deals. Several research articles (Cantor and Packer, 1996; Kamin and von Kleist, 1999; Kleimeier and Megginson, 2000) have analysed this indicator. However, spreads are only one component of the true economic cost of a syndicated credit facility that the borrower has to pay, with the rest corresponding mostly to a variety of fees. The pricing structure of a syndicated credit is described in detail in Table 2.1 (p. 9). In the loan pricing analysis the so-called *drawn return* is considered; this is a proxy for the full economic cost of loans priced over LIBOR. The drawn return, which can be calculated for 5,010[3] observations in the sample, is the annual return expressed in basis points (spread plus utilization fee, participation fee, facility fee and underwriting fee) that will accrue to a senior fund provider if the facility is drawn throughout its life.

Macroeconomic explanatory variables

The macroeconomic variables can be classified into six subgroups: indicators of (1) solvency, (2) liquidity, (3) economic growth and its sustainability and (4) economic openness for the country of the borrower; (5) outside economic factors, (6) sovereign ratings.

Solvency of the borrower's country

The ratios of *external debt*[4]*/GDP* and of *debt service/exports of goods and services* are solvency measures that gauge the burden of a country's debt relative to its earnings. The higher this ratio, the more likely the country is to be distressed and therefore to default. Hanson (1974), Harberger (1980), Eaton and Gersovitz (1981), Edwards (1983) and Sachs (1984) discuss how higher debt/export or debt/output ratios result in higher sovereign loan spreads. Boehmer and Megginson (1990) further find that developing countries' deteriorated solvency can reduce the secondary market price of their debt. The ratio of external debt to GDP is therefore expected to raise the pricing of syndicated credits. An indicator of whether the borrower's country has received *assistance from the IMF* is also employed – this is defined as *use of Fund credit by operating the General Resources Account (GRA)* during the year in which the syndicated credit was granted – as a proxy for potential problems in the economy of the country concerned. This indicator is expected to be positively related to the pricing of loans. The use of this variable is equivalent to testing the effects on pricing of a *sovereign debt rescheduling history* or *debt repudiation*, which several authors have done. Gooptu and Brun (1992) find that the declaration of a moratorium on commercial bank debt-service payments has a negative impact on the availability of short-term credit lines. Besides, the existence of a current World Bank or IMF adjustment programme is a significant determinant of the amounts of short-term trade lines that are available during a given year from commercial banks. Boehmer and Megginson (1990) find that the level of incurred payment arrears, the unilateral debt moratoriums by Brazil and Peru and the loan loss provisions by US banks have a significantly negative impact on secondary loan prices on these borrowers' debt. The adoption of legislation for debt conversion programmes is associated with a decline in secondary market loan prices for the sovereign debt of the countries concerned.

Liquidity of the borrower's country

Relatively high values of the ratio of *short-term external debt/total external debt* indicate that a country can be the victim of a liquidity crisis if it cannot roll over existing credits – especially if its short-term debt exceeds its foreign currency reserves. This ratio is expected to be positively associated with the pricing of syndicated loans. The ratio of *reserves/debt* or *reserves/short-term debt* is also used as an indicator of such vulnerability. The *ratio of international reserves/GDP* measures the relative level of international liquidity held by a sovereign borrower and is determined to have a negative effect on spreads (Edwards, 1983). However, Gersovitz (1985) argues that in a willingness-to-pay (WTP) framework, a country can choose not to use reserves for debt service if it can protect them from seizure. The very liquidity of resources in the form of reserves may make them ideal for surviving sanctions after a default. The first period after repudiation may find the country most vulnerable since it will take time to set up alternatives to the banks for facilitating international trade. A foreign exchange war chest can be especially important in this transition period. In the early 1980's, rumours that developing countries were choosing to rebuild reserves rather than service debts were viewed as particularly ominous in this context. Argentina, for instance, appeared prepared to threaten its creditors with having to classify its loans as non-performing rather than use its increased reserves for debt service (Gersovitz, 1985). Therefore under a WTP approach to foreign borrowing, higher international reserves may reduce creditworthiness and will result in an increase in the country risk premium. High values of the ratios of *investment/GDP* and *credit/GDP* can forecast a future improvement in the country's general economic situation and are also signs of confidence on the part of banks and investors, provided they do not spill over into an unsustainable credit boom. The *investment/GDP* ratio captures the country's prospects for future growth. As shown in Sachs (1984) and Edwards (1983), it is negatively related to spreads. However, the WTP approach also applies to *economic investment*. Gersovitz (1985) argues that borrowers may use foreign funds to reduce the cost of the penalty in case of a default. Thus, higher investment ratios will reduce creditworthiness and increase spreads. As for the ratio of *credit/GDP*, it can be best thought of, in a cross-section, as an indicator of financial depth or development.

Economic growth and its sustainability

Real GDP growth is an indicator of the evolution of the country's wealth, and relatively high values can point to the debt burden becoming easier to bear in the future. Eichengreen and Mody (2000) find that high country *growth rates* enhance the ability to repay and reduce spreads; highly variable export growth, on the other hand, raises the risk of non-payment and increases the spread. At low levels of financial development and low growth rates, policy measures to improve financial intermediation bring value and reduce the costs of external borrowing. Even so, when they spill over into unsustainable credit booms, they are regarded by the markets with alarm and worsen the terms of access to external funds. To all intents and purposes, high values of the real GDP growth variable are supposedly associated with relatively cheaper syndicated credits, unless they reach unsustainable levels. In order to control for the sustainability of growth, *inflation* was also included as an explanatory variable in the model. As Cantor and Packer (1996) explain: 'a high rate of inflation points to structural problems in the government's finances. When a government appears unable or unwilling to pay for current budgetary expenses through taxes or debt issuance, it must resort to inflationary money finance [i.e. to printing money]. Public dissatisfaction with inflation may in turn lead to political instability.' The inflation rate is expected to be positively associated with the pricing of syndicated credits.

Economic openness

Relatively high values of the ratio of *imports/exports* and *imports/GDP* can point to excessive foreign dependence of the country in the sense that it has to import a relatively high amount of goods and services in order to export a given amount of goods and services or to generate a unit of domestic economic wealth. As suggested by Frenkel (1983) and Balassa (1986), to the extent that more open economies are more vulnerable to foreign shocks, higher values of the ratio of imports/GDP are expected to raise loan pricing. Balassa (1986) notes that, between 1973 and 1983, outward-oriented countries suffered considerably larger external shocks than inward-oriented ones in the first instance.[5]

Outside economic factors

Provision was made for the *country's purchasing power parity (PPP) share of world GDP*: this is an indicator of the country's economic weight in the world. *Growth in world trade* was also controlled for: if world trade is booming, one could expect that there will be more competition for funds as these are more difficult and therefore more expensive to come by. The *yield on three-year US Treasury bills* was also included in the regression models in order to control for the price of the alternative, risk-free investment available to the lenders. The extent to which lenders are willing to extend funds to potentially riskier borrowers from developing countries instead of investing in US Treasuries is an indicator of their appetite for risk. In a study of the evolution and determinants of US banks' claims on developing countries, Goldberg (2001) suggests that foreign claims of US banks are correlated with real US interest rates, but generally uncorrelated with foreign real interest rates. Tighter real lending conditions in the US are associated with lower real claims on industrialised countries and higher claims on Latin American countries. Finally, the JP Morgan Emerging Market Sovereign Bond Index was incorporated as a proxy for general market sentiment towards the emerging markets. Higher values of this index correspond to adverse market sentiment and are expected to result in higher loan prices, and vice versa.

Sovereign ratings

Cantor and Packer (1996) find that a number of rated countries' macroeconomic characteristics are reflected in their sovereign ratings, especially *per capita* income, GDP growth, inflation, external debt, level of economic development and default history. For the purposes of econometric analysis, the Standard & Poor's sovereign ratings were converted into five rating classes, using the conversion table shown in Appendix 4.1 to this chapter (p. 60). These rating classes were associated with the credits based on the nationality of the borrower and the date of the loan facility. The resulting distribution is shown in Table 4.3. The good rating classes are expected to be negatively associated with the pricing of syndicated credits, and vice versa.

Table 4.3 Number of syndicated loan facilities corresponding to each sovereign rating class

Rating class	**Ratings included**[a]	**No. of observations**
Missing	–	281
Default or not rated or not disclosed	SD, NR, R	1,257
Poor	CC to BB–	1,823
Speculative	BB to BBB–	2,832
Investment grade	BBB to A	2,856
Best	A+ to AAA	1,255
	Total	**10,304**

Note: [a] See Appendix 4.1 for more detail.

Sources: Standard & Poor's; Dealogic.

Microeconomic explanatory variables

The microeconomic explanatory variables pertain to loan maturity and size, the existence of risk mitigants, business sector and loan purpose, as well as the structure of the market for syndicated loans granted to developing countries.

Maturity indicates the lifetime of the loan, expressed in years, and hence the period for which the lender is exposed to credit risk. Kleimeier and Megginson (2000) report that loan maturity and spread are significantly and positively related, except for project finance loans. The effect of maturity on the pricing of loans is generally not found to be uniform in the academic literature (see, for instance, Smith, 1980).

The natural logarithm of *loan size* (and the resulting bank exposure) was also included, expressed in million US dollars. Kleimeier and Megginson (2000) confirm a negative and significant relationship between loan prices and size for most syndicated credits in their sample, except for project finance loans. This could point to the ability of more creditworthy borrowers to arrange larger loans or to the presence of economies of scale when banks arrange syndicated credit facilities.

Dummies were computed to indicate the presence of *risk mitigants*, such as the loan being *secured* (notably on an asset or receivables the borrower might have), *sponsored* or *explicitly guaranteed* by a third party. Eichengreen and Mody (2000) do not control for the presence of risk mitigants. Kleimeier and Megginson (2000) do include dummies for the existence of a third-party repayment guarantee or of collateralizable assets; these are explicit guarantees, though. While the authors find the presence of a *third-party guarantee* to reduce the spread on most syndicated credits, the effect of collateralisable assets depends on the type of credit. As an innovation in the Kleimeier and Megginson (2000) article, a distinction was made between *explicit guarantees* (written pledges from a third party to guarantee the loan) and *implicit guarantees* (e.g. when the borrower is a developing country subsidiary of a multinational firm from an industrialized country) and examine their effects separately. In the rest of the existing empirical literature, the findings about the effects of risk mitigants on the pricing of loans are mixed (Smith and Warner, 1979; Smith, 1980; Bester, 1985; Besanko and Thakor, 1987; Berger and Udell, 1990).

Dummies were also calculated to identify subsamples within the dataset that corresponded to particular *borrower business sector* and *loan purpose* groups that one might expect to have different risk characteristics and therefore incur different pricing of their loans. The control for the borrower business sectors and the industrial structure of borrowing countries is more refined than in Kleimeier and Megginson (2000), who determine a dummy variable for the existence of collateralizable assets based on the borrower's industry, and Eichengreen and Mody (2000), who control for only four industrial sectors (manufacturing, financial services, other services, government). The authors report that when *financial institutions* borrow on the syndicated loan market, they seem to be able to obtain lower spreads than non-financial borrowers. This is consistent with the emphasis some observers have placed on the tacit or explicit guarantees provided to financial institutions by the monetary authorities (lenders of last resort, LOLR). Ten *business sector* subcategories were created: construction and property, financial services (banks), financial services (non-banks), high-tech industries, infrastructure-related industries, services provided to the population, services provided by the state, traditional industry, transportation and utilities firms, based on the 188 groups described in Appendix 4.2 to this chapter (pp. 61–2). The *loan purpose* classifications are partially based on Kleimeier and Megginson (2000), who notably report that M&A purpose loans are relatively more expensive than others. Eichengreen and Mody (2000) further find that spreads on loans to finance infrastructure projects are usually higher than on other types of loans. A distinction was made between the following loan purposes: corporate control, capital structure, general corporate purpose, project finance, property, transport, other or not available and multipurpose. For a full list of purpose codes included in the various groupings, refer to Appendix 4.3 (p. 63).

Market structure indicators

Variables were included to control for the *structure of the loan market*, an approach which has not been adopted so far in the literature on the pricing of developing country syndicated credits. First, a dummy was included showing whether the credit facility is *transferable* or not. This is an indicator of the market's liquidity, i.e. the extent to which the loan can be traded on the secondary market. It may be easier for a bank to offload loans from its balance sheet and manage its exposure to certain developing country borrowers if the loans concerned are transferable.[6] This may have an impact on the pricing of the loans. Second, a dummy was used to indicate if the amount of the loan has been *increased* from the original amount. When this dummy is equal to 1, it can indicate that the market had a positive reaction to the deal during syndication or that the banks have shown flexibility in adapting their financing package to a change in the borrower's needs. Third, the *size of the syndicate* of lending banks was controlled for each facility. A first dummy was defined to indicate the case when the number of fund providers was greater than two, and a second one to indicate that the deal is a *club deal* or a *bilateral deal*.[7] The conditions of bilateral or club deals are expected to reflect the relationship of the borrower to its core banks and may therefore be more favourable than on other deals. Fourth, the *share of the borrower's country in total lending to all countries during the year concerned* was included: this ratio indicates the relative presence of the country on the market for syndicated credits relative to others. A high country share may indicate relatively high financing needs for a nation, possibly leading to more expensive credits but also, conversely, to an established presence on the market, resulting in more favourable financing conditions.

Descriptive statistics

As an exploratory analysis, some descriptive statistics are now presented to help understand the characteristics of the sample[8] of loans and its subsamples, in particular in terms of average, median and dispersion.

As Table 4.4 shows, with the exception of 1996, the mean and the median of the drawn return in the sample have been generally following an upward trend, peaking in 1999 – the mean was then 252 basis points, possibly reflecting higher risk premia demanded from developing country borrowers in the aftermath of the Asian and Russian financial crises. Loan prices subsequently levelled off. The mean and the median are quite close to each other, suggesting a symmetrical statistical distribution of the data. Higher drawn returns have generally been associated with higher dispersion. Table 4.5 further suggests that loan size has been increasing over time; even so, the relatively high standard deviation indicates dispersion in loan sizes, although the coefficient of variation is relatively stable.

Loan size and drawn return seem to differ significantly according to the borrower's industry (Table 4.6), with the highest median loan size

Table 4.4 Evolution of drawn return in basis points over time, 1993–2001

Year	N	Mean	Median	Standard deviation	Coefficient of variation
1993	317	120.4	100.0	74.7	0.62
1994	400	125.3	111.2	74.7	0.60
1995	615	124.0	95.0	105.7	0.85
1996	945	111.9	79.5	95.0	0.85
1997	1,132	132.5	92.8	116.5	0.88
1998	558	180.4	145.0	137.6	0.76
1999	412	252.2	225.0	181.0	0.72
2000	552	190.6	150.0	133.1	0.70
2001[a]	79	204.8	187.5	139.1	0.68
Total	**5,010**	**149.0**	**106.7**	**125.3**	**0.84**

Note: [a] First-quarter data only.

Source: Dealogic.

Table 4.5 Evolution of loan size over time, 1993–2001, $m

Year	*N*	Mean	Median	Standard deviation	Coefficient of variation
1993	317	62.2	35.0	104.2	1.68
1994	400	84.1	42.6	166.2	1.98
1995	615	83.7	50.0	167.0	2.00
1996	945	77.8	44.3	123.1	1.58
1997	1,132	107.4	50.0	244.4	2.28
1998	558	126.7	66.3	209.9	1.66
1999	412	129.2	77.6	217.1	1.68
2000	552	140.8	99.3	172.7	1.23
2001[a]	79	162.7	75.0	390.2	2.40
Total	**5,010**	**102.6**	**50.0**	**194.1**	**1.89**

Note: [a] First-quarter data only.
Source: Dealogic.

Table 4.6 Distribution of loan size and drawn return, by industry

	Loan size ($m)			
Industry	***N***	**Mean**	**Median**	**Standard deviation**
Construction and property	170	46.2	30.0	42.1
Financial services – banks	897	83.5	50.0	109.4
Financial services – non-banks	501	63.0	30.0	110.7
High-tech industries	825	104.9	56.8	156.4
Infrastructure	17	89.1	70.0	70.0
Population-related services	149	86.9	50.0	123.0
State-provided services	249	191.4	90.0	354.3
Traditional industry	866	94.2	50.0	170.7
Transport	521	75.7	39.7	207.6
Utilities	794	163.1	91.2	282.3
	Drawn return (bp)			
	N	**Mean**	**Median**	**Standard deviation**
Construction and property	170	131.1	100.0	94.5
Financial services – banks	898	140.6	96.2	134.3
Financial services – non-banks	501	124.0	100.0	96.2
High-tech industries	826	150.3	105.0	132.1
Infrastructure	17	233.0	188.0	163.1
Population-related services	149	258.6	203.6	180.0
State-provided services	249	139.0	100.0	113.5
Traditional industry	866	171.9	130.8	126.6
Transport	522	98.3	75.0	79.6
Utilities	794	164.3	137.5	120.6

Source: Dealogic.

associated with the utilities sector ($91 m) and the lowest one with the construction, property and non-bank financial services sectors ($30 m). The highest median drawn returns are observed for infrastructure- and population-related services, more than twice as high as the median return observed for the transport industry (the sector with the lowest median drawn return).

Table 4.7 shows that better borrower country sovereign ratings correspond to lower drawn returns. Besides, except for the worst Standard &

Table 4.7 Summary statistics, by borrower country sovereign rating and year, 1993–2001

	Median drawn return (bp), by borrower country, sovereign rating and year								
Rating class	**1993**	**1994**	**1995**	**1996**	**1997**	**1998**	**1999**	**2000**	**2001[a]**
Default or not rated or not disclosed	150.0	160.0	172.3	150.0	138.3	82.0	105.0	117.7	
Poor	136.3	150.0	170.0	155.0	182.5	220.8	250.0	200.0	249.6
Speculative	142.8	138.6	120.6	90.0	76.4	158.0	255.6	190.0	236.0
Investment grade	97.5	100.0	100.0	82.5	80.0	85.0	132.5	106.6	74.0
Best	70.8	66.0	55.0	61.1	53.2	63.0	85.0	73.7	77.2
	Median loan size ($m equivalent) by borrower country, sovereign rating and year								
	1993	**1994**	**1995**	**1996**	**1997**	**1998**	**1999**	**2000**	**2001[a]**
Default or not rated or not disclosed	32.0	40.0	36.0	40.3	50.0	120.0	100.0	100.0	
Poor	43.5	50.3	80.8	60.0	50.0	61.8	60.0	95.0	72.5
Speculative	50.0	42.8	67.5	75.0	50.0	75.0	83.0	100.0	70.0
Investment grade	29.0	31.0	40.0	40.0	48.4	52.7	86.5	91.9	95.0
Best	40.0	50.0	33.4	30.0	56.3	60.0	52.5	77.0	60.0
	Median maturity (years), by borrower country, sovereign rating and year								
	1993	**1994**	**1995**	**1996**	**1997**	**1998**	**1999**	**2000**	**2001[a]**
Default or not rated or not disclosed	5.0	5.0	4.0	5.0	5.0	7.0	8.4	7.0	
Poor	1.5	2.0	1.1	1.5	1.0	1.0	2.0	3.3	3.0
Speculative	5.0	2.5	4.2	5.0	5.0	3.0	4.5	3.3	4.0
Investment grade	5.0	5.0	5.0	5.0	5.0	5.0	3.0	3.0	3.0
Best	3.0	5.0	5.0	3.0	5.0	5.5	3.0	3.0	3.0

Note: [a] First-quarter data only.

Source: Dealogic.

Poor's rating class, the median maturity of poor rating classes (e.g. class 1 – 'poor') is typically short (never above two years between 1993 and 1999), potentially indicating that lenders are reluctant to extend funds to poorly rated borrowers for longer periods of time. This may leave these countries in a 'maturity trap', if the maturity of fresh loans is always sufficient only to refinance maturing credits.

The methodology used to further analyse these data patterns is now presented.

Methodology

As many of the independent variables are qualitative dummies, a *hedonic* (i.e. quality-adjusted) model seems particularly useful for the task at hand. Hedonic prices are the implicit prices of attributes of a differentiated product. Following the approach of Linneman (1980),[9] the equations are of the form:

$$\ln DRAWN_i = \alpha + \Sigma_k \beta_k X_{ik} + \Sigma_m \gamma_m Y_{im} + \Sigma_n \phi_n Z_{in} + U_i$$

where:

$\ln DRAWN_i$ represents the natural logarithm of the drawn return on loan i, α is a constant

$(x_1, \ldots, x_k)$ is a vector of k continuously measurable microeconomic characteristics of the loan or the borrower (e.g. maturity, natural logarithm of loan size)

$(y_1, \ldots, y_m)$ is a vector of m continuously measurable macroeconomic measures for the performance of the borrower's country (e.g. ratio of debt/GDP, of debt service/exports of goods and services)

$(z_1, \ldots, z_n)$ is a vector of n qualitative characteristics (e.g. loan purpose dummies, borrower business sector dummies)

U_i = is a random disturbance.

$(\beta_1, \ldots, \beta_k)$, $(\gamma_1, \ldots, \gamma_m)$ and $(\phi_1, \ldots, \phi_n)$ are parameters to be estimated.

ϕ_j $(j = 1, \ldots, n)$ can then be interpreted as the hedonic price attached to qualitative characteristic j.

The results of the regressions are presented and interpreted in the next section.

Results and discussion

Insofar as sovereign ratings are expected to be correlated with the other indicators of countries' macroeconomic performance, the effects of these two sets of independent variables were analysed separately in the first instance (for more on this, however, see n. 16 at the end of the volume, p. 212). Models combining different sets of variables were estimated, allowing us to gauge the relative importance of macroeconomics and microeconomic factors influencing loan pricing.

The effect of sovereign ratings

Table 4.8 shows that the drawn return is statistically different for each rating class from 'poor' to 'best' (the 95 per cent confidence intervals for the mean do not overlap). In accordance with Kamin and von Kleist (1999), it is found that the pricing of loan issues increases as sovereign ratings deteriorate, suggesting that lenders price sovereign ratings properly into their loan offerings. This is the straightforward result one would expect. Borrowers from countries with a 'poor' sovereign rating are having to pay a drawn return of 238.3 bp on their loans on average, almost four times the average drawn return of the borrowers from countries with the 'best' sovereign ratings (65.7 bp).

The relative effect of macroeconomic and microeconomic variables

The relative effect of macroeconomic and microeconomic factors on the pricing of developing country syndicated credits is now analysed. The results of the standard ordinary least squares (OLS) estimation, where the drawn return is the dependent variable, are shown in Table 4.9.

First, a model is estimated with only macroeconomic explanatory variables (left-hand column of Table 4.9) and loan maturity. The significant and positive coefficients on the ratio of debt/GDP and of debt service/exports are in accordance with the results of the academic literature (Feder and Just, 1977; Sachs, 1984; Eichengreen and Mody, 2000): lenders seem to be concerned about the weight of countries' debt service as a proportion of their income and therefore charge higher prices to borrowers from countries whose ratios of debt or debt service/income

Table 4.8 Drawn return, by broad sovereign rating category, basis points

Rating class	*N*	Mean	Median	Standard deviation	95% conf. interval	
Default or not rated or not disclosed	324	169.4	147.3	116.7	156.6	182.1
Poor	860	238.3	182.5	159.4	227.7	249.0
Speculative	1,617	166.0	125.0	134.7	159.4	172.6
Investment grade	1,509	106.1	93.3	67.0	102.8	109.5
Best	614	65.7	60.0	27.7	63.5	67.9

Source: Dealogic.

Table 4.9 The relative effect of macroeconomic and microeconomic factors on syndicated loan pricing

Three specifications of the model below were estimated, using standard OLS, one with macroeconomic variables only, another with microeconomic ones only, and a third with the two sets of variables combined.

$$\begin{aligned} \ln drawn = {} & \beta_0\, Intercept + \beta_1\, maturity + \beta_2\, debtgdp + \beta_3\, tdstoxgs + \beta_4\, gra + \beta_5\, restogdp + \beta_6\, st\_tdebt + \beta_7\, invgdp \\ & + \beta_8\, credgdp + \beta_9\, growth + \beta_{10}\, cpi + \beta_{11}\, impexp + \beta_{12}\, pppsh + \beta_{13}\, trade + \beta_{14}\, trsyld + \beta_{15}\, embi\_svg \\ & + \beta_{16}\, c\_share\_w + \beta_{17}\, lnsize\_l + \beta_{18}\, nbprov3 + \beta_{19}\, clubilat + \beta_{20}\, secured + \beta_{21}\, spgtr + \beta_{22}\, g\_implic \\ & + \beta_{23}\, transfer + \beta_{24}\, increase + \beta_{25}\, constrpt + \beta_{26}\, finservb + \beta_{27}\, finservn + \beta_{28}\, hightech + \beta_{29}\, infrastr \\ & + \beta_{30}\, popserv + \beta_{31}\, state + \beta_{32}\, tradind + \beta_{33}\, transpor + \beta_{34}\, cc + \beta_{35}\, cs + \beta_{36}\, gen + \beta_{37}\, oth + \beta_{38}\, prj + \beta_{39}\, pty \\ & + \beta_{40}\, tr + \varepsilon \end{aligned}$$

where:

- **ln *drawn*** = natural logarithm of drawn return, in bp
- ***maturity*** = maturity of loans, in years
- ***ln size_l*** = natural logarithm of loan size, converted into millions US dollars

Macroeconomic independent variables

Solvency indicators for the country of the borrower

- ***debtgdp*** = ratio of debt/GDP for country of the borrower, for year concerned (end-year)
- ***tdstoxgs*** = ratio of debt/service exports of goods and services for country of the borrower, for year concerned
- ***gra*** = dummy for assistance received by the country of the borrower from the IMF – use of Fund credit by operating the GRA – during the year concerned

Liquidity indicators for the country of the borrower

- ***restogdp*** = ratio of reserves/GDP for country of the borrower, for year concerned (end-year)
- ***st_tdebt*** = ratio of short-term external debt/total external debt for borrower's country, for year concerned (end-year)

Economic growth and its sustainability in the country of the borrower

- ***invgdp*** = ratio of investment/GDP for country of the borrower, for year concerned
- ***credgdp*** = ratio of bank credit/GDP for country of the borrower, for year concerned

Table 4.9 (Continued)

- ***growth*** = real GDP growth in the borrower's country, for year concerned
- ***cpi*** = inflation in the borrower's country, for year concerned

Trade and share of the borrower's country in world GDP

- ***impexp*** = ratio of imports/ exports for country of the borrower, for year concerned
- ***pppsh*** = PPP share of world GDP of the borrower's country for year concerned (end-year)
- ***trade*** = growth in world trade for year concerned

Risk-free rate of interest and proxy for overall emerging market risk

- ***trsyld*** = yield on the three-year US Treasury bill, for month concerned
- ***embi_svg*** = JP Morgan emerging market sovereign bond index, for month concerned

Borrower country's relative dependence on international syndicated loan market

- ***c_share_w*** = share of the borrower's country in world syndicated lending, for year concerned

Microeconomic independent variables

Syndicate structure

- ***nbprov3***; ***clubilat*** = dummies for deals with more than two provider banks; for club or bilateral deals

Guarantees and collateral

- ***secured*** = dummy for secured deals
- ***spgtr***, ***g_implicit*** = dummy for deals explicitly guaranteed or sponsored by a third party; dummy for implicitly guaranteed deal (e.g. borrower is a developing country subsidiary of a major US concern)

Loan transferability and size increase

- ***transfer*** = dummy for loan transferability
- ***increased*** = dummy to indicate that the original amount of the deal has been increased

Table 4.9 (*Continued*)

Sectoral and loan purpose dummies

- ***constrpty*, *finservb*, *finservn*, *hightech*, *infrastr*, *popserv*, *state*, *tradind*, *transpor*** = sectoral dummies for construction and property, financial services (banks), financial services (non-banks), high-tech industry, infrastructure, population-related services, state, traditional industry, transport. Note that the dummy for the utilities sector was excluded from the equation as the case by default as its inclusion would have overspecified the model. See Appendix 4.2 for the full list of sectors included in each broad grouping.
- ***cc*, *cs*, *gen*, *oth*, *prj*, *pty*, *tr*** = purpose dummies for corporate control, capital structure, general corporate purpose, other, project finance, property, transport finance. Note that the multipurpose dummy has been excluded from the equation as the case by default as its inclusion would have overspecified the model. See Appendix 4.3 for the full list of purposes included in each broad grouping.

Dependent variable: natural logarithm of drawn return

	Macro only		Micro only		Macro and micro	
Variable	**Coefficient**	**Standard error**	**Coefficient**	**Standard error**	**Coefficient**	**Standard error**
Maturity	0.002	(0.003)	−0.0131‡	(0.003)	0.001	(0.003)
Debt/GDP	0.0054‡	(0.001)			0.004‡	(0.001)
Debt/service exports	0.0061‡	(0.001)			0.0054‡	(0.001)
IMF assistance	0.234‡	(0.033)			0.2391‡	(0.032)
Reserves/GDP	0.0124‡	(0.002)			0.0102‡	(0.002)
Short-term/total debt	–0.001	(0.001)			−0.0001	(0.001)
Investment/GDP	−0.0038	(0.003)			−0.0043*	(0.003)
Credit/GDP	−0.0054‡	(0.001)			−0.0048‡	(0.001)
GDP growth	−0.0339‡	(0.004)			−0.0318‡	(0.004)
Inflation	0.0004†	(0.000)			0.0004†	(0.000)
Imports/exports	0.0008†	(0.000)			0.0004	(0.000)
Share of world GDP	0.0667‡	(0.007)			0.054‡	(0.007)
Growth in world trade	−0.0046	(0.005)			−0.0094*	(0.005)
Treasury yield	−0.0652‡	(0.018)			−0.0472‡	(0.017)
EMBI sovereign spread	0.0004‡	(0.000)			0.0004‡	(0.000)
Share of syndicated lending	0.3405‡	(0.056)			0.3075‡	(0.054)
Log (loan size)			−0.0688‡	(0.01)	−0.0867‡	(0.010)

Table 4.9 (Continued)

Dependent variable: natural logarithm of drawn return

Variable	Macro only		Micro only		Macro and micro	
	Coefficient	Standard error	Coefficient	Standard error	Coefficient	Standard error
Syndicate size ≥ 3			0.0021	(0.028)	0.0778‡	(0.027)
Club or bilateral deal			−0.1684‡	(0.028)	−0.1748‡	(0.026)
Secured deal			0.2779‡	(0.028)	0.1979‡	(0.028)
Sponsored or guranteed			−0.0784‡	(0.026)	−0.0843‡	(0.025)
Implicitly guaranteed			0.0299	(0.042)	−0.0583	(0.042)
Transferable			−0.0227	(0.038)	0.1127‡	(0.036)
Increased			0.2159‡	(0.037)	0.1845‡	(0.037)
Construction or property			−0.0789	(0.064)	0.1285†	(0.061)
Financial services – banks			−0.1892‡	(0.038)	−0.090†	(0.038)
Financial services – non-banks			−0.0709	(0.043)	0.1193‡	(0.043)
High-tech			−0.0828†	(0.036)	0.0083	(0.036)
Infrastructure			0.3759†	(0.179)	0.2849	(0.183)
Population-related services			0.4662‡	(0.065)	0.4058‡	(0.063)
State			−0.0834	(0.053)	0.004	(0.052)
Traditional industry			0.0605*	(0.036)	0.0699†	(0.035)
Transport			−0.1402†	(0.059)	0.0578	(0.057)
Corporate control			0.1337*	(0.072)	0.2401‡	(0.072)
Capital structure			−0.3241‡	(0.048)	−0.2402‡	(0.050)
General corporate purpose			−0.1777‡	(0.046)	−0.1547‡	(0.048)
Other purpose			−0.4653‡	(0.044)	−0.2475‡	(0.047)
Project finance			−0.1593‡	(0.048)	−0.0118	(0.051)
Property finance			−0.1366	(0.175)	0.0021	(0.160)
Transport finance			−0.6764‡	(0.070)	−0.4138‡	(0.072)
Intercept	4.4786†	−0.138	5.3585‡	(0.070)	4.9406‡	(0.149)
N	4,198		4,921		4,195	
Adjusted R^2	0.2201		0.1466		0.2971	

Notes: * = Significant at the 10% level; † = Significant at the 5% level; ‡ = Significant at the 1% level.

are higher. The dummy controlling for assistance from the IMF is also positive and significant: likewise, Eichengreen and Mody (2000) find that loans granted to countries with a history of debt rescheduling are more expensive than those to countries with no such history. Lenders seem to regard with suspicion the necessity of the borrower's country to rely on assistance from the IMF. They impose a penalty for this.[10]

The ratio of reserves/GDP is significantly and positively related to drawn returns: although sovereign borrowers normally default only in extreme circumstances, the WTP argument developed by Gersovitz (1985) seems to prevail in creditors' eyes over any possible good impression conveyed by relatively high reserves about borrower countries' finances or prospects (Edwards, 1983).[11]

The significant and negative coefficients on real GDP growth and the ratio of domestic credit/GDP are also in accordance with Eichengreen and Mody (2000): investors seem to grant a discount on loans to borrowers from countries whose fortunes may be expected to improve, presumably at least as long as the situation does not spill over into an unsustainable inflationary credit boom (the coefficient on the inflation variable is significant and positive).

Although the ratio of imports/exports of the borrower country does show up as a significantly positive determinant of loan pricing, growth in world trade does not. This may point to the fact that (1) only a limited portion of syndicated loans granted to developing countries does in fact accompany their participation in world trade, and that (2) the participation of developing countries in world trade is significantly lower than that – one would suspect – of industrialized countries.

Countries' PPP share of world GDP is significantly and positively related to the pricing of syndicated loans: lenders seem to extract a premium from relatively 'wealthier' borrowers. Financial institutions granting syndicated credits to developing country borrowers may have been exploiting their market power.[12]

The yield on the three-year US Treasury bill, the alternative, risk-free investment to extending credit to potentially riskier borrowers from developing countries, is significantly and negatively related to the pricing of syndicated credits. One interprets this as survival bias in the sense that only the best developing country borrowers are able to obtain credits in a time of higher industrialized country interest rates. The coefficient on the JP Morgan Emerging Market Sovereign Bond Index is significant and positive, suggesting that developing country borrowers are penalized by higher loan prices when there is general adverse market sentiment towards emerging markets.

Countries' share in syndicated lending to the whole world is significantly and positively related to the loan prices in this regression: investors seem to interpret high country shares as relatively high and/or more urgent financing needs for a nation and therefore demand a higher price for extending credit. This could point to the market power of lenders being exploited, or banks charging more for a higher perceived concentration of risk.

When microeconomic factors are examined on their own (middle column of Table 4.9), the coefficient on loan size is negative, as in Kleimeier and Megginson (2000), suggesting either that banks extending syndicated credits to developing country borrowers are enjoying economies of scale, or that safer borrowers are able to arrange larger loans, or both. Longer loan tenors result in lower pricing; this is unusual, but in accordance with Fons (1994). In reference to the junk-bond market, Fons argues that for good-quality borrowers, the passage of time only offers an opportunity for a deterioration of creditworthiness, while very poor credit risks that survive during the tenor of the bond are likely to experience an improvement in their creditworthiness.[13]

Bilateral loans and club deals are relatively cheaper than others, possibly reflecting more favourable conditions stemming from borrowers' relationship with their core banks. Large syndicate sizes do not appear to reduce loan pricing, indicating that competition among banks bidding for the facility does not lower the pricing of loans.[14] Loans whose amount has been increased from the original amount are relatively more expensive, possibly because banks have found their pricing attractive. The causality may also play in the opposite direction, with the interpretation then being that if the borrower needs to increase the original amount of the loan because of increased financing needs, the lenders may raise the price. In sum, the previous two arguments can point to bank market power potentially being exploited: (1) discounts appear on club and bilateral deals, rather than on facilities where a large number of lending institutions bid for the loan, and (2) despite the fact that larger loans are cheaper, the pricing of loans may no longer be competitive if their original amount has been increased.

In accordance with Kleimeier and Megginson (2000), the results also indicate that loans sponsored or explicitly guaranteed by a third party cost less, although the ones that are secured actually carry a premium, potentially because they are very risky. The latter finding is in accordance with Smith and Warner (1979) and Berger and Udell (1990) on collateral. The presence of implicit guarantees attached to syndicated credits does not seem to lower loan pricing, possibly because lenders regard them as insufficient (non-binding).

Turning to the effects of borrower sector, in the same way as Eichengreen and Mody (2000), it is found that banks enjoy cheaper pricing on their loans. Loans granted to borrowers involved in infrastructure projects carry a premium, although this is also the case in traditional industry. There is a small discount on loans to the high-tech and transport sectors. The insignificance of the sectoral dummy for the state[15] and the positive and significant coefficient in population-related services may be related to the insufficiency of state and public and population-related services provided in these countries and the unwillingness of international lenders to grant relatively better conditions on loans geared to fund such services.

Regarding the effects of loan purpose, corporate control loans are pricier than other loans, meaning that the borrower is prepared to pay a premium if a facility is urgently needed for an acquisition – this is in accordance with the rest of the academic literature. Further, it is found that loans arranged for transport finance, general corporate, project finance and capital structure purposes are cheaper than others (for a definition of these purposes, see Appendix 4.3), with transport finance loans carrying the steepest discount.

When microeconomic variables are combined with indicators of countries' macroeconomic performance (right-hand column of Table 4.9), the signs of the coefficients are mostly the same as when these two sets of independent variables are not combined (left-hand and middle columns). As already noted, though, the dummy for large syndicate sizes of three banks or more now shows up as significant and positive, indicating that large syndicate sizes do not lower loan pricing. Note that a number of purpose and sectoral dummies (high-tech industry, infrastructure, transport, project finance) are rendered insignificant in this model, possibly because indicators of macroeconomic performance for the borrowers' countries take away some of their information content, at least in the eyes of the lenders.[16]

The dummies for loan transferability and non-bank financial sector borrowers appear significant and positive in this model. One can reasonably surmise that loan transferability seems unattractive in lenders' eyes once macroeconomic conditions prevailing in the borrower's country are taken into consideration. It may be the case that loan buyers do not trust the group of potential buyers of loan tranches sold by other members of the syndicate in the event of distress. Besides, macroeconomic indicators may deteriorate lenders' perception of the riskiness of non-bank financial institutions. Monetary authorities of developing countries experiencing dire economic straits may be expected only to a limited extent to perform their lender of last resort (LOLR) functions and bail out insolvent financial institutions that are critical to the country's financial system. Appendix 4.5 (p. 70) provides direct tests for these hypotheses by estimating a loan pricing model with microeconomic variables and interaction terms between loan transferability and non-bank financial sector borrower, on the one hand, and the presence of a junk sovereign rating for the borrower's country, on the other. The model is the same as in the middle column of Table 4.9 but two cross-term dummies have been added which are, respectively, the products of the loan transferability and the non-bank financial sector borrower variables with 'junk' (dummy equal to 1 if the borrower's country has a Standard & Poor's sovereign rating worse than BBB at the time of signing). The model shows that when the loan transferability and non-bank financial sector borrower dummies are considered on their own, they command discounts. One can surmise that this is because implicit government financial safety nets exist and since loan transferability represents an option held by the lender. However, when the two dummy variables interact with the presence of a junk sovereign rating for the borrower's country at the time of signing, the coefficients become significant and positive. This confirms the behaviour of the stand-alone non-bank financial sector and transferability dummy variables in Table 4.9, which compares the effects of the macroeconomic and microeconomic variables on their own and in combination.

The LIBOR spread alone does not represent the full economic cost of the loans. Three other specifications of the main model were therefore estimated, using components of the drawn return (i.e. the LIBOR spread, drawn fees and undrawn fees separately) as dependent variables. The third model is estimated with undrawn fees, i.e. fees that are charged to the borrower as long as the facility is not drawn, such as the participation fee, as well as the facility and/or commitment fee. The results are shown in Appendix 4.4. The findings of the model using the drawn return on the left-hand side are largely confirmed when the LIBOR spread is used. As far as drawn fees are concerned, they are significantly and negatively related to loan maturity. The relationship is significant and positive between maturity and LIBOR spreads, and drawn fees contribute to reversing it when total drawn return is used as the dependent variable. Drawn fees show sensitivity to macroeconomic variables, but not to the share of the country in total syndicated borrowing. The sensitivity of drawn fees to sectoral and purpose dummies is weaker than that of the total drawn return. Undrawn fees can be thought of as contracting costs that serve to compensate the lenders for tying up regulatory capital while the facility is not drawn. The undrawn fees show little sensitivity to macroeconomic and microeconomic factors.

Conclusion

In this chapter, hedonic models were estimated to analyse the macroeconomic and microeconomic determinants of the pricing of syndicated credits granted to developing country borrowers using the risk–return framework. The following conclusions can be drawn from the findings. Indicators of countries' economic weakness (high ratios of debt/ GDP, of debt service/ exports, assistance from the IMF) are found to raise the cost of borrowing, while indicators of economic strength (high real GDP growth, high ratio of domestic credit/ GDP) lower it. This is in accordance with the previously existing academic literature. It is further found that higher reserves/GDP ratios raise the pricing of loans granted to developing country borrowers, in keeping with the willingness-to-pay (WTP) approach developed by Gersovitz (1985).

Evidence is presented that corporate control loans granted to developing country borrowers are more expensive than other loans. In accordance with Kleimeier and Megginson (2000), the results also indicate that loans sponsored or explicitly guaranteed by a third party cost less, although those that are secured actually carry a premium, potentially because they are very risky. The latter finding is in accordance with Smith and Warner (1979) and Berger and Udell (1990) on collateral. The presence of an implicit guarantee attached to syndicated credits does not lower loan pricing, possibly because lenders regard it as insufficient (non-binding).

Certain microeconomic characteristics of developing country syndicated loans thus generally affect their pricing in the expected way (i.e. risk raises pricing), albeit more weakly when macroeconomic conditions are also controlled for. In particular:

- First, as in Eichengreen and Mody (2000), banks are shown to enjoy cheaper pricing on their loans than borrowers from other sectors. However, when macroeconomic conditions prevailing in the borrowers' countries are explicitly controlled for, loans to non-bank financial institutions appear to cost more than other loans. Macroeconomic indicators may deteriorate lenders' perception of the riskiness of non-bank financial institutions. Furthermore, monetary authorities of the developing countries experiencing economic difficulties may be limited in performing their LOLR functions. This result can be related to the findings of Martinez Peria and Schmukler (2001), who note that market discipline is present among insured depositors in

selected Latin American countries, demonstrating that deposit insurance schemes are not always fully credible.
- Second, absolute values of the coefficients on microeconomic variables are often lower when macroeconomic variables are also present in the model. This suggests that loan purpose and the borrower's business sector have a weaker effect on the pricing of syndicated credits granted to developing country borrowers once indicators of macroeconomic performance of the countries concerned are controlled for.
- Third, loan transferability appears to raise loan pricing once macroeconomic conditions prevailing in the borrower's country are taken into consideration.

Banks are shown potentially to exploit their market power in syndicated lending in three respects:

- Borrowers from 'wealthier' developing countries (countries with relatively higher PPP shares of world GDP), or countries that use the world market for syndicated loans more intensely, are having to pay more for their credits. This could be a result of lender market power being exploited, lender brand name recognition, or (in the case of the share of the borrower in world syndicated lending) penalties being charged for a higher perceived concentration of risk.
- Discounts are granted to developing country borrowers on bilateral or club deals rather than on deals where a large number of lending institutions bid (compete) for the loan.
- Syndicated credits whose initial amount has been increased may not be priced competitively.

Lastly, the results reflect the relatively low participation of developing countries in world trade, or at least the low contribution of syndicated credits to supporting such participation. The weak or non-existent discounts on the pricing of loans intended to fund state-provided or transport services may not help improve the quality of such services, let alone enhance the relatively limited role of the state in some developing countries. Some of the most poorly rated developing countries further face a 'maturity trap' because they are able to obtain only short-term loans, which they can then use only to refinance existing credit lines instead of genuinely improving state services. The role of syndicated loans in financing distressed developing economies is analysed in greater detail in Chapter 8. However, before this is done, some supply-side issues of syndicated lending are analysed in Chapters 5 and 6.

Appendixes

Appendix 4.1 Conversion of the Standard & Poor's sovereign ratings into rating classes

Sub-investment grade		Investment grade	
Rating	**Rating class**	**Rating**	**Rating class**
SD NR R	Default or not rated or not disclosed	BBB BBB + A − A	Investment grade
CC CCC– CCC CCC + B− B B+	Poor	A + AA − AA AA + AAA	Best
BB− BB BB+ BBB−	Speculative		

Notes: SD = Selective default; NR = Not rated; R = Rated.

Appendix 4.2 Full list of borrower business sectors contained in each broad grouping

Construction and property

Construction/Building, Products–Commercial Building, Construction/Building Products–Maintenance, Construction/Building Products–Miscellaneous, Construction/Building Products–Residential Building, Construction/Building Products–Retail/Wholesale, Property/Real Estate, Property/Real Estate-Development, Property/Real Estate–Diversified, Property/Real Estate–Operations, Property/Real Estate–REIT, Construction/Building.

Financial services (bank)

Finance–Commercial and Savings Banks, Finance–Student Loan, Finance–Mortgages/Building Societies, Finance–Investment Bank, Finance–Credit Cards, Finance–Development Bank.

Financial services (non-bank)

Insurance, Finance–Investment Management, Insurance–Property and Casualty, Insurance–Multi-Line, Insurance–Life, Insurance–Brokers, Insurance–Accident and Health, Holding Companies–Conglomerates, Finance–Leasing Companies, Finance–Brokers and Underwriters, Finance, Holding Companies–Special Purpose Financial Vehicles, Holding Companies.

High-tech

Aerospace and Defence–Aircraft, Chemicals–Fibres, Chemicals–Diversified, Chemicals, Agribusiness–Agriculture, Aerospace and Defence–Products and Services, Aerospace and Defence, Healthcare–Genetics/Research, Chemicals–Plastic, Agribusiness, Services–Management Consulting, Telecommunications– Wireless/ Mobile, Telecommunications–Telephone, Telecommunications– Services, Telecommunications– Satellite, Electronics, Telecommunications, Computers, Services–IT, Healthcare–Products, Computers–Internet, Telecommunications–Equipment, Computers–Hardware, Healthcare–Medical/Analytical Systems, Computers–Software, Electronics–Electrical Equipment, Healthcare–Drugs/ Pharmaceuticals, Healthcare–Instruments/Surgical Supplies.

Infrastructure

Transportation–Airport, Transportation–Logistics/Distribution, Construction/ Building Products–Infrastructure.

Population services

Dining and Lodging–Hotels and Motels, Healthcare–Nursing Homes, Automobile–Repair, Automobile–Sales, Dining and Lodging, Services–Funeral and Related, Retail–Home Furnishings, Retail–Jewellery Stores, Retail–Mail Order and Direct, Dining and Lodging–Restaurants, Retail–Pharmacy, Healthcare–Professional Services/Practices, Retail–Supermarkets, Services, Retail–Department Stores, Services–Advertizing/Marketing, Retail–Miscellaneous/Diversified, Services–Legal, Services–Personnel, Services–Printing, Services–Schools/Universities,

Services–Security/Protection, Services–Travel, Telecommunications–Cable Television, Telecommunications–Radio/TV Broadcasting, Services–Accounting, Healthcare– Miscellaneous Services, Healthcare, Healthcare–Hospitals/Clinics, Retail– Specialty, Healthcare–Management Systems, Retail–Convenience Stores, Healthcare–Outpatient Care/Home Care, Leisure and Recreation, Leisure and Recreation–Film, Leisure and Recreation–Gaming, Leisure and Recreation–Services, Publishing, Publishing–Books, Publishing–Diversified, Publishing–Newspapers, Publishing–Periodicals, Retail, Retail–Apparel/Shoe, Retail–Computers and Related, Leisure and Recreation–Products.

State

Finance–Export Credit Agencies, Government–Provincial Authority, Government–Local Authority, Government–Central Bank, Government–Central Authority, Finance–Multilateral Agencies, Government.

Traditional industry

Air Conditioning and Heating, Forestry and Paper, Automobile, Automobile–Manufacturers, Automobile–Mobile Homes, Automobile–Parts, Chemicals–Fertilisers, Metal and Steel–Products, Forestry and Paper–Packaging, Forestry and Paper–Pulp and Paper, Forestry and Paper–Raw Materials, Machinery, Machinery–Electrical, Construction/Building Prods–Cement/Concrete, Machinery–General Industrial, Food and Beverage–Wholesale Items, Machinery–Material Handling, Machinery–Printing Trade, Food and Beverage–Miscellaneous, Metal and Steel–Distributors, Machinery–Farm Equipment, Mining, Mining–Excavation, Oil and Gas–Equipment and Services, Oil and Gas–Exploration and Development Onshore, Oil and Gas–Exploration and Development Offshore, Textile, Textile–Apparel Manufacturing, Textile–Home Furnishings, Textile–Mill Products, Textile–Miscellaneous, Metal and Steel, Consumer Products–Footwear, Construction/Bldg Prods–Engineering, Construction/Building Prods–Wood Products, Machinery–Machine Tools, Consumer Products–Cosmetics and Toiletries, Food and Beverage–Sugar and Refining, Consumer Products–Furniture, Consumer Products–Glass, Consumer Products–Home Improvement, Consumer Products–Miscellaneous, Consumer Products–Office Supplies, Consumer Products–Precious Metals/Jewellery, Consumer Products–Rubber, Consumer Products–Tobacco, Consumer Products–Tools, Food and Beverage, Food and Beverage–Alcoholic Beverages, Food and Beverage–Canned Foods, Food and Beverage–Confectionery, Food and Beverage–Dairy Products, Food and Beverage–Flour and Grain, Food and Beverage–Meat Products, Food and Beverage–Non–Alcoholic Beverages, Consumer Products–Soap and Cleaning Preps, Consumer Products.

Transport

Transportation, Transportation–Ship, Transportation–Road, Transportation–Airline/Aircraft, Transportation–Equipment and Leasing, Transportation–Rail.

Utilities

Utility–Water Supply, Oil and Gas, Oil and Gas–Diversified, Oil and Gas-Pipeline/Distribution, Oil and Gas-Refinery/Marketing, Utility and Power, Utility–Diversified, Utility–Electric Power, Utility–Hydroelectric Power, Utility–Nuclear Power, Utility–Waste Management.

Appendix 4.3 Full list of loan purposes contained in each broad grouping

Corporate control

Leveraged or Management Buyout (LBO/MBO), Employee stock option plan, Acquisition, Acquisition line.

Capital structure

Refinancing, Debtor in possession financing, Recapitalization, Receivable backed financing, Debt repayment, Securitization, Standby/Commercial Paper (CP) support.

General

General corporate, Private placement, Public finance, Trade financing, Working capital.

Project

Project financing.

Property

Mortgage lending, Property.

Transport

Shipping, Aircraft.

Other

Spin-off, Empty purpose code.

Multipurpose code

More than one purpose for the same loan.

Appendix 4.4 Loan pricing models with alternative dependent variables

Table 4A.1 Loan pricing model, dependent variable: natural logarithm of LIBOR spread

Variable	Macro only		Micro only		Macro and micro	
	Coefficient	Standard error	Coefficient	Standard error	Coefficient	Standard error
Maturity	0.0197‡	(0.003)	0.0012	(0.004)	0.0148‡	(0.004)
Debt/GDP	0.0038‡	(0.001)			0.0021†	(0.001)
Debt service/exports	0.0075‡	(0.001)			0.0064‡	(0.001)
IMF assistance	0.2466‡	(0.034)			0.2512‡	(0.034)
Reserves/GDP	0.0113‡	(0.003)			0.0096‡	(0.002)
Short-term/total debt	−0.0032†	(0.001)			−0.0024*	(0.001)
Investment/GDP	−0.0033	(0.003)			−0.0043	(0.003)
Credit/GDP	−0.0049‡	(0.001)			−0.0043‡	(0.001)
GDP growth	−0.036‡	(0.004)			−0.034‡	(0.004)
Inflation	0.0003	(0.002)			0.0003	(0.000)
Imports/exports	0.0006*	(0.003)			0.0004	(0.000)
Share of world GDP	0.0474‡	(0.007)			0.0353‡	(0.007)
Growth in world trade	−0.0036	(0.005)			−0.0085	(0.005)
Treasury yield	−0.0554‡	(0.019)			−0.0394†	(0.018)
EMBI sovereign spread	0.0004‡	(0.000)			0.0004‡	(0.000)
Share of syndicated lending	0.4112‡	(0.058)			0.3844‡	(0.056)
Log (loan size)			−0.0669‡	(0.011)	−0.09‡	(0.011)
Syndicate size ≳ 3			−0.0371	(0.030)	0.0461	(0.029)

Variable	Macro only		Micro only		Macro and micro	
	Coefficient	Standard error	Coefficient	Standard error	Coefficient	Standard error
Club or bilateral deal			−0.1611‡	(0.029)	−0.166‡	(0.028)
Secured deal			0.2787‡	(0.029)	0.195‡	(0.029)
Sponsored or guaranteed			−0.0848‡	(0.027)	−0.0769‡	(0.026)
Implicitly guaranteed			0.0509	(0.044)	−0.0358	(0.044)
Transferable			−0.0449	(0.040)	0.0935†	(0.038)
Increased			0.1423‡	(0.039)	0.1248‡	(0.039)
Construction or property			−0.0725	(0.068)	0.151†	(0.064)
Financial services – banks			−0.2652‡	(0.040)	−0.1525‡	(0.039)
Fin services – non-banks			−0.2015‡	(0.046)	0.0163	(0.045)
High-tech			−0.0735*	(0.038)	0.0217	(0.038)
Infrastructure			0.3867†	(0.187)	0.2978	(0.191)
Population-related services			0.5014‡	(0.068)	0.4371‡	(0.066)
State			−0.1004*	(0.056)	−0.0029	(0.054)
Traditional industry			0.0651*	(0.038)	0.0781†	(0.037)
Transport			−0.1645‡	(0.061)	0.0479	(0.060)
Corporate control			0.1841†	(0.075)	0.2881†	(0.075)
Capital structure			−0.3011‡	(0.051)	−0.2098‡	(0.053)
General corporate purpose			−0.169‡	(0.048)	−0.1347‡	(0.050)
Other purpose			−0.4459‡	(0.046)	−0.2156‡	(0.050)
Project finance			−0.1522‡	(0.051)	0.0244	(0.053)
Property finance			−0.2188	(0.183)	−0.0494	(0.168)
Transport finance			−0.669‡	(0.074)	−0.3813‡	(0.075)
Intercept	4.3773‡	(0.144)	5.222‡	(0.074)	4.9024‡	(0.156)
N	4,183		4,905		4,180	
Adjusted R^2	0.2252		0.1470		0.2978	

Notes: * = Significant at the 10% level; † = Significant at the 5% level; ‡ = Significant at the 1% level.

Table 4A.2 Loan pricing model, dependent variable: natural logarithm of drawn fees

	Macro only		Micro only		Macro and micro	
Variable	**Coefficient**	**Standard error**	**Coefficient**	**Standard error**	**Coefficient**	**Standard error**
Maturity	−0.1317‡	(0.004)	−0.1502‡	(0.005)	−0.1276‡	(0.005)
Debt/GDP	0.008‡	(0.001)			0.0083‡	(0.001)
Debt service/exports	−0.0014	(0.001)			−0.0003	(0.001)
IMF assistance	0.0767*	(0.045)			0.0681	(0.045)
Reserves/GDP	0.0015	(0.003)			0.0019	(0.003)
Short-term/total debt	0.0117‡	(0.002)			0.0106‡	(0.002)
Investment/GDP	−0.0124‡	(0.004)			−0.0118‡	(0.004)
Credit/GDP	−0.0020*	(0.001)			−0.0032‡	(0.001)
GDP growth	−0.0287‡	(0.006)			−0.0291‡	(0.005)
Inflation	0.0079‡	(0.001)			0.0063‡	(0.001)
Imports/exports	−0.0003	(0.001)			−0.0005	(0.001)
Share of world GDP	0.1081‡	(0.095)			0.0995‡	(0.009)
Growth in world trade	−0.0005	(0.007)			−0.0042	(0.007)
Treasury yield	−0.1053‡	(0.025)			−0.0932‡	(0.025)
EMBI sovereign spread	0.0004‡	(0.000)			0.0004‡	(0.000)
Share of syndicated lending	0.127	(0.078)			0.0947	(0.077)
Log (loan size)			−0.0743‡	(0.016)	−0.063‡	(0.016)
Syndicate size $\gtrsim 3$			−0.0362	(0.051)	0.0214	(0.048)
Club or bilateral deal			−0.0327	(0.042)	−0.036	(0.040)
Secured deal			0.1501‡	(0.041)	0.1309‡	(0.040)

Variable	Macro only		Micro only		Macro and micro	
	Coefficient	Standard error	Coefficient	Standard error	Coefficient	Standard error
Sponsored or guaranteed			0.0983‡	(0.037)	0.0033	(0.036)
Implicitly guaranteed			−0.0373	(0.063)	−0.0341	(0.062)
Transferable			0.1524‡	(0.051)	0.2405‡	(0.048)
Increased			0.2912‡	(0.047)	0.237‡	(0.047)
Construction or property			−0.0406	(0.090)	0.1242	(0.085)
Financial services – banks			0.2043‡	(0.054)	0.1645‡	(0.053)
Fin services – non-banks			0.3276‡	(0.060)	0.3643‡	(0.059)
High-tech			−0.1112†	(0.053)	−0.007	(0.052)
Infrastructure			0.0576	(0.330)	0.1126	(0.294)
Population-related services			0.2074†	(0.105)	0.2364†	(0.100)
State			0.052	(0.075)	0.0739	(0.073)
Traditional industry			−0.037	(0.054)	−0.0155	(0.052)
Transport			−0.0764	(0.088)	0.1316	(0.087)
Corporate control			−0.0185	(0.111)	0.1109	(0.114)
Capital structure			−0.4224‡	(0.069)	−0.2824‡	(0.070)
General corporate purpose			−0.0725	(0.066)	−0.0155	(0.067)
Other purpose			−0.3744‡	(0.063)	−0.1628†	(0.066)
Project finance			−0.0112	(0.071)	0.0435	(0.073)
Property finance			0.1583	(0.221)	0.0538	(0.199)
Transport finance			−0.2168†	(0.105)	−0.1472	(0.106)
Intercept	2.7006‡	(0.195)	3.5018‡	(0.106)	2.9818‡	(0.218)
N	2,787		3,173		2,786	
Adjusted R^2	0.3959		0.3511		0.4379	

Note: * = Significant at the 10% level; † = Significant at the 5% level; ‡ = Significant at the 1% level.

Table 4A.3 Loan pricing model, dependent variable: natural logarithm of undrawn fees

	Macro only		Micro only		Macro and micro	
Variable	**Coefficient**	**Standard error**	**Coefficient**	**Standard error**	**Coefficient**	**Standard error**
Maturity	0.0364	(0.031)	0.0217	(0.045)	0.0735*	(0.044)
Debt/GDP	0.0127	(0.009)			0.0106	(0.010)
Debt service/exports	0.0092	(0.029)			0.0043	(0.033)
IMF assistance	0.2926	(0.458)			0.3681	(0.447)
Reserves/GDP	−0.0369	(0.035)			−0.1301‡	(0.038)
Short-term/total debt	−0.0081	(0.018)			−0.0428*	(0.023)
Investment/GDP	0.0841*	(0.044)			0.0547	(0.050)
Credit/GDP	0.0168	(0.011)			0.0278*	(0.015)
GDP growth	0.001	(0.043)			−0.0191	(0.052)
Inflation	−0.0093	(0.008)			−0.0154*	(0.009)
Imports/exports	0.0084	(0.009)			0.007	(0.009)
Share of world GDP	−0.1202	(0.087)			−0.2536†	(0.098)
Growth in world trade	−0.1056*	(0.063)			−0.1484†	(0.075)
Treasury yield	0.1888	(0.199)			0.0407	(0.187)
EMBI sovereign spread	−0.0001	(0.000)			0.0002	(0.004)
Share of syndicated lending	0.0285	(0.756)			−0.3566	(0.793)
Log (loan size)			−0.0358	(0.127)	0.1458	(0.145)
Syndicate size $\gtrsim 3$			−0.0533	(0.294)	0.0116	(0.317)
Club or bilateral deal			0.0635	(0.294)	0.0065	(0.284)
Secured deal			0.327	(0.312)	0.5947*	(0.345)
Sponsored or guaranteed			0.9077†	(0.361)	0.5884	(0.363)

Variable	Macro only		Micro only		Macro and micro	
	Coefficient	Standard error	Coefficient	Standard error	Coefficient	Standard error
Implicitly guaranteed			0.4749	(0.651)	0.4542	(0.860)
Transferable			0.177	(0.344)	0.224	(0.360)
Increased			−0.2024	(0.306)	0.0631	(0.359)
Construction or property			0.0636	(0.878)	1.0121	(1.109)
Financial services – banks			0.0244	(0.595)	1.2715*	(0.689)
Fin services – non−banks			0.9269	(0.588)	2.8477‡	(0.682)
High-tech			−0.6213	(0.587)	0.9233	(0.647)
Infrastructure						
Population-related services						
State			0.4325	(0.572)	2.8404‡	(0.727)
Traditional industry			0.2363	(0.642)	1.3758*	(0.712)
Transport			0.1836	(0.733)	1.3834	(0.995)
Corporate control			2.3608†	(1.177)	1.591	(1.323)
Capital structure			0.2783	(0.406)	0.3893	(0.517)
General corporate purpose			−0.2706	(0.348)	−0.2151	(0.451)
Other purpose			−0.4159	(0.404)	−0.2383	(0.511)
Project finance			−1.3568†	(0.568)	−1.4652†	(0.633)
Property finance						
Transport finance						
Intercept	−0.8638	(2.557)	2.7167‡	(0.926)	1.8797	(2.674)
N	118		143		118	
Adjusted R^2	0.1751		0.1612		0.4016	
F-test	F(16; 101) = 2.55		F(21; 121) = 2.30		F(36; 81) = 3.18	

Notes: * = Significant at the 10% level; † = Significant at the 5% level; ‡ = Significant at the 1% level.

Appendix 4.5

Table 4A.4 Interaction between junk sovereign rating, loan transferability and non-bank financial sector, dependent variable: natural logarithm of drawn return

Variable	Coefficient	Standard error
Maturity	−0.0124‡	(0.003)
Log (loan size)	−0.0722‡	(0.010)
Syndicate size $\gtrsim 3$	0.0135	(0.028)
Club or bilateral deal	−0.1725‡	(0.028)
Secured deal	0.2698‡	(0.028)
Sponsored or guaranteed	−0.0796‡	(0.026)
Implicitly guaranteed	0.0236	(0.042)
Transferable	−0.1098†	(0.044)
Increased	0.2147‡	(0.037)
Construction or property	−0.0712	(0.064)
Financial services – banks	−0.1861‡	(0.038)
Financial services – non-banks	−0.0949†	(0.047)
High-tech	−0.0831†	(0.036)
Infrastructure	0.3908†	(0.179)
Population-related services	0.4708‡	(0.065)
State	−0.0827	(0.053)
Traditional industry	0.0595*	(0.036)
Transport	−0.1454†	(0.058)
Corporate control	0.1248*	(0.072)
Capital structure	−0.3213‡	(0.048)
General corporate purpose	−0.1747‡	(0.046)
Other purpose	−0.4541‡	(0.044)
Project finance	−0.1487‡	(0.048)
Property finance	−0.1138	(0.174)
Transport finance	−0.6618‡	(0.070)
Junk×transferable	0.3718‡	(0.085)
Junk× (fin services – non-banks)	0.1947†	(0.085)
Intercept	5.354‡	(0.070)
N	4,921	
Adjusted R^2	0.1507	
F-test	F(27; 4,893) = 33.33	

Notes: * = significant at the 10% level; † = Significant at the 5% level; ‡ = Significant at the 1% level.

5
Lender Behaviour and the Structure and Pricing of Syndicated Loans

Introduction

In 2004, international syndicated lending represented more than one-third of new international capital market financing, and is deemed to have generated more underwriting revenue in recent years than either the equity or the bond market (Madan, Sobhani and Horowitz, 1999). In particular, *leveraged lending* has been growing rapidly, as commercial borrowers have increasingly displayed a preference for leveraged borrowing over junk-bond financing (Jones, Lang and Nigro, 2000).[1] Specific tranches of such syndicated loans are purchased by non-bank investors. These non-bank tranches are in most cases equivalent to public bonds and subject to an 'arm's-length' relationship in the case of problems (Altman and Suggitt, 2000). This means that banks arranging syndicated credits, especially at the leveraged end of the credit quality spectrum, have *de facto* been acting as investment banks, collecting fees for putting together syndicates, but not always warehousing the loans themselves, leaving that activity to commercial banks or even non-banks.[2] Indeed, in the aftermath of the banks' reduced lending following the Russian crisis, BIS locational banking statistics show a marked decline after 1995 of banks' international loan portfolios relative to their total foreign claims including holdings of securities (Figure 5.1). In other words, banks have increasingly been investing in publicly marketable securities in relative terms at the expense of traditional intermediation and monitoring activities. The question therefore arises as to which market participants ultimately act as the main risk-takers in the syndicated lending market. Their level of knowledge about risk raises important

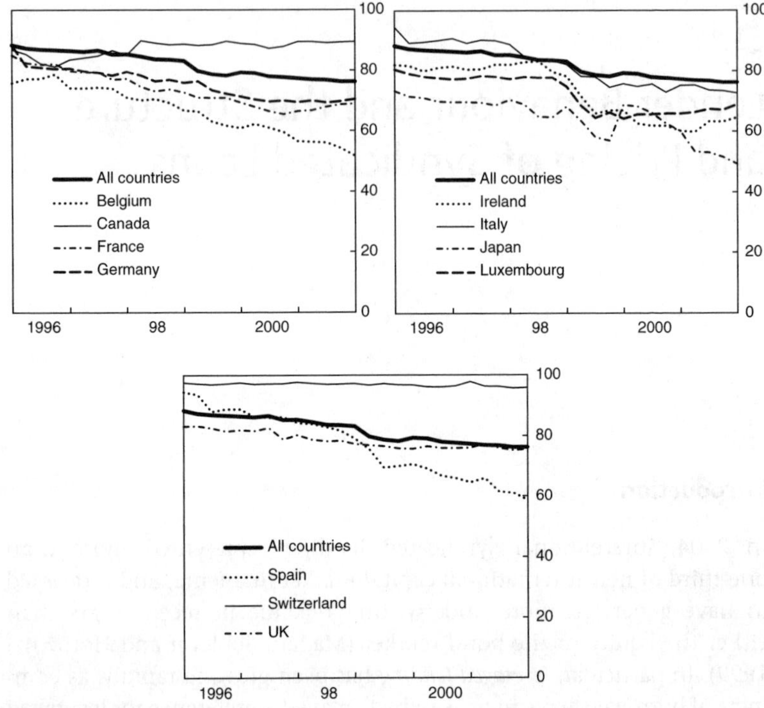

Figure 5.1 Evolution of banks' international loan portfolios relative to their total foreign claims including holdings of securities, by country of residence of the banks, 1996–2000, per cent

source: BIS locational banking statistics.

concerns for financial stability, and one aspect that this chapter aims to examine is the extent to which international syndicated lending over the 1990s contributed to risk transfer from banks with insider knowledge of borrowers to less well informed outsiders.

Based on the evolution of the international market for syndicated lending from 1993 to 2001, this chapter examines the following:

- First, the effect of *banks' capital and liquidity situation* on the pricing of syndicated credits is analysed from 1993 to 2001, controlling for a series of borrower, loan and other bank characteristics.[3] Thakor (1996) has reported that capital requirements linked solely to credit risk are shown to increase equilibrium credit rationing and lower aggregate lending. With the new Basel Accord linking capital requirements even more closely to risk, this issue has important policy implications and involves the issue of the international 'level playing field' (Chen, Mazudmar and Yan, 2000).

- Second, the extent to which capital- or liquidity-constrained banks engage in *opportunistic behaviour* by originating and subsequently selling low-quality loans about which they hold privileged information as senior banks is assessed. From this type of activity the senior banks gather syndication fees but do not hold the loans on their balance sheets (i.e. they do not warehouse the loans). The transfer of risk in the economy, in such a way or by other means – via credit derivatives, for instance – to market participants who may have limited knowledge about the risk, is a serious issue for policy-makers. Most empirical studies in this area (e.g. Dennis and Mullineaux, 2000; Jones, Lang and Nigro, 2000) have drawn on US data, mainly from regulatory returns. However, data from Dealogic Loanware, a commercial data provider, shows that 51 per cent of the funds for syndicated loans arranged for US borrowers in 2001 were provided by non-US banks who do not necessarily complete US regulatory returns; 54 per cent of those loans were arranged by non-US banks. A unique international dataset is compiled, combining the specifications of individual loan contracts such as size, maturity and pricing with lenders' balance sheet and income statement information. This allows us to undertake the first analysis of this kind at an international level.
- Third, the effects of *local knowledge* on loan characteristics are examined. As underlined by Boot and Thakor (2000), interbank and capital market competition can either leave banks to act like capital market underwriters and originators of transaction loans or make them return to their roots as relationship lending experts. The greater and more timely availability of borrower credit records, as well as the greater ease of processing them, makes it easier for banks to originate transaction loans even when they are at a great distance from the borrower (Petersen and Rajan, 2000). As an extension of the first two research questions outlined above this chapter also seeks to determine whether there is still an advantage – reflected in loan terms – for a bank to operate in the same country as the borrower or to be domiciled or headquartered in the country in whose currency the loan is made.

In keeping with the credit rationing hypothesis developed by Thakor (1996), it is shown that the pricing of loans is likely to be lower as banks participating in those loans become less liquidity-constrained or better capitalized. The relationship between bank characteristics and loan pricing generally appears to be stronger in the case of senior banks than of junior banks. This confirms the stronger pricing power of senior banks when arranging loans, while junior participants tend to act more as price-takers. Contrary to the existing literature, there appears to be evidence of senior banks offloading riskier loans to outsider junior banks with little knowledge of the borrower. They also tend to hold higher portions of loans they arrange when they are better capitalized. In addition, as information about the borrower becomes less transparent, junior banks appear to rely more on the reputation of the senior bank to determine their level of participation in the syndicate than when borrower information is widely available to the public. Finally, this chapter highlights the importance of local knowledge by senior syndicate banks about the most informationally opaque borrowers if those borrowers are to access international syndicated credit markets.

Studies in lender behaviour

This section reviews the literature dealing with (1) how banks' capital constraints are reflected in loan terms, (2) the possible occurrence of opportunistic behaviour by senior banks who arrange syndicates of banks and sell low-quality loans to junior syndicate participants and (3) whether some borrowers can still benefit from lending by syndicates of banks where senior banks have local or insider knowledge about borrowers.

Capital constraints and loan syndications

In an article exploring the effects capital regulations have on aggregate bank lending and monetary policy, Thakor (1996) demonstrates how binding capital constraints can result in *credit rationing*. According to Thakor, the most heavily regulated banks have the highest incentive to ration credit. Several authors investigate how loan syndications or loan sales can alleviate banks' financing costs under such constraints. Pennacchi (1988) argues that loan sales allow some banks to finance loans less expensively than by traditional deposit or equity issue because bank funds received via loan sales can avoid the costs associated with required reserves and capital. Other banks with substantial market power in deposit financing, but with limited loan-origination opportunities, may choose to hold marketable assets. These assets can take the form of loan shares purchased from those banks facing competitive financing.

Banks that have capital–asset ratios below or close to regulatory minima or that are liquidity constrained may not want to increase assets by adding large loans to their balance sheets and may choose, instead, to share them with other banks by selling them (Pavel and Phillis, 1987) or by syndicating them (Simons, 1993). Furthermore, Simons (1993) points out that banks are limited in the size of the loan that they can make to any one borrower (exposure to a single borrower cannot exceed 15 per cent of a bank's capital under US regulation). Participating in a syndicate thus allows small banks to acquire exposure to large borrowers which they would otherwise not be permitted to have. While loan sales or syndications from banks with higher capital requirements to banks with lower requirements may take place in some instances, one main function of loan sales and syndications is to reduce the concentration of risk.

Finally, Chen, Mazumdar and Yan (2000) explore how regulatory differences faced by banks can affect loan pricing. Following Thakor (1996), less heavily regulated banks may charge a premium on loans to borrowers which might otherwise fall victim of a credit crunch (i.e. would be denied credit by the more heavily regulated banks). In accordance with these hypotheses, Chen, Mazumdar and Yan (2000) show that Japanese banks operating in the US seem to have been extracting such premiums from US borrowers who might otherwise not have been lent to by US banks.

The interaction between senior and junior banks

Some lead banks originating syndicated credits, especially when they are capital- or liquidity-constrained, may exploit the procedure during their behaviour *vis-à-vis* junior participants in the syndicate. Flannery (1989) shows how certain bank examination procedures may induce banks to hold only certain risk classes of loans while profitably selling the rest (i.e. that portion which cannot be efficiently funded by the bank itself). Pennacchi (1988) demonstrates that the extent of banks' loan selling is limited by a moral hazard problem that arises from the diminished incentive by banks to efficiently monitor and service loans after they have been sold. But this problem can be alleviated by optimally designing the loan sales contract.

In Pennacchi's model, if the bank sells a proportion b_i of loan i, then it gets only $(1 - b_{ih})$ of the return on the loan. In other words the marginal benefit of its monitoring effort will be discounted by factor $(1 - b_{ih})$. Rational loan buyers will infer the diminished level of monitoring that this entails and hence expect a smaller state-contingent loan cash flow.

However the structure of the contract can be made incentive-compatible by giving the selling bank a disproportionate share of the loan, assuming certain loan distributions (notably that the bank's monitoring effort increases the 'fatness' of the lower tail of the distribution of the borrowing firm's value). The contract is characterized by penalizing the bank if low loan outcomes occur and rewarding the bank if high loan outcomes occur. Giving the bank a disproportionate share of the risk allows the bank to reap a disproportionate share of the gains from monitoring, enabling a greater amount of the loan to be sold while maintaining monitoring-incentive efficiency. A practical illustration of this type of contracting can be found in banks' loan sales from a pool of credit card receivables where the seller retains an equity position in the pool equal to twice the historical default level of the receivables. To summarize, a bank's ability to sell loans depends on the loan buyer's perception of the bank's incentive to monitor those loans. Besides, by designing the loan sales contract in a way that gives the bank a disproportionate share of the gains to monitoring, Pennacchi (1988) shows that a greater share of the loan can be sold – and, hence, a greater level of bank profits can be attained.

The model of Banerjee and Cadot (1996) offers another example of how lead banks may have exploited insider knowledge when arranging syndicated credits. The authors relate that large syndicates lending to Latin American debtors were organized and managed by a couple of large banks who negotiated loan contracts and sold participations to smaller banks worldwide. The same group of banks could be found organizing most of the large syndications in the late 1970s and early 1980s, and could be considered real 'insiders' of the country-risk business. Those large banks, being in close contact with officials in the borrowing-country governments, had private – albeit imperfect – information on the true level of credit risks in any particular country, and might even have got advance warning of repayment difficulties. Whether they had any incentive to pass that information on to other market participants is another matter. Such a situation makes junior participants vulnerable to a certain degree of opportunistic behaviour by the agent bank, which could withhold information about borrower or loan quality or possibly 'cherry-pick' the high-quality syndicated loans for its own portfolio. It could do so by either not syndicating them at all or retaining a larger share of them on its books in case of a syndication. The agent may even be tempted to deliberately sell bad loans. Banerjee and Cadot (1996) develop a game theory model to show that prior to the 1982 international debt crisis, it was possible for banks with heavy exposure to troubled debtors to attract rational newcomers into syndicated loans which were, with a positive probability, bailout loans. They use a model in which lenders enter the market sequentially in two rounds of lending. Between the two rounds, a shock separates borrowers into good ones and bad ones, and early entrants acquire information about individual borrower type, while late entrants only know the distribution of borrower types. The asymmetric information structure gives rise to both signalling and screening issues. The authors note that there is always a pooling perfect Bayesian equilibrium in which late entrants lend to both good and bad types, without the borrower type being exposed before final clearing at the terminal phase, at which borrower types are revealed.

Several researchers have produced empirical work in this area. Working with a 1991 sample of US loans, Simons (1993) finds that agent banks who are more capital-constrained are also more likely to retain a smaller share of syndicated loans. She demonstrates that the agent bank's capital–asset ratio is positively and significantly related to the share of syndicated loans retained on the agent's books. However, agent banks typically hold greater shares of real estate loans, which in 1991 were typically more risky than other types of loans. Therefore, there is no indication of opportunistic behaviour on agent banks' behalf in 1991 as they are found to keep a smaller share of higher-quality loans on their books.

Dennis and Mullineaux (2000) show that lead banks which have established a reputation through a large volume of repeat business (or are rated better) are able to sell off larger portions of syndicated loans. Longer maturity makes a loan more saleable, presumably because longer-term loans save on duplicative monitoring costs for the syndicate banks. Unsecured loans are as likely to be syndicated as secured ones. A loan is more likely to be syndicated as the managing agent is more heavily involved in repeat business, as the agent's credit rating improves and as the agent is a bank rather than a non-banking institution. The identity of the managing agent also influences whether a particular loan will be syndicated. Moreover, according to the authors, although banks are more likely to engage in syndication when they are capital-constrained, managing agents of syndicates hold larger proportions of information-problematic loans on their portfolios. This is in keeping with the standard view that the saleability of a debt contract depends on the scale and scope of information asymmetries, and that financial intermediaries engage in relationship-oriented finance that draws on their specialized monitoring skills.

Working with a sample of syndicated loans from the US Shared National Credit Programme, Jones, Lang and Nigro (2000) find evidence that capital constraints significantly influence the share of loans held by agent banks. The authors also show that agent share tends to be lower if the borrower is a public company and the loan is large (i.e. in cases where the agent's informational advantage is smaller). Finally, while agent banks generally hold a larger share of their low-quality loans, agent banks that have a greater portfolio concentration of lower-quality credits hold a smaller share of their loans. That is, some banks specialize in originating low-quality loans and these banks are relatively successful in finding participants for such loans.

Angbazo, Mei and Saunders (1998) conduct an empirical investigation of the relationship between credit spreads and the seniority of the bank in the syndicate that retains the largest share in the loan. They find that spreads are lowered by the presence of a *lead lender* who retains a large share of the loan (and thus bears broad monitoring responsibilities). Other members of the syndicate then supposedly perceive that the risk is lesser and hence are prepared to earn a lower margin. Conversely, if large portions of the loan are sold down to junior syndicate members, then this should entail an increase in spreads, insofar as the junior syndicate members have narrower oversight authorities and lower incentives to monitor the borrower.

Local presence effects

The potential importance of relationship lending for smaller borrowers who would otherwise be unable to access funds has been underscored by Simons (1993). She points out that, in the US, limitations on interstate banking closely link the fortunes of small and mid-sized banks to those of their local and regional economies (the McFadden Act of 1927 puts geographical restrictions on bank branching). Participating in syndicated loans can give banks a chance to lend to borrowers in regions or industries to which they might otherwise have no convenient access.

Sirmans and Benjamin (1990), Jones, Lang and Nigro (2000) and Sommerville (2001) make the case that conditions on local or relationship loans are really different from those on other types of loans. In a study of the Louisiana mortgage market between 1985 and 1987, Sirmans and Benjamin (1990) argue that the product cost functions of national, regional and local mortgage banks are different – because of differing economies of scale and scope – and that, furthermore, local banks may have comparative cost advantages in originating and servicing mortgages compared to national financial institutions, because they can process geographically specific information about the creditworthiness of borrowers and the condition of local real estate markets.[4] The authors provide empirical evidence that national lenders, on average, have higher mortgage interest rates than local lenders. Jones, Lang and Nigro (2000) argue that since it is more likely that the agent bank has special knowledge of local firms, the agent is expected to retain larger shares of loans made to such to firms. In a comparison of the behaviour of local and national banks that finance the housing market in British Columbia, Sommerville (2001) presents evidence that local lenders offer cheaper loans – and, more importantly, are more likely to extend credit to more marginal or less well-capitalized borrowers (they are better at relationship banking, while with their economies of scale or scope, larger national lenders focus on lending to bigger borrowers).

An alternative view is developed in Petersen and Rajan (2000). The authors conjecture that greater, and more timely, availability of borrower credit records, as well as the greater ease of processing these, may explain why in the US the distance between smaller lenders and firms considerably increased between 1973 and 1997. Distant firms no longer have to be observably the highest-quality credits, suggesting that a wider cross-section of firms can now obtain funding from a particular lender. These findings are interpreted as evidence that there has been substantial development of the financial sector, even in areas such as small-business lending that have not been directly influenced by the growth in public financial markets. From a policy perspective, the fact that small firms can now obtain wider access to financing suggests that the consolidation of banking services may now not raise as strong anti-trust concerns as in the past.

Degryse and Ongena (2002) summarize the various considerations involved in distance and bank lending.[5] They note that developments in technology and travel may ultimately diminish the relevance of the borrower–lender distance in European banking, and they find that proximity branching remains very important to ensure credit at accessible rates, particularly for small firms and entrepreneurs.

Data and methodology

The purpose of this chapter is to analyse the relationships between banks' characteristics participating in syndicated loans and the conditions on those loans, as reflected by the price and share of the loan retained by the senior bank. A sample of credit facilities granted by syndicates of banks between 1993 and 2001 is used. These data were extracted from the Dealogic Loanware database, a primary market information provider on individual syndicated credit facilities, in particular the characteristics of the loans (amount, maturity, currency, pricing) and the borrowers (name, nationality, business sector). A large part (80 per cent) of the facilities were contracted in US dollars. The database provides detailed information on the composition of the syndicate, the respective roles of senior participants such as arrangers, administrative agents or senior managers, as well as junior participants. In addition, information is provided on the amounts committed by each institution. The individual loan transaction data were combined with balance sheet and income statement information on syndicate participants available from the BankScope IBCA database. This unique dataset, linking international loan transaction data with individual bank characteristics,[6] allows us to perform an analysis of supply-side issues in syndicated lending for the first time.

To allow for time effects, the relationship is examined between loan specifications and bank characteristics for the year of the transactions as well as for the year before. In order to explore the relationship between the characteristics of each participant and loan specifications, each transaction is introduced into the regression as many times as there were banks participating in the loan at various levels of seniority, provided that balance sheet and profit and loss statement information was available about these banks. Each observation then corresponds to the same transaction but to the various characteristics of each participating bank.[7]

The effects of specific lender characteristics on loan pricing are first explored. Junior and senior banks are analysed separately through separate model specifications. The indicators of capital, liquidity and loan-quality constraints facing senior banks are similar to those used by Simons (1993), Dennis and Mullineaux (2000) and Jones, Lang and Nigro (2000):

- *Capital and liquidity constraints*, reflected, respectively, by the ratio of equity[8] capital/assets, the ratio of liquid assets/deposits and money market funding
- *Specialization in investment banking versus commercial banking-type activities*, gauged by the ratio of interest income/total assets. Low values of this ratio reflect investment banking-type behaviour while high values would mean more traditional intermediation activity

- *Quality of the loan portfolio*, proxied by the ratio of loan loss reserves/loans gross of reserves (discussed, for instance, in Berger, 1995)
- *Efficiency*, measured by the cost-to-income ratio (personnel costs divided by net income) and by size (natural logarithm of total assets is used as a proxy for scale efficiency, as suggested, among others, by Berger and Humphrey, 1997)
- *Profitability*, reflected by the return on assets.

Attention is then turned to the effects of reputation and business mix, plus liquidity, capital and portfolio-quality constraints faced by senior banks on the share of the loan they retain on their books.[9] Bank regulations require participants to be responsible for their own credit analysis and evaluation (Jones, Lang and Nigro, 2000). In principle, though, junior banks often rely on the reputation of the senior bank with a view to determining their decision to join the syndicate or their level of commitment, hence the inclusion of a proxy for the reputation of the senior bank into the model. This was calculated as the position in the arranger league tables, i.e. the percentage of total loans arranged by the bank concerned within total loans arranged worldwide, for the year under consideration. Higher percentages correspond to a better reputation, and vice versa.

Finally, location of lender versus borrower issues are discussed. In most of the models, the following loan characteristics are controlled for:

- size
- maturity
- guarantees (implicit or explicit; implicit, for instance, in the sense that the borrower is the subsidiary of another major concern, without the parent providing a formal written guarantee)
- collateral (dummy variable for secured loans)
- loan purpose (purpose dummy for corporate control loans)
- Standard & Poor's rating of borrower at time of signing.

In order to reduce the effects of heteroscedasticity resulting from the inclusion of banks with different asset sizes in the sample, least squares with robust standard errors are used as the estimation methodology in all the models where loan pricing is the dependent variable. As far as the share of the loan retained by senior banks is concerned, it has a lower boundary of zero and an upper limit of 100 per cent. As such, it is estimated using a censored Tobit model with a lower limit of zero and an upper limit of 100.

Table 5.1 Number of observations, by borrower Standard & Poor's rating and year, 1993–2001

Rating	1993	1994	1995	1996	1997	1998	1999	2000	2001	Unknown	Total
Default	10	10	9	9	11	14	26	28	10	3	**130**
CC to BB–	228	260	223	198	285	295	450	464	222	69	**2,694**
BB to BBB–	90	172	156	177	212	215	253	336	195	34	**1,840**
BBB to A	175	273	290	242	314	318	377	451	318	57	**2,815**
A + to AAA	79	164	164	180	134	127	155	172	90	23	**1,288**
Total	582	879	842	806	956	969	1,261	1,451	835	186	**8,767**

Source: Dealogic.

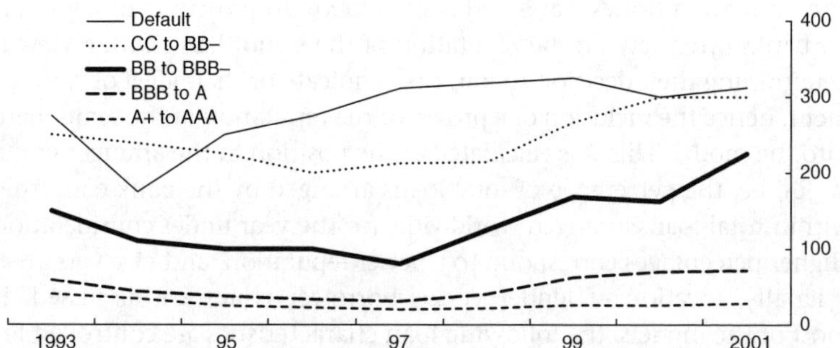

Figure 5.2 Evolution of loan pricing, LIBOR spread + fees, medians, by rating class, basis points, 1993–2001

Results and discussion

The sample comprises 8,767 loan facilities granted to industrialized and developing country borrowers between 1993 and 2001. Table 5.1 shows the distribution of the observations by year and rating and Figure 5.2 the evolution of loan pricing by year and rating. Worse ratings appear to have systematically faced higher loan prices than better ratings – this is the straightforward result that one would expect – and loan prices have generally been edging up for all borrower ratings since 1997–98, which roughly reflects the adverse influence of the Asian crisis.

Senior versus junior bank characteristics and loan pricing

To investigate banks' characteristics that influence pricing, tests are now performed regarding the effects of quantitative variables such as capital and liquidity constraints, specialization (investment-versus commercial banking-type activities reflected by the relative weight of loans in the total activities of the bank), quality of the loan portfolio, efficiency and profitability. The variables used are explained and detailed in Table 5.2. The effect of senior and junior banks' characteristics on the pricing of loans is tested separately to allow for the hypothesis that the former may have more power in determining loan pricing during the arrangement phase and also earn more fees for putting together the facility, while the latter may act more as pure risk holders and price-takers. The lender characteristics considered mainly use changes in various

Table 5.2 The effect of bank characteristics on loan pricing

The following equation was estimated separately for junior and senior banks, (OLS with robust standard errors):

$$\textbf{lndrawn} = \beta_0\, \textbf{\textit{Intercept}} + \beta_1\, \textbf{\textit{lnsize}} + \beta_2\, \textbf{\textit{maturity}} + \beta_3\, \textbf{\textit{g\_implic}} + \beta_4\, \textbf{\textit{g\_explic}} + \beta_5\, \textbf{\textit{secured}} + \beta_6\, \textbf{\textit{cc}} + \beta_7\, \textbf{\textit{spn}} + \beta_8\, \textbf{\textit{deqas}} + \beta_9\, \textbf{\textit{dllr}} + \beta_{10}\, \textbf{\textit{dci}} + \beta_{11}\, \textbf{\textit{dliq}} + \beta_{12}\, \textbf{\textit{lnasts}} + \beta_{13}\, \textbf{\textit{dROA}} + \beta_{14}\, \textbf{\textit{diita}} + \varepsilon$$

Dependent variable: loan price

- **ln*drawn*** = natural logarithm of drawn return (spread over LIBOR plus fees)

Control variables – loan and borrower characteristics

- **ln*size*** = natural logarithm of facility size converted to US dollars
- ***maturity*** = maturity of loans, in years
- ***g_implic, g_explic*** = dummies for implicitly or explicitly guaranteed loan (implicitly in the sense for instance that the borrower is the subsidiary of another major firm)
- ***secured*** = dummy for secured loan
- ***cc*** = dummy for corporate control loans (LBO, acquisition)
- ***spn*** = numerical conversion of borrower's Standard & Poor's rating (onto a scale of 0 to 28, with 0 standing for default and 28 for AAA)

Senior or junior bank characteristics

- ***deqas*** = change between year preceding the signature of the loan (t_{-1}) and the year of signature (t_0) in the ratio of equity to assets, in per cent (proxy for capital constraints)
- ***dllr*** = change between (t_{-1}) and (t_0) in the ratio of loan loss reserves loans/ gross of reserves, in per cent (loan quality)
- ***dci*** = change between (t_{-1}) and (t_0) in personnel costs divided by net income, per cent (efficiency)

Continued

Table 5.2 Continued

- ***dliq*** = change between (t_{-1}) and (t_0) in the ratio of liquid assets/deposits and money market funding, per cent (proxy for liquidity constraint)
- **ln*asts*** = natural logarithm of total assets (in USD) (measure of size, proxy for scale efficiencies) at the end of the year when the loan was signed
- ***dROA*** = change between (t_{-1}) and (t_0) in return on assets, per cent (measure of profitability)
- ***diita*** = change between (t_{-1}) and (t_0) in ratio of interest income to total assets, per cent (measures the weight of lending in bank's total activities)
- **ε** is a random disturbance

Dependent variable is *ln_drawn*. Type of estimation: OLS with robust standard errors. (natural logarithm of drawn return = LIBOR pricing + fees). Variables are defined above.

Variable	**Senior bank characteristics**		**Junior bank characteristics**	
lnsize	−0.1198‡	(0.005)	−0.1113‡	(0.005)
maturity	0.0100‡	(0.002)	0.0119‡	(0.002)
g_implic	−0.0505†	(0.025)	−0.0080	(0.022)
g_explic	−0.0903‡	(0.030)	−0.2346‡	(0.030)
secured	0.4218‡	(0.014)	0.3853‡	(0.013)
cc	0.2461‡	(0.014)	0.2140‡	(0.016)
spn	−0.1372‡	(0.002)	−0.1500‡	(0.002)
deqas	−0.0102‡	(0.003)	−0.0012	(0.002)
dllr	0.0815‡	(0.008)	0.1168‡	(0.011)
dci	0.0002‡	(0.000)	−0.0003†	(0.000)
dliq	−0.0006	(0.001)	−0.0022‡	(0.001)
lnasts	0.0374‡	(0.005)	−0.0086†	(0.004)
dROA	0.2312‡	(0.017)	0.0393‡	(0.015)
diita	0.0032	(0.007)	−0.0166‡	(0.006)
intercept	6.8533‡	(0.104)	7.9614‡	(0.082)
N	15,934		16,391	
R^2	0.60		0.64	

Notes: Robust standard errors in parentheses.
† Significant at the 5% level; ‡ Significant at the 1% level.

ratios between the year when the loan was signed and the year before. This approach – also used by Kishan and Opiela (2000) – has the advantages of reducing (1) the effects of individual banks in the sample, and (2) the autocorrelation between the residuals, and particularly between the different explanatory variables.

The results of the model estimation are shown in Table 5.2. All coefficients on loan and borrower characteristics except the one on the dummy for the presence of an implicit guarantee are strongly significant and have the expected signs. Loan pricing decreases with the amount loaned, reflecting economies of scale in originating the loan or the ability of less risky borrowers to arrange larger loans or both. It also increases with maturity, translating the premium demanded by the lender for incurring risk for a longer period of time. Explicit guarantees significantly reduce loan pricing, while secured loans are more expensive than non-secured ones, potentially because they are very risky.[10] There is a premium on corporate control loans possibly because of the borrower's urgent need to arrange funding quickly and discreetly. The numerical conversion of the borrower's Standard & Poor's rating is strongly and negatively associated with loan pricing, with better-rated borrowers incurring lower loan prices and vice versa.

Capital and liquidity constraints and loan pricing

Evidence is found that an improvement in senior lenders' capitalization and an improvement in junior lenders' liquidity position are significantly and negatively associated with loan pricing (the coefficient on the *deqas* variable is significant and negative in the case of senior banks, the coefficient on the *dliq* variable is significant and negative in the case of junior banks). One may surmise that as their capital or liquidity cushions become larger, banks can accept lower prices for the same risk. Equity seems to play a more important role for senior banks, while the focus is more on the liquidity position for junior banks.

Loan loss reserves and loan pricing

A deterioration in the quality of the lenders' portfolio (reflected by an increase in the ratio of loan loss reserves/loans) is positively and significantly associated with loan pricing, reflecting a demand for more compensation to take on additional risk. This effect is weaker in the case of senior banks than in the case of junior banks, as the latter are more likely to be the ultimate risk-takers.

Bank specialization and loan pricing

A relationship between changes in the ratio of interest income to total assets (*diita*) is found only for junior banks, not for senior banks. Participating in syndicated loans has a greater impact on junior banks' size of traditional intermediation activities relative to their total assets. When senior banks put together syndicates of lenders, this is more of an investment banking-type activity.

Bank efficiency, size, profitability and loan pricing

Bank size (*lnasts*) as well as increases in the personnel costs to net income ratio (*dci*) are strongly and positively associated with more expensive loans in the case of senior banks, but not in the case of junior banks (indeed for junior banks the relationship is negative[11]). The positive relationship between senior bank size and loan pricing may reflect large senior banks' market power in setting loan prices. In the case of junior and senior banks, higher loan prices significantly boost return on assets (ROA), although this effect is stronger in the case of senior banks.

To summarize, in accordance with the credit rationing hypothesis developed by Thakor (1996) it has been shown that the pricing of loans where less capital- or liquidity-constrained banks are present is likely to be lower than that of other loans. With regard to the relationship between bank characteristics and loan pricing, it is found that in several instances this relationship (capitalization, size, return on assets), is stronger (in significance, magnitude, or both) in the case of senior banks than of junior banks. This confirms the stronger pricing power of senior banks when arranging loans, while junior participants tend to act more as price-takers.

The effect of capital and liquidity constraints on the share of loans retained by senior banks

Senior banks who arrange the loan may know more about the borrower and may or may not pass that information on to junior participants (Banerjee and Cadot, 1996). The focus is now on the proportion of loans arranged by senior banks that subsequently gets passed on to junior banks in the syndicate. If liquidity- or capital-constrained senior banks sell off relatively larger shares of the loans that they arrange to junior participants than senior banks without such liquidity or capital constraints, then this can constitute evidence of opportunistic behaviour on senior banks' behalf. Likewise, opportunistic behaviour can take place if the proportion of loans sold down by senior banks to junior participants is higher in the case of low-quality loans than in the case of high-quality loans.

A model is constructed to express the share of the loan retained by senior banks as a function of loan and senior bank characteristics. In the case where there are several senior banks for the same facility, the same facility is entered as many times into the model as there are senior banks, each time with the retained share and bank characteristics specific to the relevant senior arranger bank. To allow for time effects, senior bank characteristics for the year of the transactions as well as the year before are analysed separately.

The loan characteristics include the borrower's rating or the natural logarithm of the drawn return – LIBOR spread plus fees – maturity, guarantees and a dummy for corporate control loans (acquisitions, LBO). The senior bank characteristics comprise liquidity and capital constraints (equity/assets, ratio of liquid assets/deposits and money market funding), loan portfolio quality (ratio of loan loss reserves/loans), specialization (interest income as a share of total assets) and reputation (position in the Loanware arranger league table expressed as the percentage of total worldwide loans arranged by the senior bank concerned for the year under study). Loan size was not included in the model as it is highly correlated with senior banks' league table position.

Four specifications of the model were tested, where the various senior bank characteristics were entered (contemporaneous with the year in which the loan was signed or lagged by one year) for rated and unrated borrowers. A censored Tobit estimation with an upper limit of 100 and a lower limit of zero was used on the share of the loan retained by senior banks. The results are displayed in Table 5.3.

The coefficient on the natural logarithm of the drawn return, a proxy for the riskiness of the loan, is negative and significant in all specifications of the model. Senior banks are more likely to keep smaller portions of riskier loans on their books, which appears to suggest that there is evidence of possibly opportunistic behaviour on their behalf – in the sense that they would offload risky loans to outsider junior banks. These results contradict Simons (1993) and Jones, Lang and Nigro (2000), who find that agent banks tend to hold a larger share of their riskier or low-quality loans. Loan maturity significantly reduces the share of the facility kept by the senior bank in two specifications, as it is necessary to call in more banks when the length of the exposure increases. Senior banks tend to hold larger portions of explicitly guaranteed or secured loans, and smaller shares of corporate control loans or implicitly guaranteed facilities.

A relatively high position of the senior bank in the Loanware arranger league table – a proxy for 'reputation' as an arranger of loans – tends to lower the share of the loan it retains on its books – this is reflected by the negative and significant coefficients on the *league* variable – in the case of unrated borrowers. It has no effect when the borrower has a rating. In other words, when information about the borrower is more opaque, junior banks joining the syndicate seem to rely on the reputation of the arranger bank when deciding which portion of the loan to purchase,

Table 5.3 The effect of bank characteristics on the share of the loan retained by the senior bank

Specifications of the following model were estimated (censored Tobit with lower limit of zero and upper limit of 100), with contemporaneous and lagged values of the senior banks' characteristics.

$$\text{sen\_shr} = \beta_0\, \textbf{\textit{Intercept}} + \beta_1\, \textbf{ln}\textbf{\textit{drawn}} + \beta_2\, \textbf{\textit{maturity}} + \beta_3\, \textbf{\textit{g\_implic}} + \beta_4\, \textbf{\textit{g\_explic}} + \beta_5\, \textbf{\textit{secured}} + \beta_6\, \textbf{\textit{cc}} + \beta_7\, \textbf{\textit{league}} + \beta_8\, \textbf{\textit{eqas}} + \beta_9\, \textbf{\textit{llr}} + \beta_{10}\, \textbf{\textit{liq}} + \beta_{11}\, \textbf{\textit{iita}} + \boldsymbol{\varepsilon}$$

- ***sen_shr*** = share of the loan retained by the senior bank (mandated arranger, non-mandated arranger, arranger, co-arranger, agent, co-agent, facility/syndication agent)
- **ln*drawn*** = natural logarithm of drawn return (spread over LIBOR plus fees)
- ***maturity*** = maturity of loan, in years
- ***g_implic, g_explic*** = dummies for implicitly or explicitly guaranteed loan (implicitly for instance in the sense that borrower is the subsidiary of another major concern)
- ***secured*** = dummy for secured loan
- ***cc*** = dummy for corporate control loans (LBO, acquisition)
- ***league*** = senior bank's share in syndicated loans arranged worldwide (obtained from Dealogic Loanware arranger league tables)
- ***eqas*** = ratio of equity/assets of the senior bank, in per cent
- ***llr*** = senior bank's ratio of loan loss reserves to loans gross of reserves, in per cent
- ***liq*** = ratio of liquid assets to deposits and money market funding of senior bank, in per cent
- ***iita*** = ratio of interest income to total assets of senior bank, in per cent
- $\boldsymbol{\varepsilon}$ is a random disturbance

Table 5.3 *(Continued)*

Dependent variable is *sen_shr* (share of loan retained by senior bank).

Variable	Senior bank characteristics contemporaneous with year of signature of the loan				Senior bank characteristics lagged by one year			
	Unrated borrowers		Rated borrowers		Unrated borrowers		Rated borrowers	
lndrawn	−0.9509†	(0.415)	−0.6762†	(0.265)	−1.9151‡	(0.435)	−0.9175‡	(0.266)
maturity	−1.5239‡	(0.092)	−0.0079	(0.092)	−1.3676‡	(0.099)	0.0046	(0.093)
g_implic	−9.2339‡	(1.315)	−2.5049†	(1.04)	−9.1766‡	(1.411)	−2.5609†	(1.045)
g_explic	10.0932‡	(0.952)	6.0661‡	(1.044)	10.4547‡	(1.029)	6.6388‡	(1.056)
secured	20.9627‡	(0.695)	5.3231‡	(0.587)	20.6555‡	(0.737)	3.7221‡	(0.597)
cc	−12.5005‡	(0.889)	−0.8085	(0.669)	−12.1934‡	(0.935)	0.2450	(0.668)
league	−1.0894‡	(0.166)	−0.0815	(0.096)	−0.7461‡	(0.166)	−0.0297	(0.095)
eqas	0.0434	(0.065)	0.0821	(0.053)	0.1571†	(0.071)	0.2278‡	(0.052)
llr	−0.0273	(0.174)	0.8559‡	(0.136)	0.1148	(0.185)	0.8763‡	(0.150)
liq	−0.1204‡	(0.013)	−0.0442‡	(0.008)	−0.1328‡	(0.015)	−0.0483‡	(0.009)
iita	0.8923‡	(0.198)	−0.2176	(0.161)	1.0447‡	(0.244)	−0.1112	(0.185)
intercept	−14.7632‡	(2.349)	−9.8872‡	(1.562)	−14.0989‡	(2.661)	−10.0220‡	(1.728)
N	41,809		20,747		36,495		18,302	

Notes: Robust standard errors in parentheses.

† Significant at the 5% level; ‡ Significant at the 1% level.

and allow the senior bank to keep a lower share of the loan on its books when that reputation is relatively high, although the monitoring incentives for the arranger bank resulting from that lower share may then also be lower. This result can be related to Dennis and Mullineaux (2000), who find a positive relationship between the degree of syndication and the senior bank's reputation.

The senior bank's equity position lagged by one year is significantly related to the share of the loan retained. Senior banks with a larger capital cushion appear to retain larger portions of loans that they syndicate. A lower-quality loan portfolio – reflected by a higher ratio of loan loss reserves to loans – raises the share of the loan retained only in the case of rated borrowers. As the quality of their loan portfolio deteriorates, senior banks prefer to take on more exposure to rated borrowers and less to unrated ones, relying more on publicly available information about borrowers. Rather surprisingly, the share of the loans retained by senior banks appears to decrease with their liquidity ratio. Finally, there is evidence (reflected by the significantly positive coefficient on the *iita* ratio in two model specifications) that higher loan shares retained reflect a behaviour on senior banks' behalf that is closer to the activities of a commercial bank (whose interest income is higher when related to its total assets) rather than to the behaviour of an investment bank.

To complement the analysis, Table 5.4 shows the results of subsequent tests of the effect of loan shares retained by senior banks in the syndicate on loan pricing. This share is negatively and significantly related to loan pricing. The results confirm the findings of Angbazo, Mei and Saunders (1998), who present evidence that junior banks participating in highly leveraged transaction loans accept that they will earn a smaller margin when a lead lender is present who retains a large share of the loan (and thus bears broad monitoring responsibilities).

Evidence is provided in the following section that senior banks' private knowledge about the borrower can also result in more favourable pricing. The advantage of these relationship lending effects is strongest in the case of unrated borrowers located in developing countries being lent to by banks operating in these countries.

Local presence and currency effects

It was demonstrated above how 'insider' knowledge of the borrower by the senior bank influences loan pricing and the syndicate structure. In this section whether closer knowledge of the borrower by the senior bank can be turned to the borrower's advantage is investigated. The sample of loans is partitioned into rated and unrated borrowers from

Table 5.4 The effect on loan pricing of the share of the loan retained by the senior bank

The following OLS regression was run with robust standard errors:

$$\ln drawn = \beta_0 \, Intercept + \beta_1 \, sen\_shr + \beta_2 \, maturity + \beta_3 \, g\_implic + \beta_4 \, g\_explic + \beta_5 \, secured + \beta_6 \, cc + \beta_7 \, spn + \varepsilon$$

Variable names are as in Table 5.3.

Variable	Coefficient	
sen_shr	−0.0006*	(0.004)
maturity	0.0068‡	(0.021)
g_implic	−0.0332	(0.023)
g_explic	−0.1112‡	(0.029)
secured	0.4073‡	(0.013)
cc	0.2346‡	(0.013)
spn	−0.1598‡	(0.002)
intercept	7.3363‡	(0.045)
N	20,910	
R2	0.56	

Note: Robust standard errors in parentheses.

* Significant at the 10% level; † Significant at the 5% level; ‡ Significant at the 1% level.

industrialized and developing countries and a distinction is made between facilities where the senior arranger bank resides in the same country as the borrower and those where this is not the case. Calculating confidence intervals for loan pricing (shown in Table 5.5), it is found that unrated borrowers located in developing countries incur significantly lower loan prices when the senior bank is operating in the country concerned. Presumably this is because, operating in the country of the borrower, it is easier for the senior bank to exploit the relationship with the borrower and to take advantage of local knowledge in the jurisdictional, legal and cultural domains. This pricing advantage materializes only in the case of non-rated borrowers from developing countries where the exclusive knowledge of the senior bank about the borrower might be highest. In fact, rated and non-rated borrowers from industrialized countries pay significantly higher spreads on facilities where the senior bank is located in the same country as the borrower. One may surmise that exclusive knowledge about the borrower is lesser in

Table 5.5 Loan pricing and senior bank versus borrower country

Borrower country and borrower rating	Senior bank versus borrower nationality	*N*	Mean	Median	95% conf. interval	
Emerging, rated	≠	456	146.4	106.3	134.8	158.0
	=	137	158.2	115.0	135.8	180.6
Emerging, not rated	≠	2,996	158.6	121.3	154.0	163.2
	=	1,325	122.3	84.0	116.4	128.1
Industrialized, rated	≠	632	116.0	70.0	107.4	124.6
	=	7,248	139.9	100.0	137.3	142.6
Industrialized, not rated	≠	2,706	161.5	144.4	157.0	166.0
	=	19,539	186.4	180.8	184.9	188.0

Notes: Loan pricing is LIBOR spread + fees.

Source: Dealogic.

industrialized countries and there may be more price savings to be achieved from economies of scale for lending syndicates by operating out of a big financial centre such as London, New York or Tokyo than out of the same country as the borrower.

In Tables 5.6 and 5.7 loan pricing confidence intervals are calculated for various subsamples of syndicated loan facilities classified according to whether the facility of the currency is the home currency of the borrower or of the senior bank. It is interesting to notice that there are no rated borrowers from developing countries who borrow in their domestic currency. The existence of a rating seems to systematically warrant borrowing in a hard currency.[12] Rated and unrated industrialized country borrowers are having to pay significantly more for loans expressed in their domestic currency. For all subsamples, facilities where the currency is the home currency of the senior bank cost significantly more than others, possibly reflecting a premium charged by the senior bank for potentially better knowledge about raising funds or inviting underwriters in its own currency than a foreign currency.

Looking at the extent to which the advent of the euro may have contributed to these currency- or residence-related pricing advantages, Tables 5.8 and 5.9 show that the median pricing of facilities granted to industrialized country borrowers where the borrower or the senior bank are from the European Monetary Union (EMU) area is lower than on facilities where they are not. The pricing advantage seems to have widened for facilities arranged by banks from the EMU area after 1999 in the case of rated borrowers.

In order to quantify these results, loan pricing is regressed on a number of loan and borrower characteristics listed in Table 5.10, together with dummies to signal 'proximity' effects. Tests are also performed for the effects of the borrower or the senior bank residing in the EMU area before or after 1 January 1999 – i.e. the date of the introduction of the single currency. Several specifications of the model are estimated, for industrialized and developing country borrowers, rated and not rated. A numeric conversion of the actual Standard & Poor's rating at signing is used in the case of rated borrowers, and purpose and sector dummies in the case of unrated borrowers.

The findings on the residence of the borrower versus that of the senior bank confirm the descriptive statistics presented earlier. Local knowledge about the borrower by the senior bank – reflected by identical residencies – can lower the pricing of loans in the case of unrated borrowers where monitoring information is not widely available to the public, the coefficient on the *bbnat* dummy is strongly significant and

Table 5.6 Loan pricing and currency of facility versus borrower's home currency

Borrower country and borrower rating	Currency of facility versus borrower's home currency	*N*	Mean	Median	95% conf. interval	
Emerging, rated	≠	608	149.1	109.4	138.9	159.2
	=	0	–	–	–	–
Emerging, not rated	≠	4,335	149.0	106.5	145.2	152.7
	=	52	168.8	128.4	127.8	209.8
Industrialized, rated	≠	566	70.5	41.6	64.1	76.9
	=	7,593	144.6	110.0	142.0	147.2
Industrialized, not rated	≠	2,038	110.4	70.0	105.8	115.0
	=	21,698	192.7	200.0	191.3	194.2

Note: Loan pricing is LIBOR spread + fees.

Source: Dealogic.

Table 5.7 Loan pricing and currency of facility versus senior bank's home currency

Borrower country and borrower rating	Currency of facility versus senior bank's home currency	*N*	Mean	Median	95% conf. interval	
Emerging, rated	≠	275	124.2	90.0	111.2	137.2
	=	318	170.6	136.3	155.4	185.8
Emerging, not rated	≠	2,995	127.0	93.3	123.1	130.8
	=	1,326	193.8	157.1	185.9	201.6
Industrialized, rated	≠	650	110.2	62.1	102.0	118.4
	=	7,230	140.5	100.0	137.8	143.2
Industrialized, not rated	≠	2,923	152.0	125.0	147.7	156.3
	=	19,322	188.2	187.5	186.6	189.7

Note: Loan pricing is LIBOR spread + fees.

Source: Dealogic.

Table 5.8 Median loan pricing and borrower residence for industrialized country borrowers, 1993–2001

	Rated borrowers		Unrated borrowers	
Year	**Not from EMU**	**From EMU**	**Not from EMU**	**From EMU**
1993	150.0	58.5	175.0	62.5
1994	75.0	42.5	150.0	50.3
1995	62.5	21.0	175.0	34.5
1996	62.2	19.5	175.0	30.0
1997	62.5	16.0	175.0	42.5
1998	75.0	24.7	187.5	75.0
1999	140.6	51.5	201.3	120.0
2000	150.0	65.0	200.0	145.0
2001	137.5	73.8	200.0	152.5

Note: Loan pricing is LIBOR spread + fees.

Source: Dealogic.

Table 5.9 Median loan pricing and senior bank residence for industrialized country borrowers, 1993–2001

	Rated borrowers		Unrated borrowers	
Year	**Senior bank not from EMU area**	**Senior bank from EMU area**	**Senior bank not from EMU area**	**Senior bank from EMU area**
1993	150.0	94.2	156.3	150.0
1994	75.0	86.3	150.0	125.0
1995	68.8	42.5	175.0	67.5
1996	62.5	44.3	175.0	99.5
1997	75.0	37.5	175.0	105.0
1998	75.0	68.8	200.0	127.5
1999	162.5	77.5	215.0	175.0
2000	175.0	122.5	215.0	162.5
2001	200.0	90.0	212.5	155.7

Note: Loan pricing is LIBOR spread + fees.

Source: Dealogic.

negative for specifications D, E and F (Table 5.10). The absolute value of the coefficient is highest in the case of specification D (non-rated borrowers from developing countries). This can be explained by relationship effects and the importance of local knowledge, notably in the legal

Table 5.10 Local presence and the advent of the euro

The following regression was estimated with robust standard errors

$$\ln drawn = \beta_0\, Intercept + \beta_1 \ln size + \beta_2\, maturity + \beta_3\, secured + \beta_4\, g\_implic + \beta_5\, g\_explic + \beta_6\, spn + \beta_7\, cc + \beta_8\, cs + \beta_9\, gen + \beta_{10}\, prj + \beta_{11}\, pty + \beta_{12}\, tr + \beta_{13}\, multi + \beta_{14}\, constrpty + \beta_{15}\, finservb + \beta_{16}\, finservn + \beta_{17}\, high\text{-}tech + \beta_{18}\, util + \beta_{19}\, infrastruct + \beta_{20}\, popserv + \beta_{21}\, state + \beta_{22}\, tradind + \beta_{23}\, transport + \beta_{24}\, bbnat + \beta_{25}\, brcur + \beta_{26}\, bkcur + \beta_{27}\, bremu98 + \beta_{28}\, bremu99 + \beta_{29}\, bkemu98 + \beta_{30}\, bkemu99 + \varepsilon$$

- ***lndrawn*** = natural logarithm of drawn return (spread over LIBOR plus fees)
- **ln*size*** = natural logarithm of facility size converted to US dollars
- ***maturity*** = maturity of loans, in years
- ***g_implic, g_explic*** = dummies for implicitly or explicitly guaranteed loan (implicitly in the sense, for instance, that the borrower is another major firm's subsidiary)
- ***secured*** = dummy for secured loan
- ***spn*** = numerical conversion of borrower's Standard & Poor's rating (on a scale of 0 to 28, with 0 standing for default and 28 for AAA)
- ***cc, cs, gen, prj, pty, tr, multi*** = purpose dummies for corporate control, capital structure, general corporate purpose, project finance, property, transport finance, multi-purpose; the residual dummy for other purposes not listed here has been excluded as it would have overspecified the model
- ***constrpty, finservb, finservn, high-tech, util, infrastruct, popserv, state, tradind, transport*** = sectoral dummies for construction and property, financial services (banks), financial services (non-banks), high-tech industry, utilities, infrastructure, population-related services, state, traditional industry, transport; the residual dummy for other sectors not specified here was excluded from the equation as the case by default as its inclusion would have overspecified the model
- ***bbnat*** = dummy to indicate that the residence of at least one senior bank in the syndicate is identical to that of the borrower
- ***brcur*** = dummy to indicate that the currency of the facility is identical to the home currency of the borrower
- ***bkcur*** = dummy to indicate that the currency of the facility is identical to the home currency of a senior bank
- ***bremu98, bremu99*** = dummies to indicate that the borrower is resident of a country of the EMU/euro zone (respectively before/after 1 January 1999)
- ***bkemu98, bkemu99*** = dummies to indicate that a senior bank is resident of a country of the EMU/euro zone (respectively before/after 1 January 1999)
- ε is a random disturbance

The sectoral dummies are correlated with borrower ratings so they were included into separate specifications of the model:

Specification A	rated borrowers from emerging economies
Specifications B, C	rated borrowers from industrialized countries

Specification D	unrated borrowers from emerging economies
Specifications E, F	unrated borrowers from industrialized countries

Dependent variable is *ln_drawn* (natural logarithm of drawn return = LIBOR pricing + fees). Variables are defined above. OLS estimation with robust standard errors.

Variable	Specification A		Specification B		Specification C		Specification D		Specification E		Specification F	
lnsize	−0.0186	(0.041)	−0.1080‡	(0.007)	−0.1121‡	(0.007)	−0.0816‡	(0.011)	−0.1746‡	(0.003)	−0.1734‡	(0.003)
maturity	−0.0331†	(0.014)	0.0139‡	(0.003)	0.0201‡	(0.003)	−0.0097‡	(0.004)	0.0079‡	(0.002)	0.0135‡	(0.002)
secured	0.3605‡	(0.121)	0.3382‡	(0.018)	0.3313‡	(0.018)	0.2489‡	(0.026)	0.3046‡	(0.009)	0.2919‡	(0.009)
g_implic	0.4674‡	(0.116)	−0.0929‡	(0.036)	−0.1087‡	(0.035)	−0.0402	(0.043)	−0.101‡	(0.028)	−0.0966‡	(0.028)
g_explic	−0.0851	(0.130)	−0.1047‡	(0.036)	−0.0744†	(0.035)	−0.1515‡	(0.025)	−0.2395‡	(0.023)	−0.2035‡	(0.022)
spn	−0.1092‡	(0.016)	−0.1331‡	(0.003)	−0.1316‡	(0.003)						
cc	0.0703	(0.174)	0.2844‡	(0.023)	0.2778‡	(0.023)	0.6082‡	(0.067)	0.3334‡	(0.014)	0.3073‡	(0.014)
cs							0.1449‡	(0.040)	−0.0382‡	(0.013)	−0.0461‡	(0.012)
gen							0.3126‡	(0.034)	−0.0062	(0.016)	−0.0280*	(0.016)
prj							0.3139‡	(0.035)	−0.0144	(0.034)	−0.0143	(0.035)
pty							0.3492†	(0.142)	0.0757	(0.048)	0.0384	(0.046)
tr							−0.1092†	(0.052)	−0.1284†	(0.059)	−0.0957	(0.059)
multi							0.4348‡	(0.047)	0.1099‡	(0.014)	0.0744‡	(0.014)
constrpty							−0.4902‡	(0.155)	−0.0233	(0.060)	−0.0265	(0.060)
finservb							−0.6762‡	(0.152)	−0.6106‡	(0.065)	−0.5484‡	(0.065)
finservn							−0.5288‡	(0.150)	−0.3455‡	(0.061)	−0.3485‡	(0.061)
high tech							−0.5408‡	(0.150)	−0.1049*	(0.059)	−0.0967	(0.060)
util							−0.5277‡	(0.152)	−0.4006‡	(0.061)	−0.3972‡	(0.062)
infrastruct							−0.1733	(0.241)	−0.1163	(0.074)	−0.1282*	(0.074)
popserv							−0.1292	(0.161)	−0.0411	(0.059)	−0.0312	(0.060)
state							−0.5512‡	(0.161)	−1.1095‡	(0.112)	−0.9574‡	(0.114)

Continued

Table 5.10 Continued

Variable	Specification A		Specification B		Specification C		Specification D		Specification E		Specification F	
trandind							−0.4528‡	(0.150)	−0.1214†	(0.059)	−0.1093*	(0.060)
transport							−0.6037‡	(0.154)	−0.2147‡	(0.063)	−0.1953‡	(0.063)
bbnat	0.1468†	(0.066)	0.0517	(0.044)	0.0088	(0.042)	−0.155‡	(0.023)	−0.0431*	(0.026)	−0.0798‡	(0.025)
brcur			0.1897‡	(0.032)	0.1292‡	(0.033)	−0.0432	(0.092)	0.4058‡	(0.021)	0.2799‡	(0.021)
bkcur	0.1608†	(0.067)	0.1026‡	(0.043)	0.1152‡	(0.040)	0.286‡	(0.027)	0.1931‡	(0.026)	0.1898‡	(0.025)
bremu98					−0.3097‡	(0.052)					−0.5488‡	(0.029)
bkemu98					−0.1495‡	(0.021)					−0.1016‡	(0.016)
bremu99					−0.1822*	(0.106)					−0.3459‡	(0.034)
bkemu99					0.2417‡	(0.020)					0.1709‡	(0.016)
intercept	6.7139†	(0.329)	7.1336†	(0.071)	7.1892†	(0.702)	5.3686‡	(0.152)	5.1479‡	(0.064)	5.3026‡	(0.065)
N	574		7,869		7,869		4,239		22,200		22,200	
R^2	0.2615		0.6153		0.6285		0.1921		0.3335		0.3595	

Note: Robust standard errors in parentheses.

* Significant at the 10% level; † Significant at the 5% level; ‡ Significant at the 1% level.

domain, being potentially most acute in the case of non-rated borrowers from developing countries. The *bbnat* dummy does not lower loan pricing in the case of rated borrowers; in fact in specification A it even increases loan pricing – a premium can be demanded on loans where the senior bank has to operate out of the country of residence of the borrower when the latter is rated. Since in such a set-up public monitoring information is widely supplied about such borrowers to the general public by rating agencies, the senior bank that has established a presence may be considered a waste of resources, resulting in higher loan pricing.

In a study of the US national mortgage market in Louisiana, Sirmans and Benjamin (1990) present evidence that national lenders, on average, have higher mortgage interest rates than local lenders. The results on an international level are similar to the authors' findings but nuance it to the extent that the pricing gain is greatest when the amount of private information about the borrower held by the senior bank is potentially highest, i.e. in the case of unrated developing country borrowers. Petersen and Rajan (2000) argue that distance does not matter any more in bank lending, at least in the US domestic market, because of the greater ease with which large national banks can access and process information about borrowers located in distant rural areas. This research provides evidence contradicting this theory for international loans, highlighting the fact that the presence of senior banks operating out of the country of residence of the borrower can lower the pricing of syndicated credits, especially in the case of the most informationally opaque borrowers such as unrated ones from developing countries. Thus the access of such borrowers to the international syndicated credit markets seems an important policy concern.

Loan facilities expressed in the home currency of the borrower are significantly more expensive than others in all cases except for rated developing country borrowers (the variable was not included in specification A, as they tend to borrow exclusively in hard currency) and for unrated developing country borrowers.

Industrialized country borrowers from the EMU area have been able to arrange relatively cheaper loans than others, but the effect seems to have been greater before the advent of the euro than after (reflected by higher absolute values of the coefficients on *bremu98* than on *bremu99*[13]). Curiously, while facilities arranged by senior banks from the EMU area are relatively cheaper than others before the introduction of the euro, they carry a premium after its introduction.

Conclusion

In an area where the literature is sparse, this chapter is the first to analyse the effects of individual bank characteristics, including non-US banks, on the structure and pricing of syndicated loans at an international level, combining individual loan transaction data from Dealogic Loanware and information on individual lenders (the supply side) from the BankScope IBCA database.

In accordance with the credit rationing hypothesis developed by Thakor (1996) it was shown that syndicated loan prices are lower when less capital- or liquidity-constrained banks participate in the syndication process. The relationship between bank characteristics and loan pricing, appears stronger (in significance, magnitude, or both) in the case of senior banks than of junior banks. This confirms the stronger pricing power of senior banks when arranging loans, while junior participants tend to act more as price-takers. In the context of the New Basel Capital Accord which ties capital requirements more tightly than before to credit risk, the use of such market power of senior banks to set loan prices is all the more important because this chapter also shows that as information about borrowers becomes less transparent, junior banks rely more on the reputation of the senior bank to determine their level of financial commitment within the syndicate. In other words, risk in the economy may end up with outsiders – even non-banks such as insurance companies, pension funds, CDO arbitrage funds or non-financial corporations – whose knowledge about the borrower may be limited, especially if, as shown, the senior banks tend to pass on higher shares of riskier loans to junior banks. This research shows that the remuneration of junior participants is influenced by the characteristics of the senior banks who arrange the credit facilities. The effect of this on loan pricing is at least as great as that of the true riskiness of the borrower.

However, one factor should assuage policy-makers' concerns about possible risk exposures associated with the price-setting practices of large senior banks arranging syndicated credits. This chapter highlights the importance of local knowledge by senior syndicate banks about the most informationally opaque borrowers if those borrowers are to access international syndicated credit markets.

What motivates banks to participate in loan syndications, despite the risks of this nature that are involved? Chapter 6 provides some answers.

6
Banks' and Financial Institutions' Decision to Participate in Loan Syndications

Introduction

This chapter sheds light on the *supply-side determinants* of syndicated loan markets, by presenting evidence on the rationale behind the decision of banks to participate in loan syndications. First, the features of loan syndications that attract banks towards this market are discussed. Secondly, the chapter investigates the impact of banks' structural characteristics on the decision to participate in loan syndications. For this purpose, a study undertaken by Altunbaş, Gadanecz and Kara (2005), which specifically focuses on the factors as to why banks engage or do not engage in syndicated lending, stands as a focal part of the chapter. Poorly performing banks – which have lower capital adequacy ratios, lower net interest margins and lower returns on equity and higher cost/income ratios – are found to be more involved on average in loan syndications. Policy-makers should perhaps focus more on monitoring the concentration of credit risk associated with syndicated loans held on the books of poorly performing banks.

Why do banks engage in syndicated lending?

The rationale for banks to engage in syndicated lending is associated with several advantages of this financial tool relative to the alternatives, such as individual relationship lending or bond underwriting. The identification of the common factors that motivate banks to participate in syndications allows us to make forecasts regarding the availability of funds on the market for syndicated loans where lending decisions are essentially group decisions. The more common factors identified, the more such decisions are likely to be subject to herding phenomena or group reactions to signals. Banks' motivations for participating in syndicated loans can be outlined as follows:

- Syndicated loans are easy to *renegotiate, liquidate and cancel*
- They constitute an effective tool for *portfolio diversification*
- They help meet *capital adequacy regulations*
- They can satisfy demand for *large loans*
- They are a product that can be offered to compete with *bonds*
- They provide *advertisement* through publicity and arranger reputation
- They provide a means of *investing excess liquidity*
- They generate extra *fee income*
- They help reduce *loan origination* costs and favour *bank specialization.*

We shall consider each of these in turn.

Easier to renegotiate, liquidate and cancel when compared to bonds

The literature regards bond issuance as an alternative source of funding to syndicated loans. As shown in Edwards (1986) and Eichengreen and Mody (2000), banks are better able to renegotiate defaulted syndicated loans than bonds. Hale (2005) underlines the fact that a syndicated loan is easier to liquidate, to renegotiate and to cancel because, unlike the bond market where a large number of uncoordinated investors are present, the syndicated loan market has a number of relatively well-coordinated lenders.

An effective tool for portfolio diversification

Dennis and Mullineaux (2001) consider loan syndications as a cost-effective way to diversify banks' loan portfolios. Syndicated loans give the opportunity to lenders to spread risks more widely to other countries and industries without using their own sources of monitoring or needing to understand the dynamics of a new economic environment.

Overcoming capital adequacy regulations

According to Simons (1993), banks are limited in the size of the loan they can grant to any one borrower (exposure to a single borrower cannot exceed 15 per cent of a bank's capital under US regulation). Participating in a syndicate thus allows small banks to acquire exposure to large borrowers which they would not be permitted to have otherwise (i.e. if they were lending bilaterally).

A tool to be part of large loans

The funding requirements of sovereign and corporate borrowers can be too large for a single bank to meet, either because of the bank's size or regulations on lending. Syndicated lending provides the opportunity for banks to take risk exposures to such borrowers without supplying the full amount needed.

An alternative to bond issuance

Syndicated lending also allows banks to compete more effectively with disintermediated debt markets (Jones, Lang and Nigro, 2001). They have limited the erosion of the banks' role as financial intermediaries which has stemmed from borrowers' increasing reliance on disintermediated finance, such as commercial paper or bonds rather than bank loans.

Advertisement through publicity and arranger reputation

Syndicated loans are only types of loan that are publicly announced. Participation provides welcome publicity for lenders, especially at a senior level, who may be able to obtain valuable ancillary business from the borrower (Howcroft and Solomon, 1985).

Excess liquidity positions

Eichengreen and Mody (2000) argue that syndicated loans are a good means of investing banks' excess liquidity. For example, according to Tucker, Madura and Chiang (1991) in the 1970s, international banks had an abundant supply of loanable funds because of recycled petrodollars; with this liquidity lending to LDC governments was a viable alternative.

Extra fee income

Banks may choose to arrange syndicated loans because of the attractive fees that can be earned through the syndication process. The syndicated loan market enables agent banks to leverage their expertise in loan origination and fee collection for structuring, distributing and servicing the larger credits (Jones, Lang and Nigro, 2001).

Reduce loan issuance costs and increase specialization

Syndicated loans allow banks to acquire risk exposures and thereby reduce selection and monitoring costs, since these activities are undertaken by the agent and arranger banks. Further, the separation of loan origination and warehousing activities enables lead banks to acquire deeper specialization and higher cost efficiency in the loan-origination business, and small banks to get exposure to borrowers, countries or sectors which regulatory constraints would not allow them to acquire.

While the previous studies mentioned have examined the factors that determine whether banks lend one-to-one or share the risk by syndicating the loan, Altunbaş, Gadanecz and Kara (2005) take a different approach from the established literature, by focusing on the structural factors of banks and financial institutions that entice them to form syndicates and extend money at a given set of terms to borrowers. The financial characteristics of the banks are related to the decision to participate in loan syndications, and this analysis is performed for banks of various types (commercial banks, investment banks, etc.) and nationalities.

Construction of data sample

To construct the dataset used for the analysis in this chapter, data was first extracted from the Dealogic Loanware database on 65,654 individual loan transactions, covering a period of nine years from 1993 to 2001. This corresponds to a yearly amount of $500 bn in 1993 and more than $2 trn in 2000. Entities resident in the US have been the recipients of more than 60 per cent of total funds between 1993 and 2001, with the rest going to borrowers in other industrialized countries to a large extent, mainly continental Europe, Canada and the UK. Emerging country borrowers represent around 10 per cent of loans every year.

The Dealogic Loanware database provides information on a large number of features of the individual loan facilities such as loan amount, maturity, collateral, borrower identity, nationality and business sector. Information is also available on the identity of the banks participating in the syndicate. This information is used to identify a total of 1,258 banks which are known to have participated in syndications in various years during the 1993–2001 period. These correspond to institutions from industrialized countries[1] whose balance sheet and profit and loss statement information was available in the BankScope IBCA database, and for which the micro-level syndicated loan data could be linked with the banks' financial characteristics.

In addition, for every year, banks which did not participate in loan syndications during that particular year are selected from the BankScope IBCA database, taking into consideration the weights of each country and each specialization area (i.e. investment banks, commercial banks, etc.) in the participating banks' data. This yielded a total population of 3,756 non-participating banks and an overall total of 5,014 banks in the sample.

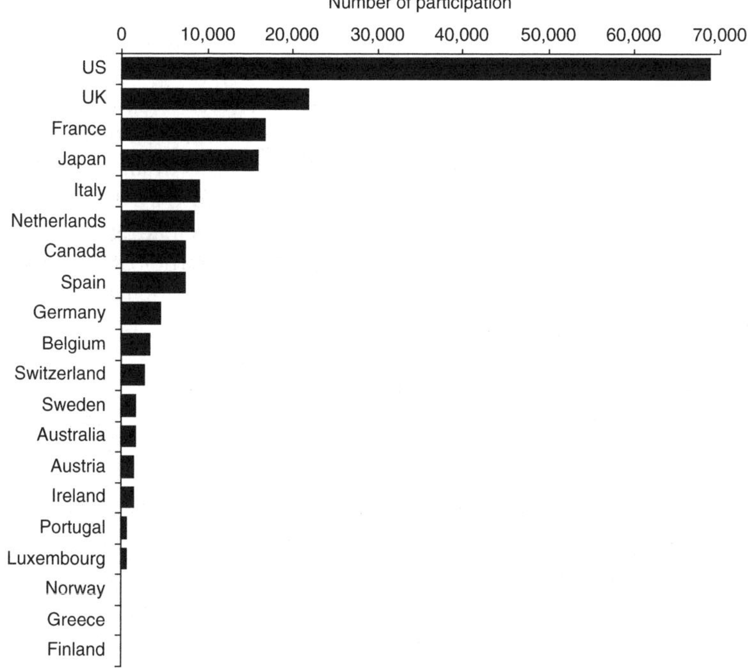

Figure 6.1 Number of participations in syndicated loans, by origin of the lender, 1993–2001

Source: Dealogic.

The number of participations according to origin of lender is presented in Figure 6.1.[2] Not surprisingly, US banks had been the foremost participants on the syndicated loans between 1993 and 2001 with over 68,000 participations followed by over 21,000 participations for UK banks. In continental Europe, French, Italian and Dutch banks were frequent participants in loan syndications, while Japanese banks stood fourth in the overall ranking. The top five syndicated providers – the US, the UK, Japanese, French and Italian banks – represent 76 per cent of the total fund suppliers to this market between 1993 and 2001.

Trends in financial indicators of participant and non-participant banks

For each type of bank, the evolution of financial characteristics is presented for the 1993–2001 period, and banks that have participated in loan syndications in a given year are compared to those that have not.

Commercial banks

The asset size – and share of loans in total assets – of commercial banks active in the syndicated loan markets has been higher than that of the non-participant banks for most of the years between 1993 and 2001 (Figure 6.2, 6.3). More significantly, participating commercial banks have had higher equity ratios than non-participating banks in all years. The loan loss provisions relative to loans, as well as the return on assets, have been comparable for the participating and non-participating commercial banks for the period under study (Figure 6.3, 6.4). Participating banks' return on equity has been lower than that of non-participating ones (Figure 6.4).

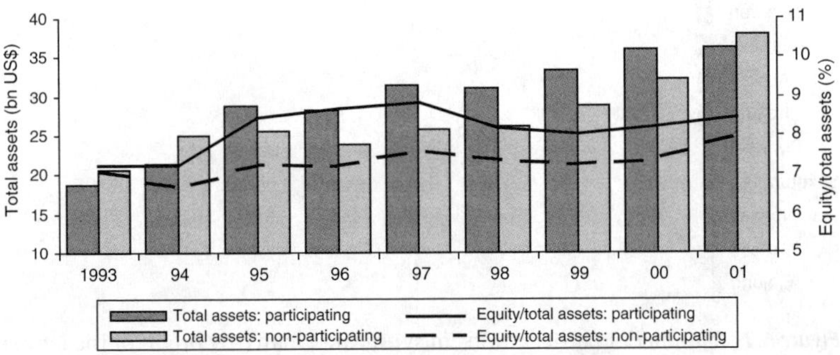

Figure 6.2 Total assets and equity/total assets ratio of participating and non-participating commercial banks, 1993–2001
Source: Thomson Analytics Bankscope.

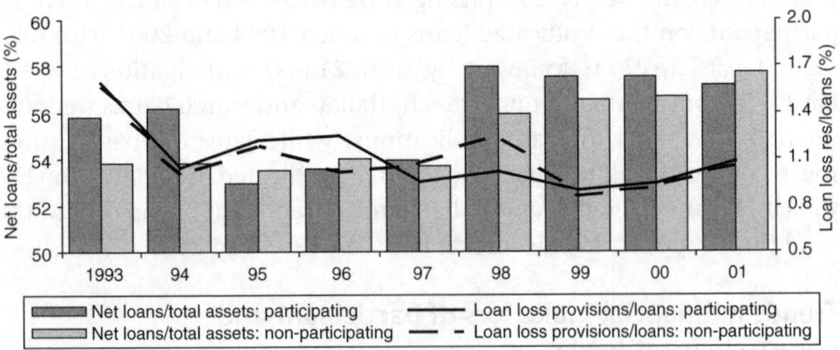

Figure 6.3 Net loans/total assets and loan loss provisions/total loans ratios of participating and non-participating commercial banks, 1993–2001
Source: Thomson Analytics Bankscope.

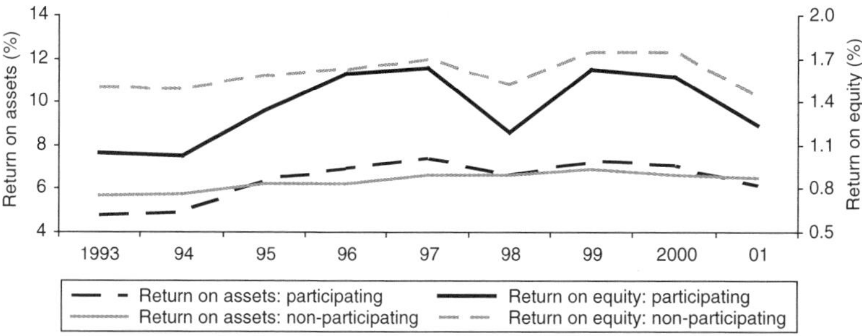

Figure 6.4 Return on equity and return on asset ratios of participating and non-participating commercial banks, 1993–2001

Source: Thomson Analytics Bankscope.

One noteworthy year is 1998, in which the participating banks' profitability declined sharply in comparison to their non-participating peers. Perhaps this significant decrease can be related to the South-East Asian financial crisis, in which banks had high credit exposures through syndicated loans.

Investment banks

The characteristics of participating and non-participating investment banks are very different for the period under study, except for 1993 and 1994. Participating investment banks have had much larger asset sizes than non-participating ones (Figure 6.5). This might indicate that the larger investment banks dominate the market as suppliers by using their brand names, experience and global distribution channels. Participating investment banks are also operating with much higher equity/total assets and loans/assets ratios when compared to non-participating banks (Figures 6.5, 6.6). Profit performance indicators of participating investment banks are higher than non-participating ones in the specified period (Figure 6.7).

Savings, mortgage and real estate banks

The asset size and equity/assets ratios, as well as the profitability (measured by return on assets and return on equity) of participating savings, mortgage and real estate banks are larger than those of non-participating ones for the whole period under study except 2001 (Figures 6.8, 6.10). Their total loans/total asset ratio is relatively higher, albeit decreasing over time (Figure 6.9).

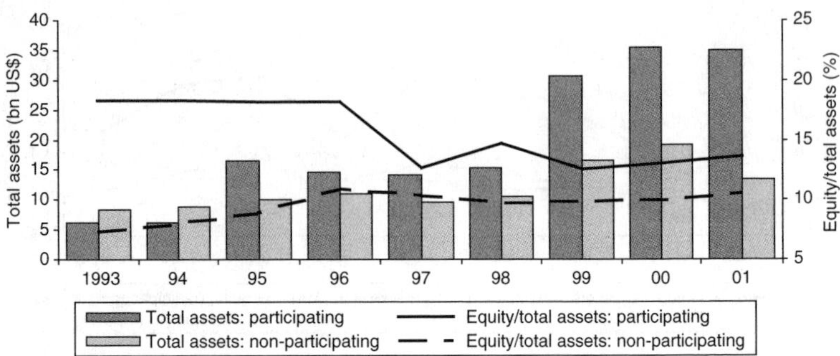

Figure 6.5 Total assets and equity/total assets ratio of participating and non-participating investment banks, 1993–2001

Source: Thomson Analytics Bankscope.

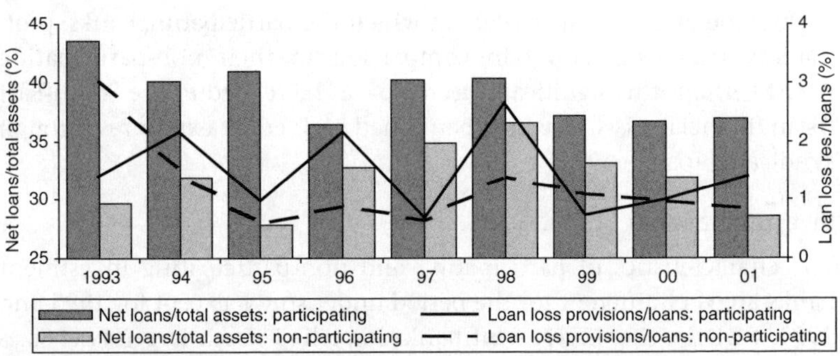

Figure 6.6 Net loans/total assets and loan loss provisions/total loans ratios of participating and non-participating investment banks, 1993–2001

Source: Thomson Analytics Bankscope.

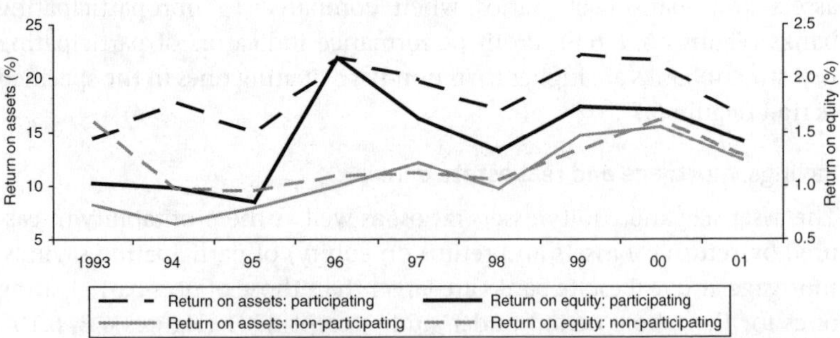

Figure 6.7 Return on equity and return on asset ratios of participating and non-participating investment banks, 1993–2001

Source: Thomson Analytics Bankscope.

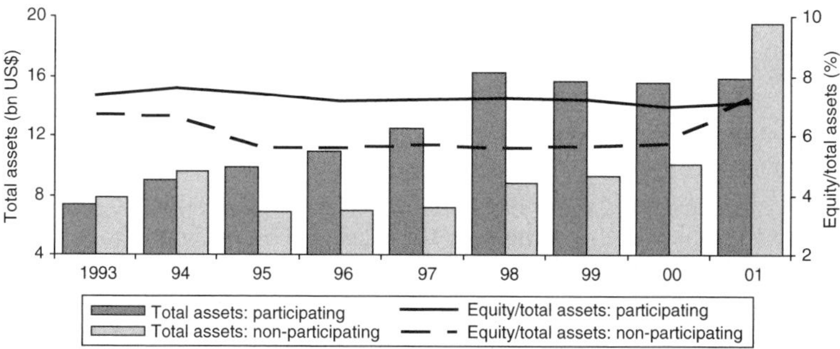

Figure 6.8 Total assets and equity/total assets ratio of participating and non-participating savings, mortgage and real estate banks, 1993–2001

Source: Thomson Analytics Bankscope.

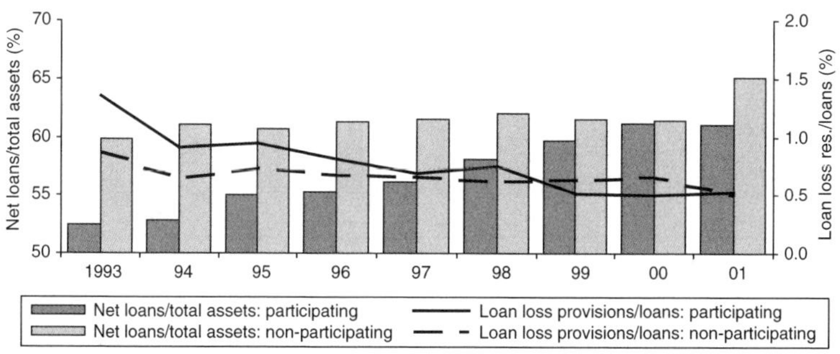

Figure 6.9 Net loans/total assets and loan loss provisions/total loans ratios of participating and non-participating savings, mortgage and real estate banks, 1993–2001

Source: Thomson Analytics Bankscope.

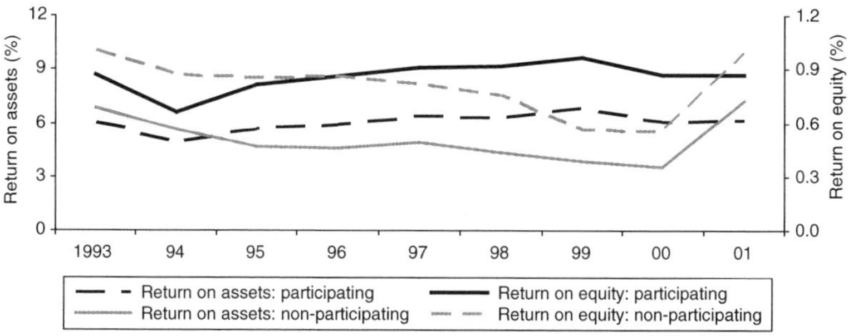

Figure 6.10 Return on equity and return on asset ratios of participating and non-participating savings, mortgage and real estate banks, 1993–2001

Source: Thomson Analytics Bankscope.

Specialized credit institutions

Such institutions active in syndicated loan markets on average have smaller balance sheets in comparison to their non-active peers, which gradually enlarged their size during this period (Figure 6.11). A remarkable fact is the trend in the equity/total assets ratio of the participating banks. They steadily strengthened their capital adequacy measures, while the opposite happened for their peers. The net loans/total assets ratios and loan loss provisions/total loans ratios of participating and non-participating institutions do not show significant differences for the period (Figure 6.12), while the profitability of participating banks surpasses that of non-participants (Figure 6.13).

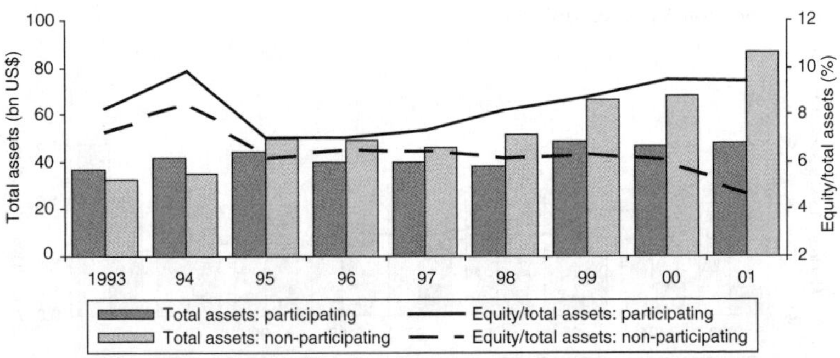

Figure 6.11 Total assets and equity/total assets ratio of participating and non-participating specialized credit institutions, 1993–2001
Source: Thomson Analytics Bankscope.

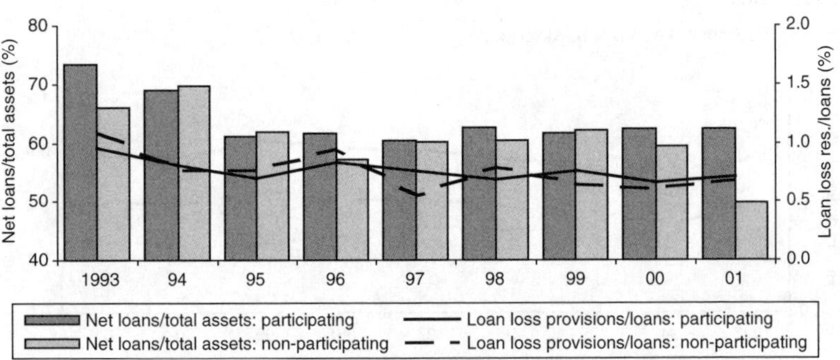

Figure 6.12 Net loans to total assets and loan loss provisions total loans ratios of participating and non-participating specialized credit institutions, 1993–2001
Source: Thomson Analytics Bankscope.

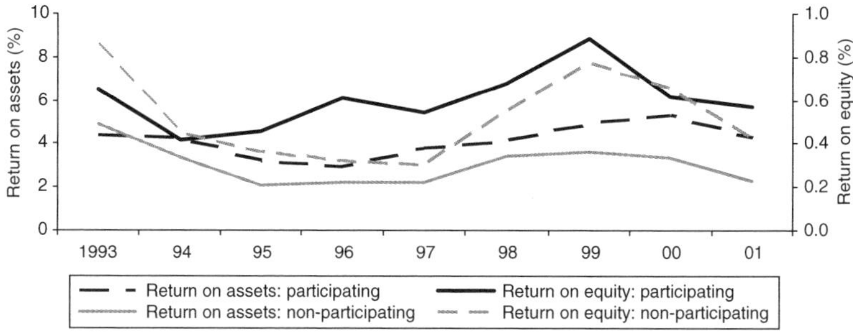

Figure 6.13 Return on equity and return on asset ratios of participating and non-participating specialized credit institutions, 1993–2001

Source: Thomson Analytics Bankscope.

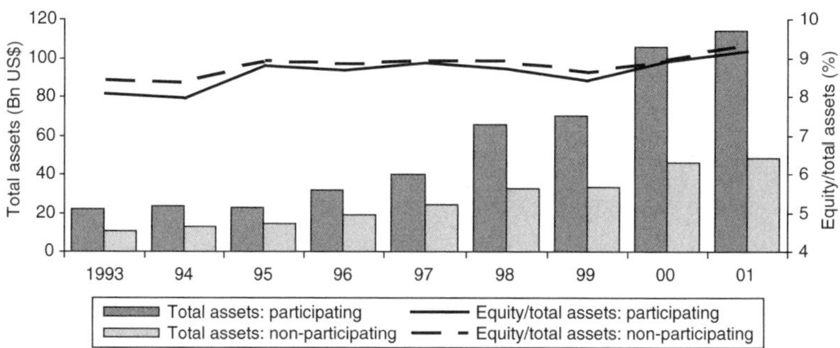

Figure 6.14 Total assets and equity/total assets ratio of participating and non-participating banking corporations, 1993–2001

Source: Thomson Analytics Bankscope.

Banking corporations

Such corporations participating and not participating in loan syndications are relatively similar as regards their financial structure and profitability. The most significant difference between the two subgroups pertains to the average size of the balance sheet (Figure 6.14) where participating bank holding corporations have been about twice the size of non-participating bank holding corporations, proportionally working with the same level of equity. Furthermore, the loan portfolios (Figure 6.15) of participating holding corporations have been larger than those of non-participants. The loan loss ratios show a similar evolution over time

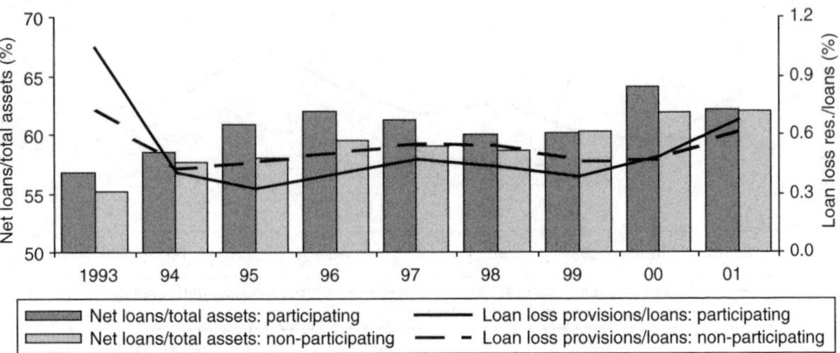

Figure 6.15 Net loans/total assets and loan loss provisions/total loans ratios of participating and non-participating banking corporations, 1993–2001

Source: Thomson Analytics Bankscope.

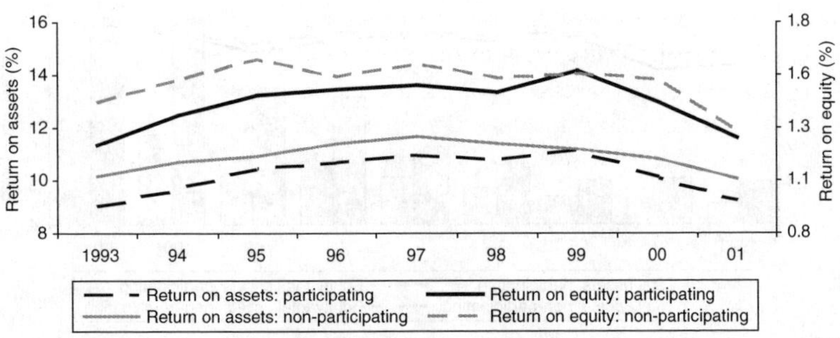

Figure 6.16 Return on equity and return on asset ratios of participating and non-participating banking corporations, 1993–2001

Source: Thomson Analytics Bankscope.

for both groups of holding corporations. Non-participant bank holdings have been slightly more profitable in the period under study than participating ones (Figure 6.16).

Non-banking credit institutions

The analysis of financial structure and profitability of non-banking credit institutions is presented in Appendix 6.3 (pp. 124–5) for reference; the indicators fluctuate over time and show a much larger degree of inter-group (participating versus non-participating) divergence than for any of the other types of banks.

Financial structure indicators and model specification

It has been shown that differences are apparent in the financial structure and profitability of banks that have and not participated in loans syndications in a given year, and these differences are now investigated further empirically. A theoretical model for analysing banks' decision to participate or not in loan syndication as a function of their financial characteristics is constructed by considering a binary variable, *Syndd*, taking the value of 1 if a bank has participated in a loan syndication in a given year, and 0 otherwise. *Syndd* is modelled as a function of the bank's financial characteristics for the previous fiscal year. Ideally, one would like to have information from the bank's monthly internal reporting system, borrower limits and so on. But given the yearly frequency of publicly available balance sheet and profit and loss statement information, values at the end of the fiscal year preceding the loan participation decision are the most accurate measure one can use to gauge the interaction between bank characteristics and lending decisions.

The following model is constructed:

$$Syndd = \beta_0 Intercept + \beta_1 llpl + \beta_2 eta + \beta_3 nim + \beta_4 roe + \beta_5 cir + \beta_6 ooita + \beta_7 ladep + \beta_8 \ln taresid + u$$

where:

$(\beta_0, \ldots, \beta_8)$ are parameters to be estimated;

Syndd = binary dependent variable for syndicated loan participation decision for a given year, 1 if the bank participates, 0 if it does not
llpl = bank's ratio of loan loss provisions/loans at the end of the year preceding the syndication participation decision
eta = ratio of equity/total assets at the end of previous year
nim = net interest margin for previous year
roe = return on equity for previous year
cir = cost/income ratio for previous year
ooita = ratio of other operating income/total assets for previous year
ladep = ratio of liquid assets/deposits at the end of previous year
lntaresid = residual obtained by regressing the natural logarithm of the bank's total assets at the end of previous year on all the above bank characteristics – this is discussed in more detail on p. 00
u = random disturbance

Lagging the bank characteristics by one year allows us to counter the effects of endogeneity – i.e. one wants to look at how bank characteristics influence the loan syndication participation decision, not the reverse. The explanatory variables pertaining to the bank's characteristics for the year preceding the year in which it decides to participate or not in a loan syndication can be thought of in the following way.

Ratio of loan loss provisions/loans

Provisions for loan losses are charged against earnings to establish a reserve to absorb loan losses. As such, they can be thought of as a proxy for *credit risk* and a measure of *loan quality* which can influence lending policies and loan syndication decisions. It is expected that the size of loan loss provisions relative to total loans in a certain year has a negative effect on the dependent variable, based on the hypothesis that banks with bad-quality loan portfolios are unlikely to want to take on more risk.

Ratio of equity/total assets

Certainly, capital adequacy is one of the criteria that are by far the most strictly followed by regulators. At all times, banks are required to maintain adequate capital. The primary function of bank capital is to support or absorb risk. The amount of a bank's capital puts a limit on the losses it can bear. Therefore the loan supply function of banks is directly related to their capital adequacy. It may be expected that banks with higher capital adequacy ratios will be able to participate in loan syndications to a greater extent, suggesting a positive coefficient. Yet, an alternative possibility is also discussed in the literature with reference to the decision of syndicating a loan versus keeping it bilateral. According to Simons (1993), a bank that finds itself constrained in its capital–asset ratio, either because of regulatory requirements or because of its own internal standards, could be reluctant to lower the ratio by putting a large bilateral loan on its balance sheet and might choose instead to syndicate a portion of the loan.

Net interest margin and return on equity

The net interest margin, which measures a bank's spread per dollar of loans, can be used to analyse its performance in its primary business of financial intermediation. The return on equity, on the other hand, gauges the overall return that the bank produces for its shareholders on a unit of equity. Lower net interest margins and returns on equity in a given year might prompt banks to participate in more loan syndications in the following year. This could be a means of boosting returns by acquiring exposure to new customers such as those in emerging markets, where it might take time to acquire expertise for banks lending bilaterally.

Cost/income ratio

This ratio is an efficiency measure for banks. As noted in James (1987), banks have a cost advantage over outsiders in producing and transforming information. Banks' decision of participating in a loan syndication can thus be thought of as a means of cashing in on this cost advantage. As pointed out by Hale (2005), the activity of lending entails *screening and monitoring costs*. In syndicated loans, unlike bilateral loans, such costs are borne by the agent and arranger banks, which reduces the cost of lending for banks participating at a lower level of seniority. To the extent that junior banks wish to save on these costs by participating, the effect on the loan participation decision dummy of the cost/income ratio is expected to be positive.

Ratio of other operating income/total assets

This ratio measures the income diversification of banks emanating from activities other than their primary business of financial intermediation. Fees for originating loans or guaranteed lines of credit are often included in this category. Banks acting as arrangers/leads, coarrangers and agents can earn substantial fees by originating syndicated loans. They can achieve higher income diversification by participating in loan syndications.

Ratio of liquid assets/deposits

The liquid assets/deposits ratio measures the proportion of deposits which can be repaid promptly if there is a sudden deposit withdrawal from the bank. It also indicates the availability of funds to meet loan demand quickly. Effective asset liability management requires banks to keep liquid assets for both sudden deposit withdrawals and loan demand. Demand for syndicated credits is a case in point. Banks are expected to participate in syndications if they have sufficient available liquid funds; one therefore expects a positive sign for this coefficient. A bank that finds itself constrained in its liquidity ratio, either because of regulatory requirements or because of its own internal standards, could be reluctant to lower the ratio by putting a large bilateral loan on its balance sheet and may choose instead to syndicate a portion of the loan (Simons, 1993).

Asset size

One reason why asset size is included in the analysis is to gauge to what extent large banks dominate the international market for syndicated loans. However, as such, asset size is highly correlated with the other balance sheet and profit and loss statement variables such as profitability and efficiency. Therefore, as an explanatory variable of the syndication participation decision, only the part of asset size which is not explained by the other bank characteristics is included. To that effect, first an auxiliary regression is run with the form:

$$\ln ta = \alpha_0 Intercept + \alpha_1 llpl + \alpha_2 eta + \alpha_3 nim + \alpha_4 roe + \alpha_5 cir + \alpha_6 ooita + \alpha_7 ladep + \boldsymbol{\varepsilon}$$

where, for the year preceding the syndication participation decision, the natural logarithm of the bank's total assets is regressed on its ratio of loan loss provisions/loans, equity/total assets, net interest margin, return on equity, cost/income, other operating income/total assets and liquid assets/deposits. The residuals estimated from this regression, noted $\hat{\varepsilon} = lntaresid$, are then taken as an explanatory variable for the main equation shown above.

Altunbaş, Gadanecz and Kara (2005) estimates the above model expressing banks' decision to participate in loan syndications as a function of their characteristics, first for all institutions in the sample of participating and non-participating banks described earlier and subsequently for specific subsamples by bank nationality and specialization.

Determinants of the loan syndication decision, by bank nationality

The results of the estimation by bank nationality are presented in Table 6.1.[3] The ratio of loan loss provisions/loans of the previous year is found to be significantly and negatively related to the syndication participation decision. Banks which already have worse quality loans in their portfolios are unlikely to participate in loan syndications and there is a possible hesitation to take on more risk in the following years. In accordance with the existing literature (Simons, 1993; Dennis and Mullineaux, 2000; Jones, Lang and Nigro, 2001) a negative relationship is established between bank participation and the ratio of equity/total assets. Banks with less capital may choose to syndicate part of their loan portfolios, in order to meet regulatory capital requirements. The equity/assets ratio is strongly significant and has the same sign in all countries analysed – with the highest coefficient for Japanese banks.

Altunbaş, Gadanecz, and Kara (2005) find a significant and negative relationship between the net interest margin and the return on equity when all banks are considered. Emphasized previously as one of the

Table 6.1 The effect of bank financial structure on the decision to participate in syndicated loans, by bank nationality
Dependent variable: syndication participation dummy (1 if participated, 0 otherwise)

Independent variables	**All countries**	**US**	**Great Britain**	**Japan**	**France**	**Italy**
Loan loss provisions/loans	−0.0372‡	−0.2965‡	−0.0154	−0.1819†	−0.0100†	0.1061
	(0.008)	*(0.033)*	*(0.014)*	*(0.075)*	*(0.005)*	*(0.087)*
Equity/total assets	−0.1072‡	−0.1152‡	−0.1333‡	−0.3732‡	−0.0907‡	−0.1000‡
	(0.004)	*(0.005)*	*(0.015)*	*(0.026)*	*(0.010)*	*(0.021)*
Net interest margin	−0.0273‡	0.0906‡	−0.1080‡	−0.4903‡	−0.4460‡	−0.0243
	(0.009)	*(0.019)*	*(0.038)*	*(0.081)*	*(0.029)*	*(0.062)*
Return on equity	−0.0068‡	0.0284‡	−0.0163†	−0.0254‡	−0.0326‡	−0.0286‡
	(0.001)	*(0.004)*	*(0.007)*	*(0.006)*	*(0.003)*	*(0.008)*
Cost income ratio	0.0180‡	0.0356‡	0.0268‡	0.0044	0.0104‡	0.0220‡
	(0.001)	*(0.002)*	*(0.004)*	*(0.004)*	*(0.002)*	*(0.005)*
Other operating income/total assets	0.3512‡	0.2905‡	0.3328‡	0.4233‡	0.4701‡	0.2071‡
	(0.007)	*(0.011)*	*(0.035)*	*(0.101)*	*(0.026)*	*(0.035)*
Liquid assets/deposits	0.0022‡	0.0071‡	0.0070†	−0.0217‡	−0.0087‡	0.0001
	(0.000)	*(0.001)*	*(0.003)*	*(0.005)*	*(0.002)*	*(0.004)*
Ln(total assets) residual	1.0427‡	0.8979‡	1.0916‡	1.4864‡	0.9860‡	0.5515‡
	(0.007)	*(0.013)*	*(0.038)*	*(0.042)*	*(0.023)*	*(0.041)*
Constant	2.3779‡	0.5480†	1.6467‡	5.6141‡	3.5450‡	1.7883‡
	(0.069)	*(0.215)*	*(0.357)*	*(0.414)*	*(0.205)*	*(0.381)*
R^2	0.4105	0.3388	0.4217	0.6590	0.4851	0.1678

Notes: ‡ Significant at the 1% level; ‡ Significant at the 5% level. Standard errors in parentheses.

key features of loan syndications, the fees earned on syndications tend to be an attractive alternative income for banks aiming to boost returns. Banks operating with low interest margins and low total returns tend to participate more in loan syndications in subsequent years with a view to achieving this goal. An exception worth noting is US banks, whose net interest margins and returns on equity are positively and significantly associated with the participation decision, reflecting an overall better performance of US banks compared to other nationalities during most of the 1990s. This is in part due to the historically more aggressive provisioning of US banks during that decade, also reflected by the highest absolute value of the coefficient on the ratio of loan loss provisions/total loans for US banks. The net interest margin also has a strong effect on the loan participation decision for British and French banks.

The cost/income ratio is found to have a positive relationship with the decision of participating in loan syndications, revealing that relatively cost-inefficient banks have a propensity to choose loan syndications as an effective tool for reducing costs. Participating banks may be aiming to reduce their screening and monitoring costs since, unlike in bilateral lending, these activities are undertaken by the agent or lead banks in loan syndications. Altunbaş, Gadanecz and Kara (2005) also note that the results may be influenced by the higher than average cost/income ratios of some agent/lead banks that dominate the syndicated loan market.

The impact of income diversification efforts on the decision to participate in loan syndications is measured by the ratio of other operating income/total assets. Banks with higher other operating income/total assets ratios are likely to participate in loan syndications in an effort to diversify their income sources away from the traditional business of financial intermediation. Banks acting as arrangers/lead banks, coarrangers and agents earn significant fees.

Liquidity, measured by the liquid assets/total assets ratio, is found to be another significant factor shaping the decision to participate. Banks tend to participate more in loan syndications when their liquidity positions measured at the end of the previous financial year are sufficiently high to permit it. However, different from all nationalities considered together are the Japanese banks with regard to their liquidity ratios, significantly and negatively related to the participation decision. For Japanese banks, the hypothesis developed by Pavel and Phillis (1987) and Simons (1993) is verified, namely that liquidity-constrained banks may not want stretch their liquidity positions further and prefer to sell or syndicate loans rather than keep them bilateral.

Table 6.2 The effect of bank financial structure on the decision to participate in syndicated loans, by bank type
Dependent variable: syndication participation dummy (1 if participated, 0 otherwise)

Independent variables	**Commercial banks**	**Savings, mortgage, real estate banks**[a]	**Investment banks**	**Non-banking credit institutions**[a]	**Specialized credit institutions**[a]	**Banking corporations**[a]
Loan loss provisions/loans	−0.0363‡	0.0103	−0.0407	−0.0744	0.0161	−0.3066‡
	(0.010)	(0.033)	(0.040)	(0.082)	(0.056)	(0.076)
Equity/total assets	−0.0635‡	−0.0613‡	−0.1738‡	−0.0582‡	−0.1748‡	−0.2462‡
	(0.005)	(0.011)	(0.017)	(0.020)	(0.018)	(0.022)
Net interest margin	−0.0611‡	0.1589‡	0.2784‡	−0.4264‡	0.0745	0.5245‡
	(0.013)	(0.026)	(0.097)	(0.059)	(0.104)	(0.041)
Return on equity	−0.0021	0.0306‡	−0.0174†	−0.0104†	−0.0176‡	−0.0316‡
	(0.002)	(0.005)	(0.007)	(0.004)	(0.006)	(0.011)
Cost income ratio	0.0230‡	0.0270‡	0.0125†	−0.0184‡	0.0026	0.0395‡
	(0.001)	(0.002)	(0.005)	(0.004)	(0.005)	(0.007)
Other operating income/ total assets	0.2792‡	0.4207‡	0.3440‡	−0.2505‡	0.6291‡	0.3791‡
	(0.010)	(0.041)	(0.036)	(0.094)	(0.181)	(0.036)
Liquid assets/deposits	−0.0083‡	0.0056‡	0.0156‡	−0.0007	0.0070†	0.0158‡
	(0.001)	(0.001)	(0.004)	(0.002)	(0.003)	(0.001)
Ln(total assets) residual	0.9170‡	1.0319‡	0.8783‡	0.5591‡	0.7507‡	1.4216‡
	(0.010)	(0.022)	(0.061)	(0.075)	(0.057)	(0.026)
Constant	2.4677‡	−0.0546	1.2229‡	3.5340‡	3.7558‡	−0.6429
	(0.104)	(0.171)	(0.439)	(0.424)	(0.287)	(0.588)
R^2	0.3155	0.2588	0.2936	0.3144	0.2074	0.5877

Notes: [a] See definition of these institution types in Appendix 6.1, p. 122.
‡ Significant at the 1% level; † Significant at the 5% level. Standard errors in parentheses.

Lastly, Altunbaş, Gadanecz and Kara (2005) point out the significant presence of large banks in the market for syndicated loans, measured by the asset size residual, indicating that larger banks tend to participate in syndicated loans more than small-size banks.

Determinants of the loan syndication decision, by bank specialization

The findings of Altunbaş, Gadanecz and Kara (2005) on bank specialization are presented in Table 6.2. Savings banks and non-banking credit institutions differ from the overall population of banks in their participation decision, often yielding significant coefficients with signs opposite to those obtained for the whole population. It is expected that these institutions will have management objectives that are different from traditional shareholder value maximization. Unlike the overall sample, investment banks tend to participate more in loan syndications when their net interest margins are high because their net interest margins probably contribute relatively little to their overall returns. Investment banks are the institution types whose decision participations are most likely to be primarily motivated by the fees earned at senior levels in syndicates.

Conclusion

The main purpose of this chapter was first to outline the main features of syndicated loans that motivate banks to participate in them and, secondly, to analyse the impact of these banks' financial characteristics on their decision to participate.

Portfolio diversification, capital constraints, liquidity, risk diversification, publicity, extra fee income, competition with bond markets and seniority can be summarized as the attractive advantages of loan syndications for banks. The chapter focused on findings of Altunbaş, Gadanecz and Kara (2005) who contribute to the existing literature by including in their analysis banks that have not engaged in loan syndications – independent of whether they have granted bilateral loans or not – to compare their characteristics with those who have. Poorly performing banks – characterized by lower capitalizations, lower net interest margins, lower profitability and efficiency – were found to be more involved in loan syndications on average than better-performing banks.

Coming back to the possibility of herding phenomena mentioned early in the chapter, in Borio (2003) it is stressed that one reason why the macroeconomic aspect of financial supervision and regulation is important is that threats to financial stability can be posed when whole banking systems are similarly hit by a single shock – e.g. currency movements hit them in the same way because they have similar currency exposures. Results suggest that policy-makers should perhaps focus more on monitoring the concentration of credit risk associated with syndicated loans held on the books of large and poorly performing banks. Any possible disruption of syndicated lending by such institutions could have dire consequences, especially for emerging market borrowers.

Appendixes

Appendix 6.1 Definition of selected bank types

Savings, mortgage and real estate banks

These are a type of financial institution that accept consumer deposits and invest these funds primarily in residential mortgages and high-grade securities. Mutual savings banks are owned by their depositors, while stock savings banks issue common stock to the public.

Non-banking credit institutions

This category comprises companies at the frontier of the banking industry. They do not collect individuals' deposits but might collect, as a minor source of funding, deposits from companies (i.e. their mother company or related companies). Their funding sources are the interbank market, borrowings, capital funds and endowment funds from their mother companies. Their main credit business is short-term.

Specialized credit institutions

This category includes public institutions acting in privileged or protected segments or benefiting from governmental guarantee or sponsoring.

Banking corporations

Bank holding companies, for instance in the US.

Appendix 6.2 Correlation matrix

Table 6A.1 Correlation between financial structure indicators

	syndd	*llpl*	*eta*	*nim*	*cir*	*ooita*	*ladep*	*roe*	*lta1resid*
Syndication participation dummy	1								
Loan loss Provisions/loans	−0.03*	1							
Equity/total assets	−0.05*	0.01*	1						
Net interest margin	−0.05*	−0.00	0.51*	1					
Cost/income ratio	0.08*	−0.02*	−0.17*	−0.18*	1				
Other operating income/total assets	0.05*	0.01*	0.68*	0.32*	−0.00	1			
Liquid assets/deposits	0.06*	0.00	−0.02*	−0.27*	0.12*	0.12*	1		
Return on equity	0.01*	−0.04*	0.11*	0.31*	−0.28*	0.21*	0.06*	1	
Ln(total assets) residual	0.53*	0.00	0.00	0.00	0.00	0.00	0.00	0.00	1

Note: * Significant at the 10% level.

Appendix 6.3 Trends in financial indicators of non-banking credit institutions

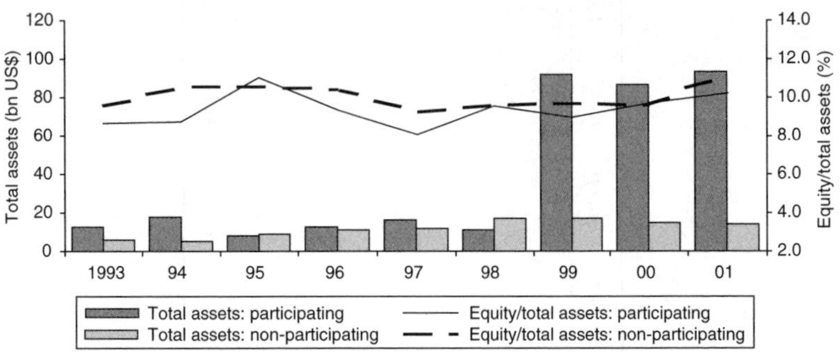

Figure 6A.1 Total assets and equity/total assets ratio of participating and non-participating non-banking credit institutions, 1993–2001

Source: Thomson Analytics Bankscope.

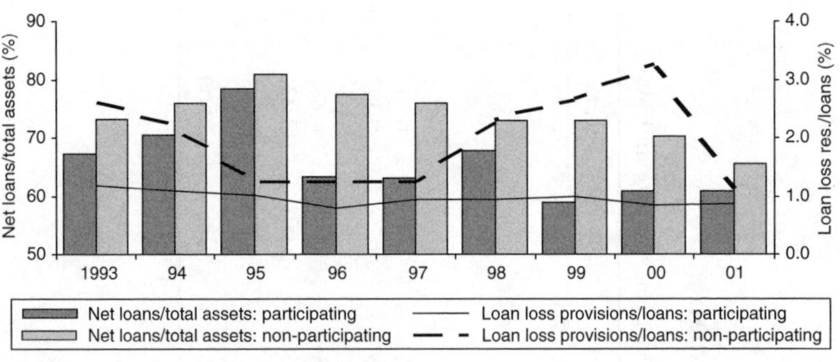

Figure 6A.2 Net loans/total assets and loan loss reserves/total loans ratios of participating and non-participating non-banking credit institutions, 1993–2001

Source: Thomson Analytics Bankscope.

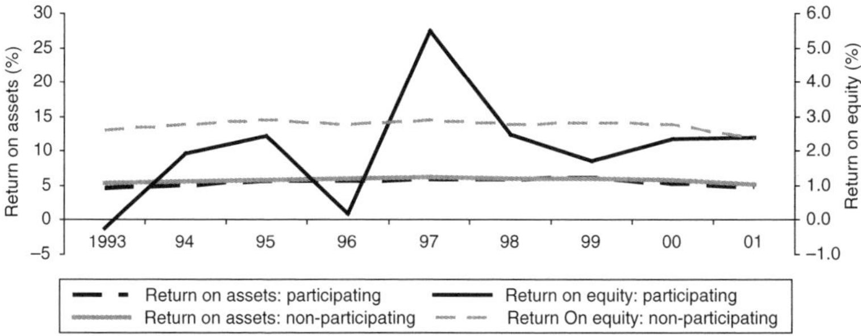

Figure 6A.3 Return on equity and return on asset ratios of participating and non-participating non-banking credit institutions, 1993–2001

Source: Thomson Analytics Bankscope.

7
Comparison of Syndicated Loan Markets with Bond Markets

Introduction

Excessive borrowing by companies, households or governments lies at the root of almost every economic crisis of the past two decades, from Mexico to Japan and from East Asia to Russia. Following the financial crises in Mexico (1995) and South-East Asia (1997, 1998) the determinants of bond and loan financing to developing countries and the pricing of these instruments have been analysed widely in the academic literature (see, for instance, Hernandez and Rudolph, 1995; Eichengreen and Mody, 1997, 1998; Kamin and von Kleist, 1999; Chowdhry and Goyal, 2000). As stressed by Hale (2005), bonds and loans compete in the market for emerging market finance and it is important to gauge the relative importance of each instrument for planning purposes by lenders and borrowers alike. Indeed, while banks can cancel loans relatively easily – posing more potential liquidity threats to emerging market borrowers – bonds are harder to restructure, not least because of the dispersion of the bondholders.

The comparison of the prices of the two instruments can also provide an indication of the degree to which the relevant markets have matured and become liquid. However, in today's globalized financial environment, emerging and industrialized country borrowers compete for funds. Cline and Barnes (1997) make the argument in the context of developing country loans and bonds competing with US junk bonds to attract investors' funds. Vine (2001) stresses that emerging market bonds lend themselves particularly well to the analysis applied to US domestic high-yield investors and to domestic high-yield borrowers. Finally, the comparison of the determinants of developing and industrialized country loan and bond characteristics is important in order to gauge the phenomena of flight to quality or contagion from one market to another during times of crisis or financial stress: financial crises in emerging markets may have made investors more wary or selective about lending to industrialized country borrowers as well. As summarised in *The Economist* (6 July 2002, p. 69). 'After Thailand devalued the baht on July 2nd 1997, capital rushed out of the region's economies, and in rapid succession most of them collapsed. The resulting panic soon spread beyond East Asia to other emerging markets and for a while it posed a serious threat to the world economy.' While most of the earlier loan and bond pricing literature has focused on developing countries or on industrialized countries separately, this chapter makes a first attempt to combine the two.

On average, it is found that developing country bonds have been riskier than developing country loans and industrialized country loans riskier than industrialized country bonds. Contagion effects are analysed between various market segments in the wake of the South-East Asian financial crisis. The influence of market structure in the respective market segments (i.e. bonds, loans, industrialized and developed countries) is also compared. Market access appears to have been more difficult for developing country borrowers in loan markets. This is the market segment where banks and investors may have exercised their market power to the greatest extent and where the penalizing effect of higher perceived risk concentration may have been most pronounced.

Some historical and theoretical background

In the case of *emerging market borrowers*, syndicated lending has been as significant as bond financing since the first half of the 1990s. While international developing country bond issues rose from negligible levels at the beginning of the 1990s to more than $120 bn in 1997 (before falling back to $82 bn in 2000 after the South-East Asian crisis) loan commitments have grown at a similar pace, reaching levels comparable to bond issuance. In fact developing country loan facilities actually exceeded bond issuance in just about every other year than 2000, totalling $96 bn in 2000.

Figures published by the BIS (see Table 7.1) indicate that, in 2001, international syndicated credit facilities granted to borrowers from *industrialized countries* were worth $1.3 trn, while gross international bond issuance by industrialized country issuers represented $1.9 trn and equity issuance $133 bn.

Table 7.1 Sources of international financing for industrialized countries, 1992–2001, US$

Gross announcements	1992	1993	1994	1995	1996	1997	1998	1999	2000	2001
International syndicated credit facilities	159.9	254.1	441.9	609.9	730.0	908.7	822.0	961.0	1,333.1	1,280.1
International bonds	n.a.	374.3	345.4	353.4	625.6	673.1	863.7	1,415.7	1,499.2	1,948.1
International equities	17.6	32.7	44.3	43.1	59.1	87.6	111.8	177.8	257.0	132.5

Note: n.a. = not available.

Sources: Dealogic; BIS (various years).

In order to understand how the choice between intermediated and disintermediated finance in developing and industrialized countries has been determined since the 1990s, one first needs to consider a series of differences between the two types of financing (see Table 7.2 for a summary):

- The costs of arranging a syndicated loan are lower than those of issuing a bond (Allen, 1990)
- The syndicated loan market generally allows borrowers to raise larger sums than they would be able to obtain through either the bond or the equity markets under a time constraint,[1]
- Syndicated credit facilities can be arranged quickly and discreetly, which may be of value with certain transactions such as takeovers
- Commitments to lend can be cancelled relatively easily, while it would be difficult to cancel borrowing in the securities markets without reducing investor confidence.

There is a number of theoretical and empirical justifications for comparing the characteristics of loan and bond instruments:

To begin with, the characteristics of bonds and loans are extensively compared in the information asymmetry literature from a monitoring/incentives perspective (Sachs and Cohen, 1982; Berlin and Loeys, 1988; Berlin and Mester, 1992; Bolton and Freixas, 2000). Eichengreen and Mody (1998) note that the determinants of risk and pricing behaviour differ between bank loans and bonds, principally because of the differences in seniority between the two instruments and the different extent to which they lend themselves to restructuring.

Secondly, a homogenous pool of loans can lend itself well to *securitization* (i.e. removal of the claims from the bank's balance sheet and purchase by a special-purpose vehicle (SPV) which issues securities that are subsequently serviced by the cash flow from the loans), allowing some tranching of the risk in the process. The characteristics of the

Table 7.2 Characteristics of syndicated credits compared to bonds

Characteristic	Syndicated loans	Bonds
Maturity	Short- to-medium-term (typically less than 3 years)	3–10 years for Eurobonds 5–10 years for US bonds
Minimal amount	As low as $1 m	$30 m for Eurobonds, higher for US bonds[a]
Targeted investor population	Banks Development banks Export credit agencies Multilateral organizations (e.g. IFC)	Banks Insurance companies Pension funds Fund managers (unit trusts, mutual funds) Individuals Corporates
Average completion time of programme	5–12 weeks	Eurobonds: 6–15 weeks US bonds: 6–20 weeks
Rate type	Floating (rarely fixed)	Eurobonds: fixed or floating US bonds: mostly fixed
Flexibility (i.e. diversity of financing options, possibility to change them if needs of borrower change)	High (e.g. multiple currency options)	Low
Information disclosure and issuance costs	Low (no US GAAP, no rating, no compulsory disclosure to the market)	Eurobonds: medium (rating and disclosure to market) US bonds: high (US GAAP, rating, disclosure to market)
Liquidity of secondary market	Low, but improving in the US	Eurobond market reasonably liquid, US market highly liquid

Note: [a] Minimal amounts also tend to be higher for bonds than for loans because of the higher costs involved, which would make it uneconomical to issue bonds for low amounts.

underlying pool of loans are derived (in terms of maturity, pricing, currency, quality) from those of the securities issued, with the SPV often engaging in some kind of transformation (by means of a currency swap or risk enhancement[2]) to make the securities more marketable to the targeted investor population. Therefore securitization is an example where financiers directly relate the characteristics of loans and bonds to one another for financial engineering purposes. As an ultimate solution to the Mexican sovereign default of 1982, some developing countries' non-performing loans were transformed into 'Brady bonds' – instruments secured on US Treasuries and purchased by creditors (Chapter 3). This was accompanied by partial debt forgiveness.

Thirdly, the issuance of certain securities is often subordinated to the arrangement of a *liquidity backstop/backup loan facility* – in fact, some rating agencies require this in order to rate the bond issue. Besides, the repayment of many syndicated loans is predicted on a bond takeout within 6–12 months (or sooner) of signing the loan. Many of the largest acquisition loans arranged in 1999 – such as those for Olivetti (€ 22.5 bn), Mannesmann (€9 bn and £8 bn), Vodafone ($10.5 bn) and Repsol ($9 bn) – were subsequently refinanced in the bond markets (Rhodes, 2000). In such financing decisions, borrowers directly compare the cost of intermediated and disintermediated financing to determine their interest expense.

Fourthly, the emergence of a relatively liquid *secondary market for loans* in the US (which had a turnover of $8 bn in 1991, $40 bn in 1996 and $118 bn in 2001 according to the Loan Pricing Corporation, a US-incorporated loan data vendor) has allowed some institutional investors – such as high-yield bond/leveraged loan mutual funds – to arbitrage between loans and bonds, picking the asset that presents the best risk–return profile (Coffey, 2000). This practice has been dominant particularly in the area of *leveraged loans*.[3] In contrast to banks which have typically been using loans to build customer relationships, these cross-over institutional investors have effectively been treating loans as an *asset class*. They weigh the attributes of bonds and loans against their yield, and will purchase the asset with the better fit. If there is a significant relative value mismatch between the two assets, investors will buy the more attractive investment and avoid the less attractive one (often forcing a repricing of the unattractive asset). In order to attract investors, many loans were repriced – worth about $11 bn in 1998 and $23 bn in 1999 according to Coffey (2000) – in order to bring them back into relative value alignment. Again, this constitutes an example of investors directly comparing the characteristics of loans and bonds in order to make investment decisions. The growing trend of institutional investors to compare relative value in the loan and bond markets is mirrored within banks' own pricing models.

Finally, Kamin and von Kleist (1999) note that bonds and loans are very different types of financial instruments. Bond issues tend to have fixed interest rates, while most loans are floating-rate instruments (i.e. have interest rates which are at a fixed initial spread over LIBOR). Additionally, many facets of the credit contract differ substantially between bonds and loans. Borrower–lender relations are also very different for bonds and loans. These considerations, taken together, would suggest that bond and loan spreads behave so differently that it would be inappropriate to analyse them together. Yet, one of the most surprising results of Kamin and von Kleist's research is that emerging market bonds and loans appear to differ only in the level of their spreads, not in the response of their spreads to changes in other factors such as credit rating or maturity.

Comparative visual analysis is now presented of bond and loan issuance over the 1990s by industrialized countries and some selected developing countries that have been affected by serious financial crises. The analysis allows us to make inferences about linkages between financing for developing and industrialized country borrowers.

To begin with, analysis of volumes shows that syndicated lending was sharply curtailed in 1998 to South-East Asia in the aftermath of the financial crises that hit the region. The crises were accompanied by a reduction of lending to borrowers in the US and in Western Europe (Figure 7A.1) (see Appendix 7.1, p. 150). The collapse of bond issuance by Asian crisis countries in 1998 and 1999 was followed by a reduction in Western European bond issuance from 1999 onwards (Figure 7A.6).

Furthermore, looking at the evolution of pricing, note that the LIBOR spreads on syndicated credit facilities granted to Asian developing countries hit by financial crises[4] peaked in 1998–9. So did launch spreads (i.e. spreads at issuance) on their bonds – for those still able to tap bond markets. These peaks were accompanied by a peaking of LIBOR loan spreads for US and Japanese borrowers (Figure 7A.2) and to a lesser extent of bond spreads in 1999 for Japanese issuers (Figure 7A.7). One could interpret this as a possible sign of contagion in financial markets, which will be tested statistically later in the chapter. Latin American loan and bond spreads peaked in 1999, while spreads demanded on Russian and Turkish bonds and loans started edging up sharply in 2000.

Lastly, the evolution of loan maturities may also provide possible evidence of contagion (Figure 7A.3). The abrupt reduction of new average facility maturities that occurred for Turkish, Russian, South Korean and Indonesian borrowers in particular, as lenders shunned further long-term exposure to crisis-hit countries, was accompanied by a less abrupt but generally protracted reduction of weighted average maturities on industrialized country syndicated loan facilities. Interestingly, as average maturities on facilities to South Korean borrowers fell in 1998 to about one-third of their average of 1997, average maturities on facilities granted to Japanese borrowers shrank by 50 per cent between 1997 and 1998. To a lesser extent, the sharp reduction in maturity for emerging country bonds issued from 1997 onwards, first in Asia and subsequently in Latin America, was accompanied by a trough in US bond maturities in 1998 (Figure 7A.8).

Finally, comparison of the sectoral breakdown of developing and industrialized country loan and bond financing allows us to highlight a few major tendencies.

In developing countries, the bulk of bank lending was channelled to banks, the high-tech industry and the utilities sector. The infrastructure and population-related service[5] sectors had to pay among the highest spreads on loans and the transport sector among the lowest (Figure 7A.4). The bulk of developing country bond issuance was made by the state sector, followed by banks and traditional industries. The construction and property sector faced among the highest bond spreads, with a peak in 1998 which could have corresponded to the peak of the Asian property bubble, while banks and the transport sector paid the lowest bond spreads (Figure 7A.9).

In industrialized countries, non-bank financial intermediaries and the high-tech industry were the most active arrangers of syndicated loans. In 1999 and 2000 borrowing by the high-tech sector peaked, boosted by large loan facilities arranged for mainly European telecoms firms to support the purchase of third-generation mobile phone licences. The state and banking sectors obtained among the lowest bond and loan spreads while the construction and property and population-related sectors faced the highest. Banks and the state sector were the most active bond issuers. Spreads on loans written to and on bonds issued by the high-tech industry were the highest in 2000 when telecoms borrowing peaked (Figures 7A.5 and 7A.10).

Figures 7A.11 and 7A.12 show the spreads and maturities on loan signings and bond issues obtained by industrialized and developing country borrowers and compare all countries in each group with the countries that obtained the largest amount of bond or loan financing in a given year. It appears from the comparisons of the various panels that the difference in spreads between the whole group and the three countries most present in the market is highest for loan signings by developing country borrowers. This finding – tested empirically later – suggests that banks may have exercised their market power to the greatest extent on this market segment by charging the highest spread supplement to developing countries more dependent on the market.

In order to prepare the statistical analysis of these issues arising from visual inspection of the figures, some of the academic literature dealing with loan and bond pricing issues is now reviewed.

The loan and bond pricing literature

Industrialized country loans are supposedly riskier than bonds

Following the logic of the 'pecking-order theory' of finance, companies use internal money (retained profits) in the first instance to finance their development and when they subsequently seek external funds, they graduate from bank finance to bond finance as information about their creditworthiness becomes more complete (Myers, 1984; Myers and Majluf, 1984; Diamond, 1991; Carey *et al.*, 1993; Bolton and Freixas,

2000). Monitoring of private debt is most efficiently delegated to a financial intermediary rather than collected directly by many intermediaries (Diamond, 1984). Bank loans tend to be relatively short term, involve extensive covenants and are frequently renegotiated. The majority of public debt contracts are longer term, involve relatively loose covenants and are almost never renegotiated. These contractual characteristics are extensively examined in the literature by Berlin and Loeys (1988), Berlin and Mester (1992) and Rajan and Winton (1995). Berlin and Mester (1992) develop a model in which bond contracts – enforced by indicators observable to anyone – tend to be either too harsh (too many good projects are liquidated) or too lenient (too many bad projects are allowed to mature). Hiring the services of a delegated monitor ensures a more efficient liquidation policy (loan contract), but providing the monitor with proper incentives is costly. The choice of contract depends on the trade-off between the inefficiencies of rigid bond covenants and the costs of hiring a delegated monitor. This trade-off depends on the firm's production technology and the information technology. Bolton and Freixas (2000) derive an equilibrium where (1) the riskiest firms (which are often start-ups) are either unable to obtain funding or are constrained to issue equity, (2) somewhat safer firms are able to take out bank loans, which provide the cheapest form of flexible financing required and (3) the safest firms prefer to tap securities markets and thus avoid paying the intermediation cost. This theoretical segmentation is consistent with practice, especially with European reality where only the safest firms are able to issue bonds on securities markets and no highly developed junk-bond market exists, as in the US.

Research conducted by Melnik and Plaut (1991) underpins the pecking-order theory. Their investigation of lending to industrialized country borrowers on the short-term Eurocredit market provides evidence that the market seems to be segmented in such a way that the highest-quality borrowers issue securities in their own names (in other words, do not require monitoring) while others have recourse to finance in the form of bank loans (i.e. are monitored). On a sample of credit contracts consisting of note issuance facilities (NIFs, instruments closer to securities than to loans) and loans that were executed for financial and non-financial borrowers in 1986, loans have a riskier average credit rating and a higher average spread over LIBOR than NIFs combined with a higher average facility amount (possibly indicating higher leverage and greater risk). Logit regression analysis shows that riskier credit ratings increase the likelihood that borrowers obtain financing through a conventional loan rather than a NIF. The inclusion of a third-party guarantee also significantly increases the likelihood that the financing is in the form of a NIF.

Developing country bonds could be riskier than loans

The above considerations apply to lending to industrialized countries, but a different analysis is warranted for developing countries. Edwards (1986) argues that the levels of risk involved in international bank loans and bonds are different. There is somewhat greater risk involved in bonds. As a result of implicit or explicit central bank guarantees on bank deposits and loans, spreads on loans would not reflect the real risk of default. Bonds, on the other hand, supposedly reflect the risk more accurately. Sachs and Cohen (1982) have argued that while bank lending is implicitly lending with an option to renegotiate, bond lending excludes the possibility of rescheduling. Consequently, in their model, bond lending is more risky – that is, for the same amount of debt, spreads are higher on bonds than on bank loans.

Monetary authorities have traditionally guaranteed bank deposits and loans. Nowadays, bank loans and deposits are, in most countries, implicitly or explicitly insured: in a way, central banks have agreed to become lenders of last resort. McKinnon (1984), Folkerts-Landau (1985) and Eichengreen and Mody (2000) have argued, among others, that the moral hazard factor has become increasingly important in bank lending. According to this view, spreads charged on bank loans do not reflect the real risk of the borrower. The bond market, on the other hand, has not been affected by the broadening of this implicit insurance scheme. Indeed, Folkerts-Landau (1985) argues that while bank loan spreads reflect the probability of *rescheduling*, bond spreads mirror the probability of *default*.

The empirical investigations of these issues in the existing academic literature confirm that spreads on developing country bonds are higher than on developing country loans (Kamin and von Kleist, 1999; Eichengreen and Mody, 1997, 1998, 2000), although the determinants of loan and bond spreads are similar.

Analysis of lending to developing countries

Determinants of the pricing of developing and industrialized country bonds and loans for the 1993 – 2001 period are now analysed in greater detail. The focus is on primary market spreads – i.e. launch spreads for bonds and LIBOR spreads for loans issued on the primary market. It is important to note that the behaviour of spreads on secondary markets, which can be quite different from that of primary spreads, is not analysed here. In particular, as underscored by Eichengreen and Mody (1997, 1998), in poor market conditions when secondary spreads rise, launch spreads generally fall.

The pricing of 2,772 developing country loans and 530 developing country bonds, issued or granted between 1993 and 2001, is regressed on a series of macroeconomic and microeconomic variables with a view to comparing the determinants of the pricing of these two instruments.

The macroeconomic[6] variables include the following measures of the economic performance of the country of the borrower:

- *Solvency*, such as the ratios of external debt/GDP, debt service/exports, assistance from the IMF, a history of debt rescheduling (see Hanson, 1974; Harberger, 1980; Eaton and Gersovitz, 1981; Edwards, 1983; Sachs, 1984; Cantor and Packer, 1996; Cline and Barnes, 1997)
- *Liquidity*, such as the total or short-term external debt positions and their relation to foreign currency reserves (Edwards, 1983; Gersovitz, 1985; Cline and Barnes, 1997; Eichengreen and Mody, 2000)
- *Economic growth and its sustainability*: economic growth rate and its variance, ratios of investment to GDP and domestic credit to GDP (Feder and Just, 1977; Edwards, 1983; Sachs, 1984; Gersovitz, 1985; Cline and Barnes, 1997; Eichengreen and Mody, 1998, 2000)
- *Economic openness*: ratio of exports to import (Frenkel, 1983; Balassa, 1986)
- *Business climate*, for which the corruption index compiled by Transparency International (TI)[7] is used as a proxy. The corruption index is standardized on a scale of 0–10, with a score of 0 corresponding to the highest degree of corruption and a score of 10 to the lowest. To the extent that lenders may be expected to charge a premium on funding to countries where a corrupt business climate prevails, it is expected to find a negative coefficient on the corruption index variable in the loan and bond pricing regressions.

General economic factors, such as the country's PPP share of world GDP, growth in world trade and the yield on the risk-free investment alternative to the loan or bond in question (the three-month US Treasury bill), are also controlled for. It is expected that the market will penalize borrowers from countries with weak macroeconomic fundamentals by charging them higher spreads, and vice versa.

The microeconomic variables include issue size, maturity, borrower business sector, the existence of guarantees, the currency of issue and market structure:

- *Issue size and maturity* can lower or increase pricing (Smith, 1980; Fons, 1994; Eichengreen and Mody, 1997, 1998; Kamin and von Kleist, 1999; Kleimeier and Megginson, 2000).

- Likewise, the effect of the presence of *collateral and third-party guarantees* are uncertain (Smith and Warner, 1979; Smith, 1980; Bester, 1985; Besanko and Thakor, 1987; Berger and Udell, 1990, Kleimeier and Megginson, 2000).
- Eichengreen and Mody (2000) report that when *financial institutions* borrow on the syndicated loan market, they seem to be able to obtain lower spreads than non-financial borrowers. This is consistent with the emphasis some observers have placed on tacit or explicit guarantees provided to financial institutions by monetary authorities (LOLR).
- Dummies were included for facilities or bonds denominated in US dollars, Japanese yen and euro (or any of its twelve predecessor currencies). Instruments denominated in yen and euro are expected to have relatively lower pricing than others, due to the low funding costs for yen-based investors and declining margins in European banking (Eichengreen and Mody, 2000) and lower benchmark yields in non-dollar currencies than comparable US Treasuries (Kamin and von Kleist, 1999).
- The indicators of market structure include a dummy to indicate if the original amount of the loan has been *increased*. When this dummy is equal to 1, it can hint that the market had a positive reaction to the deal during syndication or that the banks have shown flexibility in adapting their financing package to a change in the borrower's needs. The *number of fund providers (for loans) or arranger banks (for bonds)* was also controlled for. The conditions on issues with a lower number of participants or issue arrangers are expected to reflect the relationship of the borrower with its core banks and may therefore be more favourable than on other deals. Finally, the *shares of the borrower's country and business sector in total lending or bond issuance to all countries and all sectors* during the year concerned were included among the control variables: these ratios indicate the relative presence of the country or the industry in the market for syndicated credits and bonds relative to others. A high country or industry share may indicate relatively high financing needs for a nation or an industry, possibly leading to more expensive funding – but also, on the contrary, to an established presence on the market, resulting in more favourable financing conditions.

Since the macroeconomic characteristics of the various countries in the sample are different, a fixed-effect panel regression model is appropriate to control for these effects. Baltagi, Griffin and Xiong (2000) argue that in the case of panel data, if intergroup heterogeneity is strong, then one can just run a time-series regression for each group. If, on the other hand, it is believed that the long-run model corresponds to cross-sectional variation then a between-group approach can be employed. While pure cross-section studies cannot control for group-specific effects, pure time-series studies cannot control for unobservable changes occurring over time. The authors suggest that even when used on relatively long time-series of panel data, heterogeneous models for individual groups tend to produce implausible estimates with inferior forecasting properties. The explanation for why pooled models outperform heterogeneous ones is based on the relative variability of data between time-series and individual panels. Efficiency gains measured by root mean square errors (particularly when one is faced with a relatively short time-series) from pooling appear to more than offset the biases due to inter-group heterogeneities.

The estimation results of the model are displayed in Table 7.3. Next, the results are discussed. Most of the results regarding the effects of microeconomic factors on loan and bond pricing are in line with the existing academic literature. Maturity is significantly and positively related to the pricing of developing country loans and bonds, with the coefficient about twice as high in the case of loans than in the case of bonds. The premium for a risk of change in the borrower's creditworthiness for longer-term instruments is thus more integrated into the pricing of developing country loans than bonds. The result is in accordance with the findings of Kamin and von Kleist (1999). Pricing is negatively and significantly related to size in the case of developing country loans (this is the same result as found by Kleimeier and Megginson, 2000, for a sample containing both developed and industrialized country loans), although this is not found for bonds. Overall, these results suggest that there are economies of scale for banks issuing loans or that better risks are created with larger loans, or both. No such effect seems to exist in the case of bonds, where banks do not monitor borrowers and do not appear to derive economies of scale from carrying out that activity. There is no negative effect of issue size on developing country bond spreads found by Eichengreen and Mody (1997, 1998) arising from economies of scale in the distribution of large issues and liquidity of the secondary market. Explicit guarantees appear to significantly lower the pricing of loans while the pricing of secured developing country loans carries a premium, possibly because they are deemed too risky;[8] conversely, guarantees or collateral seem to have no effect on bond pricing. These differences may be related to the greater seniority of loans over

Table 7.3 Loan and bond pricing regressions for developing countries

The following fixed effects panel regression was estimated, considering each borrower country as a group.

$$\begin{aligned}\ln(\boldsymbol{spread}) = {} & \beta_0\, Intercept + \beta_1\, maturity + \beta_2 \ln\_size + \beta_3\, nbrov + \beta_4 g\_explic \\ & + \beta_5 g\_implic + \beta_6\, secured + \beta_7\, increase + \beta_8\, constrpt + \beta_9\, tradind \\ & + \beta_{10}\, finservb + \beta_{11}\, finservn + \beta_{12}\, high\text{-}tech + \beta_{13}\, infrastr \\ & + \beta_{14}\, popserv + \beta_{15}\, state + \beta_{16}\, transpor + \beta_{17}\, debtgdp + \beta_{18}\, debtgdp_{-1} \\ & + \beta_{19}\, brent + \beta_{20}\, brent_{-1} + \beta_{21}\, treas + \beta_{22}\, treas_{-1} + \beta_{23}\, pppsh \\ & + \beta_{24}\, pppsh_{-1} + \beta_{25}\, growth + \beta_{26}\, growth_{-1} + \beta_{27}\, wrgdp + \beta_{28}\, wrgdp_{-1} \\ & + \beta_{29}\, trade + \beta_{30}\, trade_{-1} + \beta_{31}\, cty\_shar + \beta_{32}\, cty\_shar_{-1} \\ & + \beta_{33}\, bus\_shar + \beta_{34}\, bus\_shar_{-1} + \beta_{35}\, restodeb + \beta_{36}\, restodeb_{-1} \\ & + \beta_{37}\, gra + \beta_{38}\, defiGDP + \beta_{39}\, defiGDP_{-1} + \beta_{40}\, curacGDP \\ & + \beta_{41}\, curacGDP_{-1} + \beta_{42}\, invGNP + \beta_{43}\, invGNP_{-1} + \beta_{44}\, tdstoxgs \\ & + \beta_{45}\, tdstoxgs_{-1} + \beta_{46}\, iegdp + \beta_{47}\, iegdp_{-1} + \beta_{48}\, credgdp \\ & + \beta_{49}\, credgdp_{-1} + \beta_{50}\, corrupt + \beta_{51}\, usd + \beta_{52}\, jpy + \beta_{53}\, eur + \varepsilon\end{aligned}$$

where:

- ln(***spread***) = natural logarithm of spread (over LIBOR for loans, over benchmark security for bonds).
- ***maturity*** = maturity of loan or bond, in years.
- ln_***size*** = natural logarithm of loan or bond issue size, in millions US$.
- ***nbprov*** = number of provider banks (for loans), or arranger banks (for bonds).
- ***g_explic, g_implic*** = dummies for explicitly, resp. implicitly guaranteed instrument (implicit guarantee in the sense, for instance, that the borrower or issuer is the subsidiary of another concern).
- ***secured*** = dummy for secured instrument.
- ***increase*** = dummy to indicate that the original amount of the bond or the loan has been increased.
- ***constrpt, tradind, finservb, finservn, high-tech, infrastr, popserv, state, transpor*** = sectoral dummies for construction and property, traditional industry, financial services (banks), financial services (non-banks), high-tech industry, infrastructure, population-related services, state, transport. Note that the dummy for the utilities sectors was excluded from the equation as the case by default as its inclusion would have overspecified the model.
- ***debtgdp*** = ratio of debt/GDP for country of the borrower/issuer, for year concerned (end-year), $_{-1}$ for previous year.
- ***brent*** = price of one barrel of Brent crude oil at time of signing (in US$), $_{-1}$ one year before.
- ***treas*** = yield on the three-month US Treasury Bill, for month concerned, $_{-1}$ one year before.
- ***pppsh*** = PPP share of world GDP of the borrower's/issuer's country for year concerned (end-year), $_{-1}$ for previous year.
- ***growth*** = real GDP growth in borrower's/issuer's country, for year concerned, $_{-1}$ for previous year.
- ***wrgdp*** = growth in world GDP for year concerned, $_{-1}$ for previous year.
- ***trade*** = growth in world trade for year concerned, $_{-1}$ for previous year.
- ***cty_shar*** = share of the borrower's (issuer's) country in world syndicated lending (bond issuance) for year concerned, $_{-1}$ for previous year.
- ***bus_shar*** = share of the borrower's (issuer's) business sector in world syndicated lending (bond issuance), for year concerned, $_{-1}$ for previous year.

Continued

Table 7.3 Continued

- ***restodeb*** = ratio of external reserves/debt in borrower's/issuer's country for year concerned (end-year), $_{-1}$ for previous year.
- ***gra*** = dummy for assistance received by the country of the borrower/issuer from the IMF – use of Fund credit by operating the (GRA) during the year concerned.
- ***defiGDP*** = ratio of government deficit/GDP in borrower's/issuer's country for year concerned (end-year), $_{-1}$ for previous year.
- ***curacGDP*** = ratio of current account/GDP in borrower's/issuer's country for year concerned (end-year), $_{-1}$ for previous year.
- ***invGNP*** = ratio of investment to GNP in borrower's/issuer's country for year concerned, $_{-1}$ for previous year.
- ***tdstoxgs*** = ratio of debt service to exports of goods and services for country of the borrower/issuer, for year concerned, $_{-1}$ for previous year.
- ***iegdp*** = ratio of imports plus exports over GDP for country of the borrower/issuer, for year concerned, $_{-1}$ for previous year.
- ***credgdp*** = ratio of bank credit/GDP for country of the borrower or issuer, for year concerned, $_{-1}$ for previous year.
- ***corrupt*** = corruption index of the country of the borrower/issuer (assigned by Transparency International).
- ***usd, jpy, eur*** = dummies for instrument denominated, respectively, in US $, Japanese yen and euro (or any of its 12 predecessor currencies).
- ε is a random disturbance.

Fixed-effects panel regression, considering each borrower country as a group.

Variable	Ln (Loan spreads)		Ln (Bond spreads)	
maturity	0.0253‡	(0.003)	0.0099‡	(0.002)
ln_size	−0.1029‡	(0.012)	−0.0001	(0.033)
nbprov	0.0025	(0.001)	−0.0088‡	(0.004)
g_explic	−0.2824‡	(0.030)	−0.0165	(0.068)
g_implic	0.0086	(0.045)	−0.0648	(0.069)
secured	0.1958‡	(0.028)	−0.2536	(0.320)
increase	0.0227	(0.040)	−0.1126	(0.073)
(sector dummies not reported)				
debtgdp	0.0052‡	(0.002)	0.0097	(0.012)
$debtgdp_{-1}$	−0.0035	(0.003)	−0.0152*	(0.008)
brent	−0.0086*	(0.004)	−0.0532‡	(0.014)
$brent_{-1}$	−0.0227‡	(0.004)	0.0179	(0.013)
treas	−0.0582	(0.037)	−0.1680	(0.127)
$treas_{-1}$	0.0052	(0.029)	−0.0030	(0.124)
pppsh	2.4651‡	(0.694)	−2.3399	(2.599)
$pppsh_{-1}$	−1.6127‡	(0.672)	2.5049	(2.302)
growth	−0.0137	(0.011)	0.0434	(0.050)
$growth_{-1}$	0.0039	(0.004)	−0.0036	(0.036)

Continued

Table 7.3 Continued

Variable	Ln (Loan spreads)		Ln (Bond spreads)	
wrgdp	−0.2297‡	(0.081)	−0.1319	(0.346)
$wrgdp_{-1}$	−0.4112‡	(0.083)	0.3025	(0.338)
trade	0.0976‡	(0.018)	0.0371	(0.109)
$trade_{-1}$	0.0838‡	(0.019)	0.0119	(0.100)
cty_shar	0.2303*	(0.135)	0.0823	(0.230)
$ctyshar_{-1}$	0.2285*	(0.123)	−0.2702†	(0.112)
bus_shar	−0.0346*	(0.018)	−0.0215	(0.014)
$busshar_{-1}$	0.0049	(0.019)	0.0167	(0.014)
restodeb	0.0001	(0.000)	0.0036	(0.002)
$resdeb_{-1}$	0.0003	(0.000)	−0.0005	(0.000)
gra	0.0946*	(0.051)	0.5579‡	(0.177)
defiGDP	0.0155‡	(0.005)	−0.0078	(0.027)
$defigdp_{-1}$	0.0246‡	(0.009)	0.0377	(0.040)
curacGDP	−0.0144*	(0.007)	0.0453	(0.029)
$curgdp_{-1}$	−0.0237‡	(0.009)	0.0048	(0.030)
invGNP	−0.0612‡	(0.009)	−0.0248	(0.031)
$invgnp_{-1}$	−0.0315‡	(0.009)	0.0705	(0.046)
tdstoxgs	0.0039*	(0.002)	0.0105	(0.009)
$tdsxgs_{-1}$	−0.0010	(0.002)	−0.0064	(0.016)
iegdp	0.0001	(0.000)	−0.0001	(0.000)
$iegdp_{-1}$	0.0090‡	(0.002)	−0.0266‡	(0.010)
credgdp	0.0000	(0.000)	−0.0000	(0.000)
$credgdp_{-1}$	−0.0000*	(0.000)	−0.0000‡	(0.000)
usd	−0.2550‡	(0.095)	0.1727	(0.141)
jpy	−0.3141‡	(0.126)	0.0081	(0.273)
eur	−0.1320	(0.107)	0.1942	(0.145)
intercept	7.0714‡	(0.443)	5.4644‡	(2.709)

Note: Standard errors in parentheses. Number of observations in loan spreads regression = 2,772, in bond spreads regression = 530. *F*-tests are significant at the 1% level.

* Significant at the 10% level; † significant at the 5% level; ‡ significant at the 1% level.

bonds. Other authors (see p. 136) who have analysed the effects of collateral and guarantees on the pricing of bonds and loans have also failed to identify a systematic relationship.

The sensitivity of bond and loan pricing to borrower sectors appears to be quite different: while several sectoral dummies seem to influence loan spreads, no sectoral dummy is significantly related to the pricing of bonds. Investors may consider developing country bonds as an asset class in themselves and therefore show less sensitivity than in the case of loans to the borrower's industry for determining the pricing (while banks seem to pay more attention to the borrower's industry when granting loans). The significant and positive coefficients on the construction and property as well as the high-tech sectors in the loan pricing regression may reflect the high risk–return or speculative profile of these industries. As in Eichengreen and Mody (2000), loans granted to banks appear to be relatively cheaper than others, possibly because of the implicit or explicit LOLR guarantees enjoyed by these institutions.

Turning to the macroeconomic determinants of loan and bond pricing, no relationship is detected between the yield on the risk-free alternative investment and the primary market pricing of developing country bonds and loans: this is in accordance with Kamin and von Kleist (1999).[9] As noted by these two authors, the implication for policy-makers is that an upturn in industrialized country interest rates may lead to a smaller than expected upturn in developing country spreads. The negative and significant coefficient on the dummy for loans denominated in Japanese yen indicates that Japanese banks' low funding costs could have resulted in lower spreads on developing country loans (Eichengreen and Mody, 2000) – this underpricing could reflect a 'search-for yield' attitude on Japanese banks' behalf.

A positive and significant coefficient is found for growth in world trade for the developing country loan pricing regression (indicating that when world trade is booming, more economic agents are competing for foreign funds, which are then harder to come by) and a negative one on growth in world GDP. The absence of a significant coefficient on either of these two variables in the bond pricing regressions underscores the important role that banks still play in supporting developing countries' participation in world trade. For policy-makers, who have put forward world trade as a means of improving developing countries' economic conditions, the availability of disintermediated foreign funds for these countries' participation in world trade therefore seems of particular relevance. Besides, the negative effect on bond pricing of a high penetration of trade into the economy of the borrower (measured by the ratio of imports plus exports divided by GDP) and its positive effect on loan pricing suggests that the financing of the participation of developing countries in world trade can be more optimal through bonds than loans, provided that the former channel is available.

The effect of market structure on pricing appears to be different depending on whether loans or bonds are considered. On the one hand, the positive coefficient on country share in world syndicated lending seems to lead to higher developing country loan spreads in the regressions, suggesting that banks charge higher than normal spreads to borrowers from countries which are excessively dependent on bank lending for their economic development. This could reflect the fact that either the banks are exercising market power or loans are becoming pricier as greater concentration of risk is perceived by investors. On the other hand, the opposite effect seems to prevail for bonds (higher country shares are associated with lower bond spreads) where banks, as underwriters and distributors of securities rather than ultimate bearers of risk, have less scope to exercise market power. Instead, a country's established presence as an issuer, albeit of junk bonds, seems to result in lower bond spreads (a reputation effect). Meanwhile, the negative and significant coefficient on sector share in world syndicated lending indicates that particular industries' established presence on the market can lower loan spreads. In the loan regression, a positive coefficient is obtained on the contemporaneous value of the purchasing parity share of world GDP of the borrower's country and a negative sign on the lagged value of the same variable. This can be interpreted as a time-effect phenomenon. Investors may regard high values of the contemporaneous share of world wealth indicator as a licence to charge suboptimal spreads while they are more inclined to regard its value from the previous year as a warranty of reputation, allowing cheaper loans.

It was not possible to analyse the effects of the corruption index in the panel regression because the index itself uniquely identifies each developing country. In a non-panel version of this regression with robust standard errors (not reported), this variable is negatively associated with developing country bond and loan pricing – the lower the level of corruption, reflected by higher values of the corruption index, the lower the price – confirming that for the purposes of determining the pricing of foreign funds, investors are sensitive to the quality of the business climate and the presence of corruption in developing countries and penalize those countries' borrowers where there is a relatively high level of perceived corruption by charging them relatively higher spreads.

A greater number of macroeconomic variables influence developing country loan pricing more than bond pricing, again confirming that developing country bonds may be considered by investors as an asset class in themselves, with less sensitivity to the macroeconomic conditions prevailing in the borrowers' country. Other coefficients have the expected signs, favourable macroeconomic indicators (favourable current account position, high ratio of investment/GNP and of domestic credit/GDP) are generally associated with lower spreads and unfavourable indicators (high ratio of debt service/exports, of government debt or deficit/GDP; assistance from the IMF) with higher spreads.

The significant and positive bond dummy in the regression where bonds and loans are pooled together (not reported) shows that spreads tend to be higher on emerging market bonds than on loans, confirming, on average, the riskier nature of the former as compared to the latter. This finding is in accordance with Sachs and Cohen (1982), Eichengreen and Mody (1997, 1998, 2000) and Kamin and von Kleist (1999) and of course also with the figures shown on pp. 151 and 156. The tests of the panel regression also indicate that loan spreads differ among countries: country effects are significant in determining the pricing of developing country bonds and loans (the *F*-test strongly suggests a rejection of the hypothesis that there are no country effects).

Analysis of lending to industrialized countries

The above results are now compared with those of a similar regression analysis on a sample of 20,365 industrialized country syndicated loans and 5,086 bond issues. The model and results are presented in Table 7.4. Again, the panel regression confirms that country effects are significant in the determination of the pricing of industrialized country loans and bonds.

Comparison of industrialized and developing country loans

Several similarities can be noted in the pricing of industrialized and developing country loans. As for developing country loans, the coefficient on the maturity is significant and positive on industrialized country loans, meaning that a premium is demanded by lenders for being exposed to a risk for a longer period of time. This is a verification, for industrialized country loans, of the results found in Kamin and von Kleist (1999). Moreover, in accordance with Kleimeier and Megginson (2000), a significantly negative relationship is found between loan size and spreads, although the coefficient is higher in absolute terms for industrialized loans than for developing country loans, suggesting that banks in the sample could have more experience in monitoring industrialized country borrowers than developing country ones, deriving more economies of scale from that activity. Lastly, most sectoral dummies on industrialized country loans are significant and have the same signs as in the case of developing countries, with the absolute values of the coefficients on the construction and property, traditional industry, high-tech, population-related services and transport sectors higher in the case of industrialized countries.

Still, despite the above similarities, the pricing of industrialized and developing country loans appears to differ in several respects. First, the number of fund provider banks had no effect on the pricing of developing country loans; here a significantly positive relationship is detected,

Table 7.4 Loan and bond pricing regressions for industrialized countries **Variable names as in Table 7.3.**

Variable	**Ln (Loan spreads)**		**Ln (Bond spreads)**	
maturity	0.0696‡	(0.001)	0.0274‡	(0.001)
ln_size	−0.2461‡	(0.004)	−0.1019‡	(0.012)
nbprov	0.0013†	(0.000)	−0.0209‡	(0.001)
g_explic	−0.0578†	(0.025)	−0.0213	(0.031)
g_implic	−0.0931‡	(0.028)	0.2246‡	(0.028)
secured	0.4116‡	(0.011)	−0.2026‡	(0.063)
increase	−0.1390‡	(0.040)	0.1708‡	(0.056)
(sector dummies not reported)				
debtgdp	−0.0068	(0.007)	0.0058	(0.006)
$debtgdp_{-1}$	0.0174†	(0.006)	−0.0001	(0.006)
brent	0.0009	(0.001)	−0.0199‡	(0.005)
$brent_{-1}$	−0.0042†	(0.002)	0.0117†	(0.005)
treas	−0.0368‡	(0.014)	−0.1112‡	(0.029)
$treas_{-1}$	−0.0268	(0.018)	−0.1654‡	(0.043)
pppsh	0.2381	(0.161)	0.1419	(0.183)
$pppsh_{-1}$	−0.2890	(0.219)	−0.0413	(0.205)
growth	0.0062	(0.017)	−0.0093	(0.022)
$growth_{-1}$	−0.0097	(0.016)	−0.1255‡	(0.023)
wrgdp	−0.1670‡	(0.047)	−0.2139†	(0.088)
$wrgdp_{-1}$	−0.2175‡	(0.051)	−0.1576	(0.097)
trade	0.0380‡	(0.010)	0.0542†	(0.026)
$trade_{-1}$	0.0315‡	(0.010)	0.1604‡	(0.020)
cty_shar	−0.0282†	(0.011)	0.0024	(0.005)
cty_shar_{-1}	−0.0164‡	(0.005)	0.0110†	(0.005)
bus_shar	0.0136	(0.008)	0.0025	(0.004)
bus_shar_{-1}	−0.0114	(0.009)	−0.0080	(0.005)
restodeb	−0.0126	(0.008)	−0.0000	(0.011)
$restodeb_{-1}$	0.0093	(0.007)	0.0177*	(0.010)
defiGDP	−0.0423‡	(0.014)	0.0007	(0.022)
$defiGDP_{-1}$	−0.0251*	(0.012)	−0.0307*	(0.016)
curacGDP	−0.0035	(0.012)	−0.0254	(0.019)
$curacGDP_{-1}$	0.0034	(0.013)	−0.0331	(0.023)
invGNP	−0.0677‡	(0.022)	−0.0593*	(0.031)
$invGNP_{-1}$	0.1154‡	(0.024)	0.1122‡	(0.033)
iegdp	0.0207‡	(0.004)	0.0057	(0.006)
$iegdp_{-1}$	−0.0111†	(0.004)	0.0126†	(0.006)
credgdp	0.0105‡	(0.002)	−0.0179‡	(0.003)
$credgdp_{-1}$	−0.0011	(0.000)	0.0063*	(0.003)
usd	0.0740†	(0.030)	0.1935‡	(0.035)
jpy	0.0061	(0.141)	−0.9792‡	(0.101)
eur	−0.0229	(0.045)	−0.1743‡	(0.036)
intercept	6.7548†	(2.644)	3.2922†	(1.666)

Notes: Standard errors in parentheses. Number of observations in loan spreads regression = 20,365, in bond spreads regression = 5,086. *F*-tests are significant at the 1% level.

* Significant at the 10% level; † Significant at the 5% level; ‡ Significant at the 1% level.

possibly because industrialized country loans requiring the presence of a high number of providers could represent more complex deals, on average, than comparable emerging market deals. Melnik and Plaut (1991) also detect a link between deal complexity and the number of managers. Second, for industrialized country loans, implicit and explicit guarantees can lower spreads; only explicit guarantees had this effect for developing countries, possibly because only they were considered binding enough. As in the case of developing countries, secured loans are more expensive than others, potentially because they are very risky[10]. Third, the dummy for increased deals – in the sense that the amount of a facility has been increased from its original amount – has a negative effect on industrialized country loan spreads, not on emerging ones, suggesting that banks wield less market power and show more flexibility to adapt to changes in industrial borrowers' financing needs.

Regarding market structure, it is found that, unlike developing countries, industrialized country borrowers with a high share of world syndicated borrowing are having to pay less for their loans relative to others. This could reflect pricing gains from the established presence of their countries on the loan market.

In the non-panel version of the estimation (not reported), unlike for developing countries the corruption index did not turn up as a significant variable for loan pricing: lenders do not seem concerned about this issue in industrialized countries, or consider at least that a legal framework exists for enforcing loan contracts.

The negative coefficient on the ratio of government deficit to GDP is worth noting in the industrialized country loan pricing regression. Investors seem to trust that when the government of an industrialized country stimulates demand and economic activity through higher budget deficits, then this is beneficial for the fortunes of the borrowers that operate to meet the extra demand. This translates into cheaper loans for such borrowers. An opposite effect is found for developing countries: borrowers of countries with higher government deficits face higher loan prices, possibly because investors do not trust the ability of the governments concerned to stimulate economic activity through higher deficits. For instance, in undemocratic or corrupt regimes, members of the government can be seen to embezzle the extra government expense for their own personal benefit, or to spend the money on 'white elephants'.

A negative relationship is found between the primary market pricing of industrialized country loans (and bonds) and the risk-free interest rate: as in Kamin and von Kleist (1999), no such a relationship is apparent in the case of developing countries.

Comparison of industrialized and developing country bonds

A number of differences can be noted between pricing mechanisms for industrialized and developing country bonds.

To begin with, the negative and significant effect of the number of arranger banks on bond pricing is more than twice as high for industrialized country issues as for developing ones, suggesting that there may be more competition between banks arranging the former, while a smaller number of banks may specialize in arranging issues for the latter.

Regarding the microeconomic factors that influence bond prices, secured industrialized issues are relatively cheaper than others; securing developing country bonds had a positive effect on pricing. The significant and positive coefficient on the presence of implicit guarantees is surprising in the case of industrialized country bonds, but again not incompatible with Smith and Warner (1979). Issuer sectors seem to be taken into account more for industrial country bonds than for developing country ones, suggesting that investors consider the former as an asset class in itself to the lesser extent than developing country bonds.

As far as macroeconomic factors are concerned, world economic growth, world trade and the share of trade in the GDP of the country of the issuer significantly affect the pricing of industrialized country bonds, which was not the case for developing country bonds, suggesting that the financing of trade in industrialized countries tends to rely both on loans and bonds while it tends to rely more exclusively on loans in the case of developing countries.

Regarding currency effects, note that unlike developing country bond issues denominated in euro, industrialized country issues denominated in euro are relatively cheaper than the others, suggesting that the liquidity of euro-denominated bond markets catering for industrialized country issues may be higher than for developing country issues[11]. The significant coefficients for issues denominated in yen and US dollars (respectively negative and positive) can be accounted for by benchmark or cheap funding effects in the case of bonds.

Finally, as in the case of industrialized country loans and unlike developing country bonds and loans, the corruption index did not turn up as a significant explanatory variable of spreads in the non-panel version of the estimation (not reported) in the case of industrialized country bonds. It is interesting to relate this result to Bilson, Brailsford and Hooper (2002), who present evidence that political risk is important in explaining stock return variation in individual emerging markets, but not in developed markets.

Analysis of the pooled loans and bonds sample

The significant and negative bond dummy in the regression where industrialized country bonds and loans are pooled (not reported) shows that spreads tend to be lower for industrialized country bonds than loans – confirming, on average, the riskier nature of the latter as compared to the former. This result is in contrast with the findings about developing countries, but consistent with the view (Diamond, 1991; Bolton and Freixas, 2000) that riskier or 'start-up' borrowers require monitoring and will use bank lending as a source of finance until they establish a credible repayment history and are able to issue securities in their own name. Furthermore, this finding is also in accordance with the empirical results of Melnik and Plaut (1991). The comparison with developing countries confirms that on average during the 1990s, developing country borrowers were issuing 'junk'-quality bonds i.e. bonds where risk premia are higher than developing country loans – while industrialized country borrowers have predominantly been occupying the higher-quality end of the bond market, where spreads are lower than on loans.

Analysis of contagion effects

In order to determine statistically if contagion could have affected industrialized country borrowers in the aftermath of the financial crises in developing countries – that is to say whether industrialized borrowers' terms of access to the primary market worsened following the crises – a dummy variable was created in the industrialized country bond and loan sample taking the value of 1 in the possible instances of contagion identified during the visual inspection (p. 131). In other words the value of 1 was assigned to the dummy during years when industrialized country bond and/or loan spreads had peaked or maturities had bottomed out simultaneously with developing country bonds or loans. The facilities concerned were:

- Japanese and US loans signed in 1999 (peaking of spreads during the Russian, Turkish and Latin American crises, see Figure 7A.2)
- Japanese bonds issued in 1999 (peaking of spreads and maturity trough, see Figures 7A.7 and 7A.8)
- Japanese loans signed in 1998 (sharp reduction of maturities during the Asian crisis,[12] see Figure 7A.3)
- US bonds issued in 1998 (maturity trough, see Figure 7A.8).

The industrialized country loan and bond pricing panel regressions were then re-run incorporating this extra dummy variable on the right-hand side. The contagion dummy was found to be strongly significant and positive in case of loans and insignificant in case of bonds (not reported). This confirms the results of the visual analysis (p. 131) which highlighted the fact that the contagion phenomenon from developing to industrialized countries had appeared to have occurred to a lesser extent in the case of bonds than of loans. Another explanation is that contagion on the bond markets (especially affecting the low-quality end of the market for industrialized country bonds) is more likely to have taken place in the secondary markets. The secondary market for loans is still much less developed than that for bonds.

Conclusion

While the academic literature suggests that it may be appropriate to apply the same model to analyse the pricing of bonds and loans, differences were found in the way the two instruments reacted to price determinants. Furthermore, there were differences in the pricing of developing and industrialized country instruments. Based on the research described in this chapter, the following conclusions can be drawn.

First, in the 1990s, investors may have considered developing country bonds as an asset class in themselves, with less sensitivity of the pricing of such bonds to macroeconomic conditions and borrower business sector than the developing country loans or industrialized country bonds issued during the same period. It is verified that on average, developing country bonds have been riskier than developing country loans and industrialized country loans riskier than industrialized country bonds. This could be evidence of the fact that, for the period under study, some industrialized country borrowers have been able to access the good-quality compartment of the bond market where no financial intermediation or monitoring by banks is needed while, on average, developing country borrowers have been able to issue junk bonds (i.e. bonds that are riskier than loans).

Secondly, the corruption index in the borrower's country is significantly related to bond and loan pricing in developing countries, but not in industrialized countries, possibly mirroring the fact that, in the latter, investors consider that the legal and regulatory infrastructure is sufficient to enforce financial contracts. This result can be related to Bilson, Brailsford and Hooper (2002), who present proof that political risk is important in explaining stock return variation in individual emerging markets, particularly in the Pacific Basin, but not in developed markets. The chapter helps partially to answer the research issue raised by these authors by presenting evidence that there is some political risk exposure in emerging markets that is different from any exposure in developed markets, and that this has implications for asset pricing and portfolio decisions in these markets.

Thirdly, as in Kamin and von Kleist (1999), no significant relationship is detected for the period under study between the primary market pricing of developing country bonds and loans and industrialized country interest rates. As noted by Kamin and von Kleist (1999), the implication for policy-makers is that an upturn in industrialized country interest rates may lead to a smaller than expected upturn in developing country spreads. However, a negative relationship is found between industrialized country interest rates and spreads on loans and bonds granted to industrialized country borrowers, which could reflect poorer credits dropping out of the market during a period of high interest rates.

The structure of industrialized and developing country loan and bond markets during the 1990s was also studied. As far as the currency composition of these markets is concerned, it was found that industrialized country bonds and developing country loans denominated in Japanese yen were relatively cheaper than others, possibly because of low interest rates in the Japanese economy (constituting low funding costs for investors based in Japanese yen). Industrialized country bonds denominated in euro or its predecessor currencies were also found to be relatively cheaper than others, which could reflect the higher liquidity of that market segment. No similar effect was detected for developing country bonds denominated in euro, possibly suggesting relatively lower liquidity in that market segment.

Five years after the Asian crisis, bond issuance by developing countries, particularly large corporations, is starting to pick up. As *The Economist* notes (6 July 2002, p. 71): 'The future will probably involve a continued shift away from bank borrowing by big companies [from emerging markets]. Having been burned once, the healthy ones have been raising capital in the equity and, even more eagerly, in the bond markets.' The liquidity of markets for developing country bonds deserves policy-makers' attention all the more because this research also provides evidence of the still relatively low reliance of developing countries on bonds – at the expense of loans – to finance their participation in world trade. Furthermore, potentially less than optimal pricing behaviour is detected on banks' behalf when lending to developing country borrowers. This is shown by the positive coefficient in the loan pricing regressions on the share of the country concerned in world syndicated lending and by the absence of a positive reaction from the market in case of loan deals whose amount has been increased from the original facility amount. Finally, this research highlights the lower occurrence of contagion in financial markets from developing to industrialized country borrowers in the case of bonds than in the case of loans.

Appendix

Appendix 7.1 Characteristics of loan and bond financing, 1993–2001

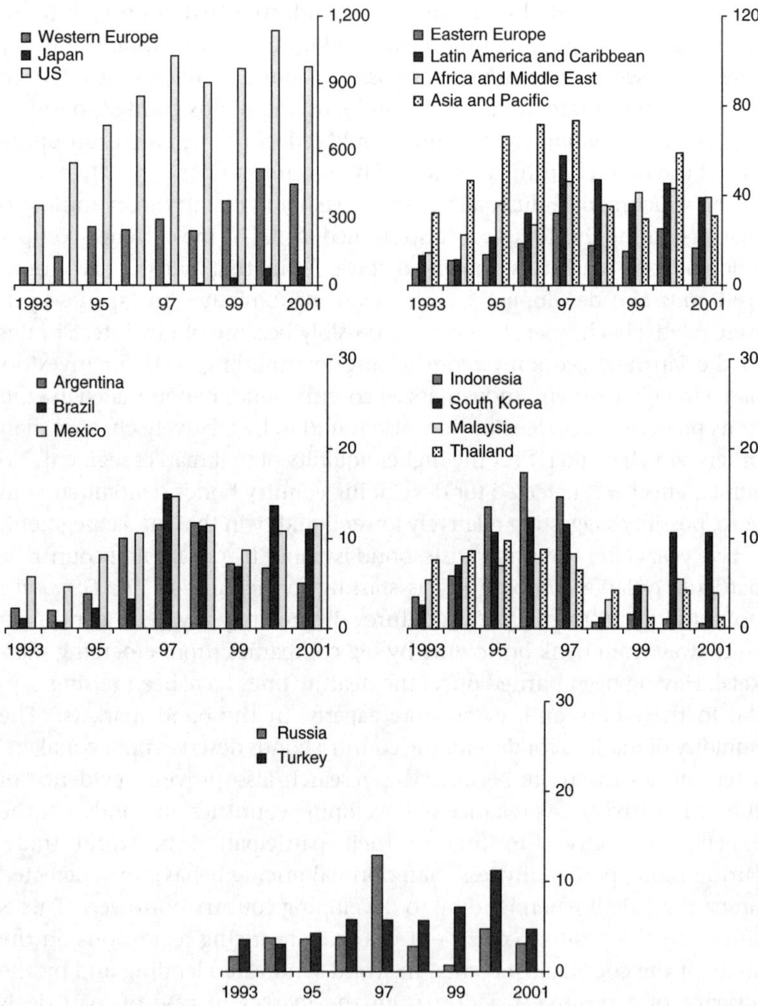

Figure 7A.1 Evolution of syndicated lending 1993–2001, industrialized countries and selected developing countries affected by financial crises, bn US$

Source: Dealogic.

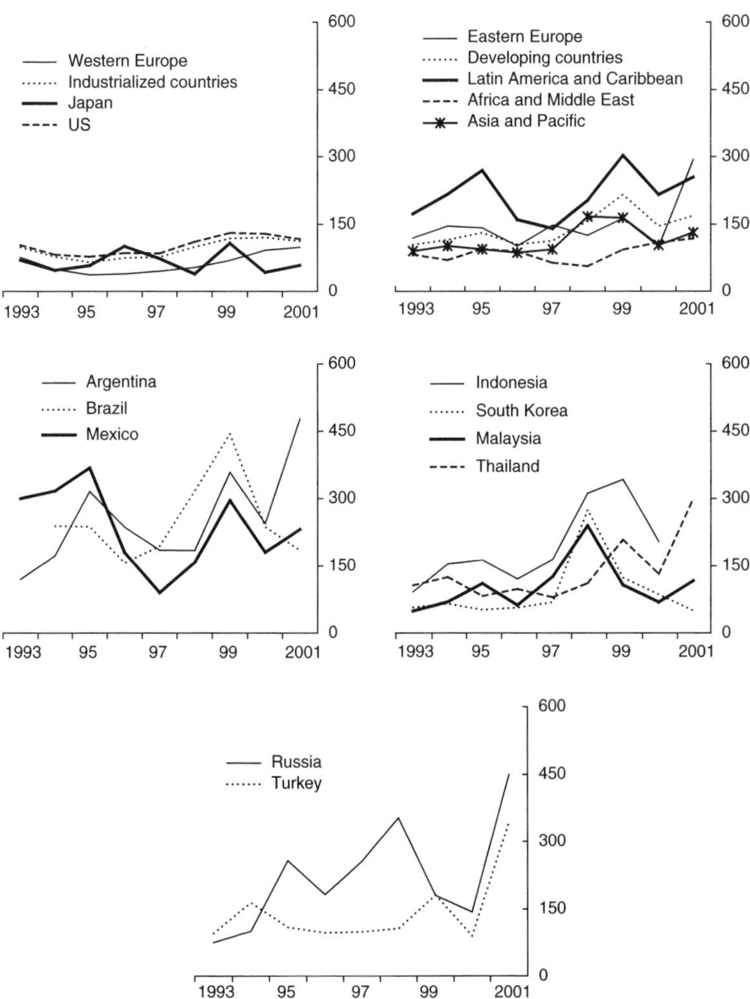

Figure 7A.2 Evolution of average LIBOR spreads weighted by facility amounts on syndicated credits granted to industrialized countries and selected developing countries affected by financial crises, basis points, 1993–2001

Source: Dealogic.

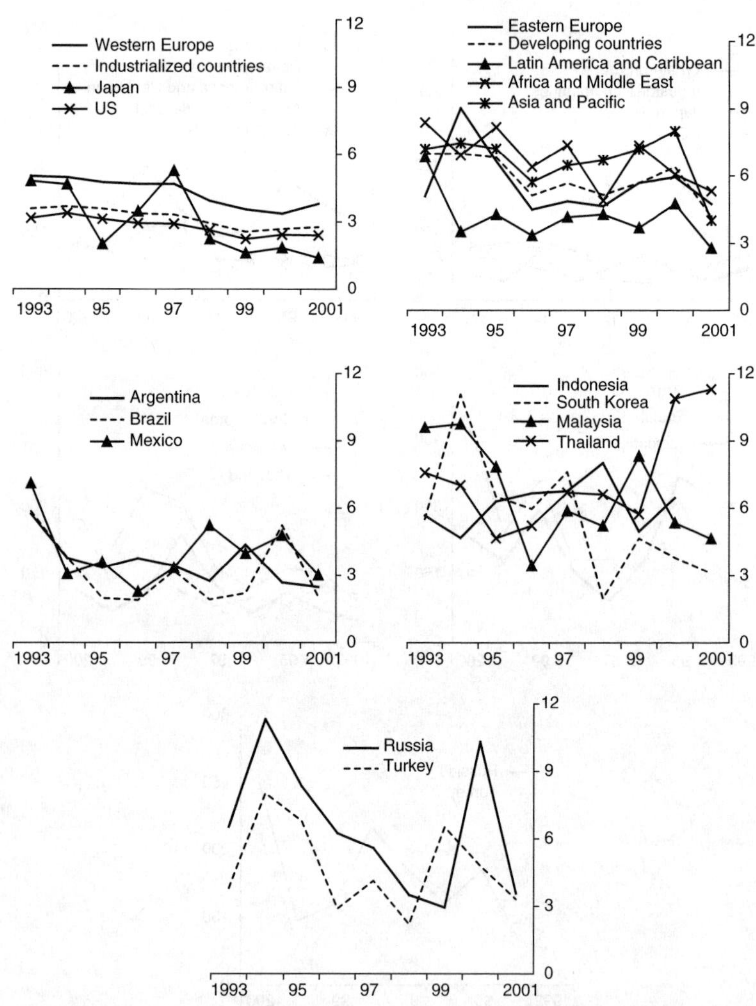

Figure 7A.3 Evolution of average maturities weighted by facility amounts on syndicated credits granted to industrialized countries and selected developing countries affected by financial crises, in years, 1993–2001

Source: Dealogic.

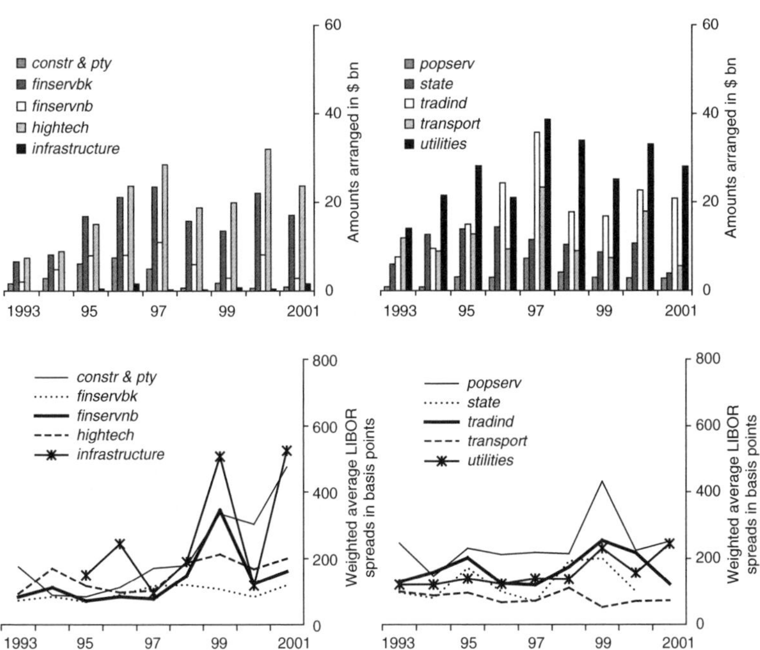

Figure 7A.4 Evolution of lending and average LIBOR spreads weighted by facility amounts on syndicated loans arranged for various business sectors in developing countries, 1993–2001

Notes: *constr&pty* = construction and property; *finservbk* = financial services – banks; *finservnb* = financial services – non-banks; *popserv* = population-related services; *tradind* = traditional industry.

Source: Dealogic.

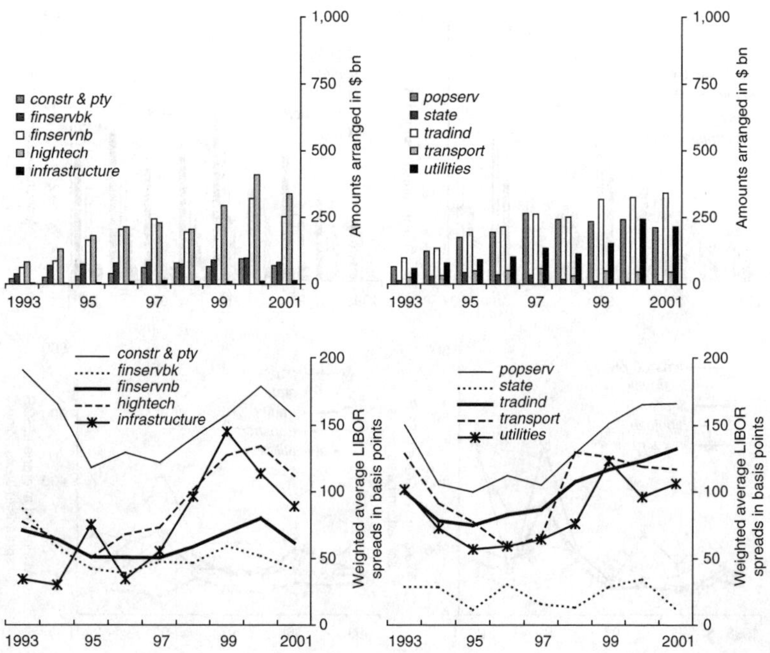

Figure 7A.5 Evolution of lending and average LIBOR spreads weighted by facility amounts on syndicated loans arranged for various business sectors in industrialized countries, 1993–2001

Notes: *constr&pty* = construction and property; *finservbk* = financial services – banks; *finservnb* = financial services – non-banks; *popserv* = population-related services; *tradind* = traditional industry.

Source: Dealogic.

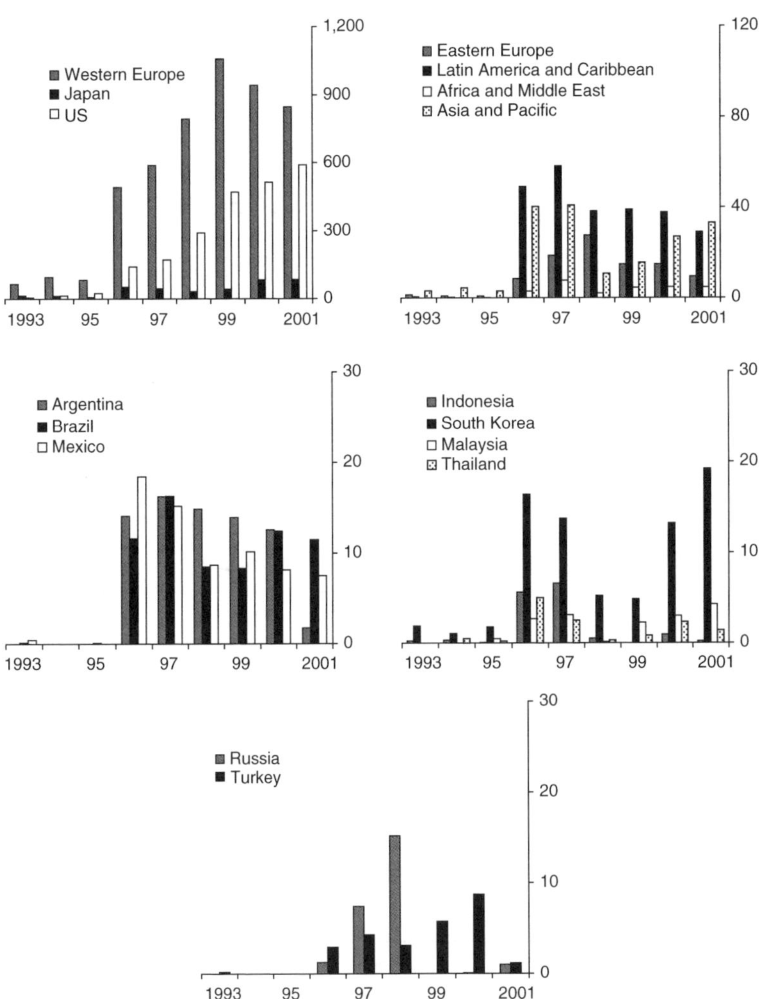

Figure 7A.6 Evolution of bond issuance by industrialized countries and selected developing countries affected by financial crises, 1993–2001, bn US$

Source: Dealogic.

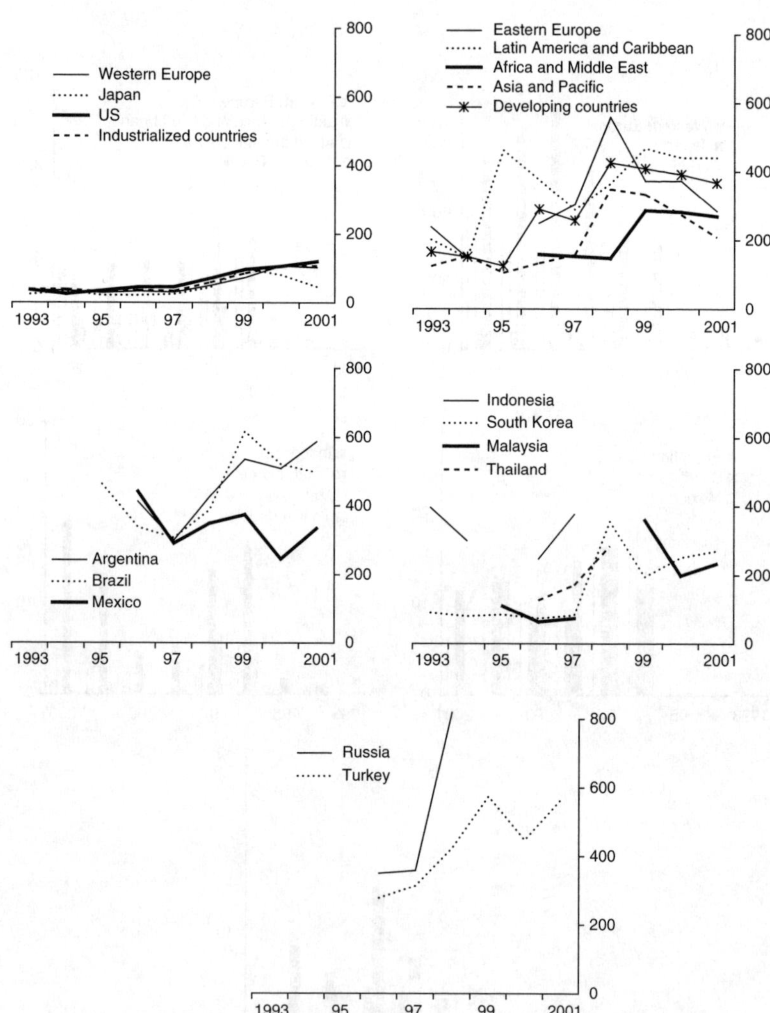

Figure 7A.7 Evolution of average launch spreads[a] weighted by facility amounts on bond issues for industrialized countries and selected developing countries affected by financial crises, basis points, 1993–2001

Note: [a] Spreads at issuance.

Sources: Dealogic.

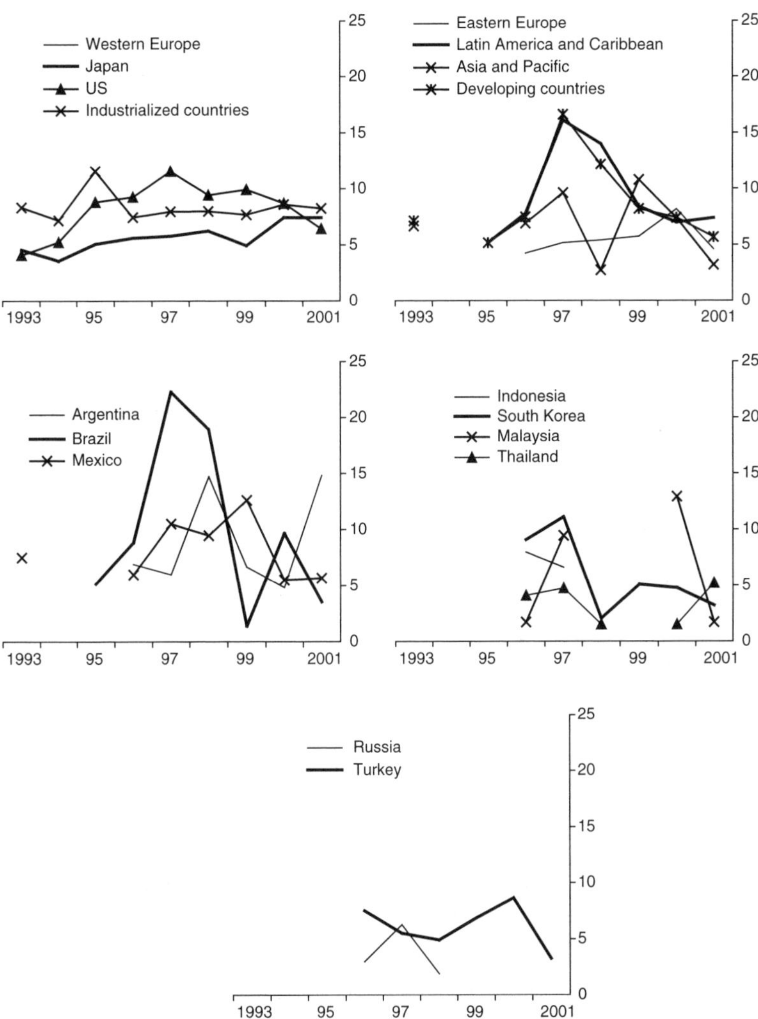

Figure 7A.8 Evolution of average maturities weighted by facility amounts on bond issues for industrialized countries and selected developing countries affected by financial crises, in years, 1993–2001

Sources: Dealogic.

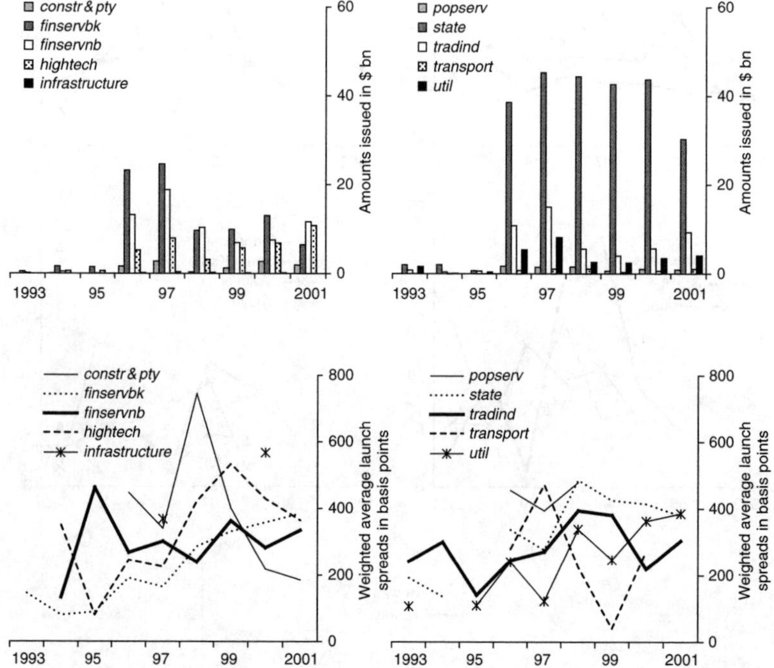

Figure 7A.9 Evolution of issuance amounts and average launch spreads[a] weighted by facility amounts on bonds issued by various business sectors in developing countries, 1993–2001

Notes: [a] Spreads at issuance.

constr&pty = construction and property; *finservbk* = financial services – banks; *finservnb* = financial services – non-banks; *popserv* = population-related services; *tradind* = traditional industry

Sources: Dealogic.

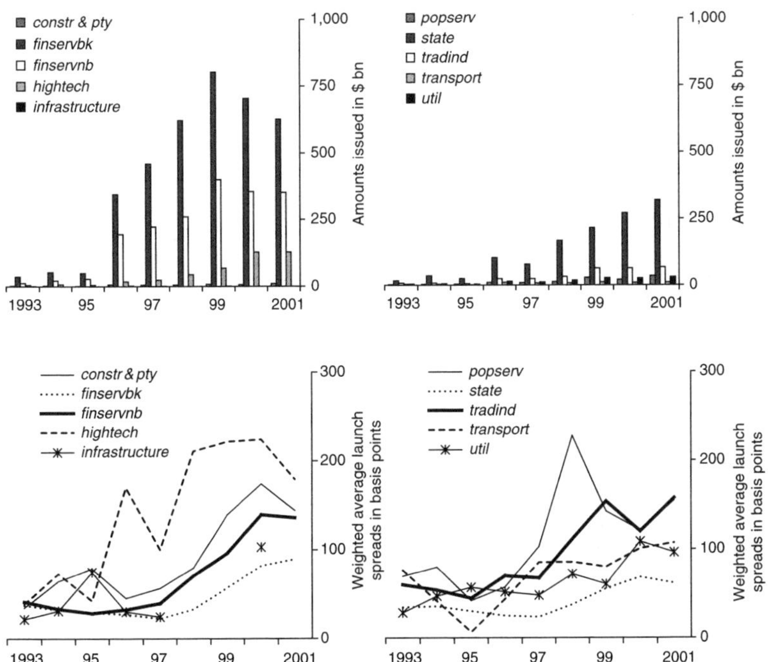

Figure 7A.10 Evolution of issuance amounts and average launch spreads[a] weighted by facility amounts on bonds issued by various business sectors in industrialized countries, 1993–2001

Notes: [a] Spreads at issuance.

constr&pty = construction and property; *finservbk* = financial services – banks; *finservnb* = financial services – non-banks; *popserv* = population-related services; *tradind* = traditional industry

Sources: Dealogic.

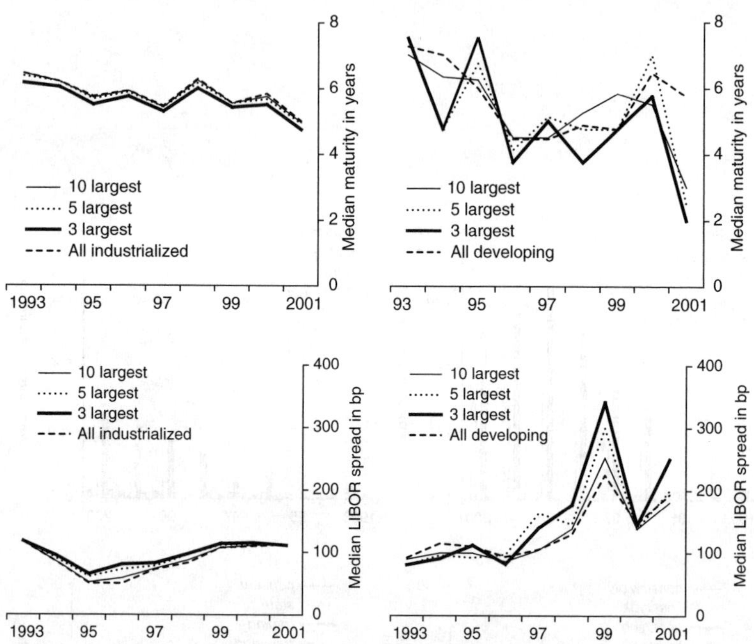

Figure 7A.11 Evolution of median maturity and pricing on syndicated loans granted to all industrialized and developing countries and countries with largest amounts of borrowings for year concerned, 1993–2001

Sources: Dealogic.

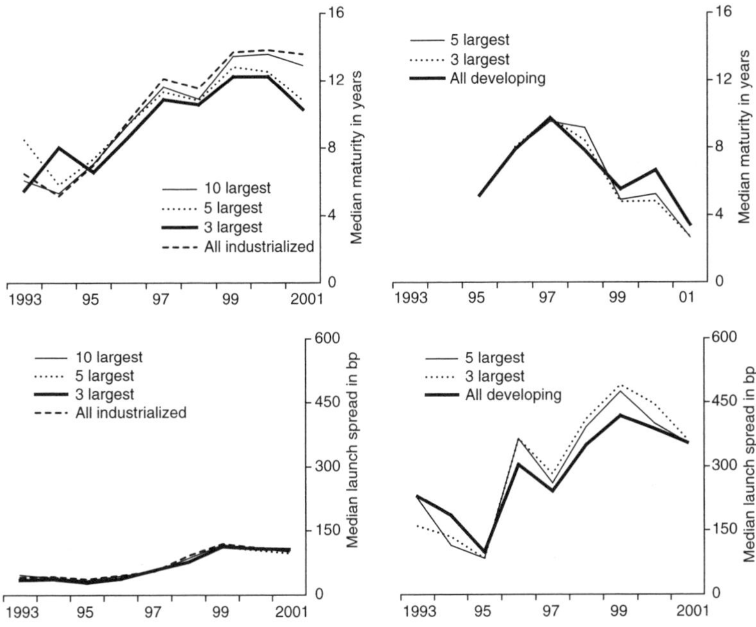

Figure 7A.12 Evolution of median maturity and launch spreads[a] on bond issues for all industrialized and developing countries and countries with largest amounts of issuance for year concerned, 1993–2001

Notes: [a] Spreads at issuance.

Source: Dealogic.

8
Syndicated Loans and the Financing of Distressed Emerging Markets

Introduction

This chapter extends the work of Altunbaş, Chakravarty and Kara (2004) and examines the effect of the IMF's *imprimatur* (seal of approval) on the cost of borrowing in the international syndicated loan markets between 1993 and 2001. It appears that the IMF-assisted countries paid higher spreads over LIBOR for short-term loans and had obtained fewer long-term loan contracts compared to their non-IMF peers for the financing of similar purpose projects. This may indicate a lack of confidence on the part of creditors that IMF prescriptions would have the desired effect in the long run on the economies of the client nations. Also, the pricing of syndicated loans for projects in these countries is inversely related to the level of short-term debt, signalling that creditors perhaps expect a bailout if a financial crisis occurs in the assisted nations. The academic critique of IMF policies and their implications for political economy, moral hazard and financial instability, is discussed first. Subsequently, an analysis of borrowing costs is undertaken by focusing on the impact of microeconomic loan characteristics and debt-distressed countries' macroeconomic indicators on loan spreads.

Critiques of the IMF

The IMF has come under increasing criticism in recent years for internal contradictions in policy. For example, it is maintained by Stiglitz (2002a, p. 107) that policies that are prescribed by the Fund to improve economic performance often have just the opposite effect on the economy. According to Edwards (1998), the world needs a major redesign of the international monetary system by abolishing the IMF – which is viewed as reactive rather than proactive – and creating new institutions with the mandate and ability to help prevent major, generalized and costly financial crises. There is also concern that the Fund's policies may not be sufficiently alert to the problems of increases in poverty, leading to avoidable political problems in economic restructuring. For example, the headcount ratio of poverty increased by 140 per cent in Indonesia between 'mid-1997 and early 1999', when the country was under IMF supervision following a major financial crisis affecting much of East Asia (Chand, 2003). The distributional effects of IMF programmes appear to depend on an indebted country's level of *per capita* income at the time of entry under the IMF umbrella. The poor in countries which have lower *per capita* income become poorer faster than their counterparts in countries with higher *per capita* income after imbibing IMF prescriptions (Grauda, 2000). Another interesting feature of income distribution is that labour's share of income is lower in countries under IMF programmes than in other countries with similar *per capita* income (Vreeland, 2002). Even the policy-makers in the IMF have begun to realise the need to address the political economy of income distribution, if restructuring is to be successful in ameliorating balance of payments constraints on growth. However, the level of understanding of these issues within the IMF may not be adequate, as observed in a report by the Fund's Independent Evaluation Unit in 2002. Finally, critics argue that the Fund may contribute to moral hazard in borrowing and lending, because it is perceived as being able to arrange lending at the last resort, and encourage risky behaviour by borrowers and private creditors in advance of crises (Joyce, 2002).

Do credit markets have faith in the IMF *imprimatur*?

The weight of the arguments underlying above criticisms is that long-term dependence on IMF prescriptions is harmful for the economic prospects of client states. Nevertheless, do financial markets also take a pessimistic view of the efficacy of IMF prescriptions? Altunbaş, Chakravarty and Kara (2004) approach this question by examining the effect of the IMF *imprimatur* on the cost of borrowing in the international capital markets by private and public sector entities located in client states, and comparing the costs for borrowers from countries that have not approached the IMF for assistance, despite the fact that they are also experiencing financial difficulties similar to those of the client states.

It is indeed the case that countries which have a history of debt rescheduling find it more expensive to borrow money in the capital markets (Ozler, 1993; Eichengreen and Mody, 2000). Some of these countries may approach the IMF for assistance following a period of financial difficulty. Any assistance that is provided is conditional on an agreement from the recipient country to revise economic policies to obtain the IMF's seal of approval. An expectation is that the financial markets will respond by making more credit available, and on terms that are more favourable, than will otherwise be the case. The literature does not provide systematic empirical evidence as to whether the above expectation is fulfilled. The literature simply suggests that a country in receipt of assistance from the IMF finds it more expensive to borrow in the private markets than developing countries in general (Altunbaş and Gadanecz, 2003).

Presumably the decision to seek assistance from the IMF is perceived as a harbinger of 'potential problems in the economy' (Altunbaş and Gadanecz, 2003). It may also be the case that private lenders may be engaging in riskier projects in counties under the IMF's umbrella in the expectation of a bailout by the Fund in case of default. However, these are not the only plausible explanations. It may also be the case that there is reluctance on the part of private lenders to put faith in the efficacy of IMF prescriptions. This particular line of investigation entails a comparison of IMF-assisted developing countries with a subset of other developing countries that are also faced with problems with balance of payments but have eschewed IMF assistance, and the object is to carry out an investigation using a large dataset on the effect of the IMF *imprimatur* on the price of loans.

Background of IMF policies

The IMF was originally set up with a mandate to provide assistance to member countries facing short-term problems in the foreign exchange markets (Goldsbrough *et al.*, 2002). Help was available to both developing and industrialized nations. But in recent years the Fund has become increasingly active in long-term development policies. Between 1971 and 2000, 29 countries out of 128 borrowers were prolonged users and another 15 were very prolonged users of IMF assistance (IMF, 2002). Stiglitz (2002b) argues that the mandate of the IMF – to provide liquidity to countries facing temporary economic downturn – is at variance with the task into which the Fund has allowed itself to be drawn. In consequence, the Fund's prescriptions, based on its traditional approach to short-term problems with currencies, are often ill advised. Short-term problems in the balance of payments can sometimes be addressed through contractionary fiscal policies, but the response to structural imbalance in an economy requires an understanding of *development policy*. Critics argue that the Fund does not have that understanding and thus resorts to prescriptions that may, at best, work to smooth out short-term difficulties in the balance of payments. The consequence is that these policies are counter-productive for making the economic adjustments needed for economic growth (Stiglitz, 2002a). For example, a study by Prezeworski and Vreeland (2000) reveals that participation in IMF programmes lowers growth rates for these countries as long as they remain under a programme.

The critics can be grouped into three categories. The first argues that the Fund does not appreciate the political consequences of policy and thus the policies that are prescribed fail to deliver economic growth. The second argues that the Fund's policies lead to greater financial instability. Finally, there is the issue of moral hazard in borrowing and lending that is not conducive to long-term prosperity. These arguments are outlined below, but without any critical evaluation of their relative merit.

Political economy

Easterly (2003) investigated the impact of various structural adjustment programmes (SAPs) and reported that they lower the impact of economic fluctuations on poverty – i.e. economic expansions following these adjustments benefit the poor less but contractions resulting from structural adjustment also hurt the poor less. According to Goldsbrough *et al.* (2002), one possible explanation as to why these policies fail to deliver growth is the linkage of aid to the acceptance of IMF-supported programmes. The linkage raises the stakes at programme negotiations to the point of putting strong pressure on both country authorities and the IMF to reach an agreement, even though both parties may have doubts about the programme's feasibility. The quality of the *imprimatur* is thus compromised by the pressure to reach an agreement.

Another aspect of the above idea – that the quality of IMF programmes is diluted due to the political exigencies of the process of reaching a decision – is examined by Gould (2003). The Fund itself provides only a fraction of the amount of money that a country needs to bring its external account into balance, and to implement the economic policies recommended by the Fund. The IMF relies on supplementary, external financing to ensure the success of its programmes. This gives the supplementary financiers leverage over the design of the Fund's programmes. Too many contradictory pressures are faced in the design of policy, and the result is less coherent than it might otherwise have been.

Financial instability

Another argument made by critics is that IMF programmes have entailed the type of financial liberalization that causes greater fluctuations in short-term capital inflows and outflows, thereby leading to greater volatility in the financial markets in the developing countries (Rodrik, 1998; Stiglitz, 2000, 2003a). Kohler (2003) categorizes the volume and complexity of these flows and explains why they raise concern about what he calls 'vulnerability to crises'.

A more favourable view of these short-term flows is taken by those who believe that the IMF's *imprimatur* has a catalyst effect on private capital flows to increase the allocative efficiency of funds. An IMF-approved loan programme, according to this view, serves as a 'good housekeeping' seal of approval, increasing the creditworthiness of debtor countries and provoking an automatic inflow of outside financing. Marchesi and Thomas (2000) finds evidence that the presence of an IMF programme serves as a signalling device of a country's willingness and ability to undertake substantive reform. Private creditors are then more willing to reschedule the country's external debt. However, it is reported in the literature that there is surprisingly little evidence that IMF lending to a country has been followed by an increase in private credit flows (Bird and Rowlands, 1997; Ergin, 1999; Edwards, 2000; Rowlands, 2001; Joyce, 2002). The literature in the above genre seldom considers the cost of credit when monies are raised in the international capital markets, and instead focuses on the size of the *private capital inflow*.

Moral hazard

Finally, there is concern about moral hazard when private institutions are brought under the umbrella of the IMF to design and implement economic reform. Private institutions may be encouraged to lend and invest more recklessly due to belief that the Fund will ensure that debtors can repay the loans (Kruger, 2001).

The literature analyses the concept of moral hazard from two perspectives, moral hazard by creditors and moral hazard by debtors. Suppose that creditors refuse to roll over maturing debt in a debt-distressed country working with the IMF. The Fund, fearing that the creditors' action could spark off a financial crisis and impose additional cost on the country and also on the credibility of the IMF, may provide extra resources that can be used to finance creditors' exit. Creditors may anticipate such a response, that the Fund will bail them out, and allocate resources with less concern about project risk, thus increasing the possibility of future crises in borrowing emerging countries (Dreher, 2004). Recent studies focusing on the Mexican, East Asian and Russian crises have found evidence on the existence of moral hazard (Zhang, 1999; Eichengreen and Mody, 2000; Tillmann, 2001; Dell'Arricia, Schnabel and Zettelmeyer, 2002; Evrensel, 2002; Kamin, 2002). The literature is not unanimous about the impact of IMF policies on the moral hazard in lending and borrowing.

Overall, the literature presented above does not directly address the issue of the IMF's impact in terms of funding costs. Altunbaş, Chakravarty and Kara (2004) take a first step to analyse this issue on debt-distressed emerging markets.

Selection procedure of debt-distressed emerging countries

Primarily, Altunbaş, Chakravarty and Kara (2004) selects debt-distressed emerging markets with a balance of payments levels defined as unsustainable and analyses the conditions on syndicated loan facilities granted to them, distinguishing between two groups. Countries with severe levels of external debt to GDP (around 40 per cent) and short-term external debt to total external debt (around 50 per cent) ratios are taken as sample countries (a comparison of the debt indicators of the two country groups is presented in Table 8.2). The first group includes countries which have availed themselves of IMF assistance by operating the GRA. The second group consists of countries that also have unsustainable external debt levels, which were not assisted by the IMF. The two groups of emerging countries selected for the analysis are described in Table 8.1. The macroeconomic conditions[1] prevailing in the two groups of countries are first compared.

Table 8.1 Selected emerging countries and total number of syndicated loans issued between 1993 and 2001

Emerging countries with IMF assistance	Emerging countries without IMF assistance
Algeria, Argentina, Brazil, Bulgaria, Croatia, Ghana, Indonesia, Mexico, Morocco, Pakistan, Peru, Philippines, Russia, Turkey	Chile, India, Malaysia, Tunisia, Sri Lanka, Thailand, Venezuela
Total syndicated loans granted 1,580	**Total syndicated loans granted** 1,085

Source: authors' calculations.

Level of debt intensity

The mean values demonstrate that the selected groups are at similar debt distress levels (Table 8.2). The two main indicators for the degree of distress of the two sample groups, *debt/GDP* and *short-term debt/total debt* ratios (measuring the imminence and intensity of potential solvency or liquidity crises, respectively) are close to each other (the differences between them are not statistically significant).

A more detailed comparison of the evolution of debt/GDP ratios is shown in Figure 8.10. In 1993, this ratio for countries with IMF assistance was around 17 per cent, but the corresponding figure for the second group of countries was around 25 per cent. In 2001, the position was reversed and the IMF-assisted countries were in a worse position. Overall, the evolution of the solvency situation of the assisted and non-assisted countries was comparable between 1993 and 2001.

A similar pattern can also be observed in Figure 8.2 for the ratio of short-term debt total debt. In 1993, the two groups had similar short-term debt/total debt levels around 51 per cent. By the end of the period

Table 8.2 Average debt intensity indicators of emerging countries with and without IMF assistance between 1993 and 2001

	IMF assistance	**No IMF assistance**
Debt/GDP	39	41
Short-term debt/total debt	48	46
T-test of difference	*P*-value	Significance
Debt/GDP	0.742	Not significant
Short-term debt/total debt	0.425	Not significant

Source: authors' calculations.

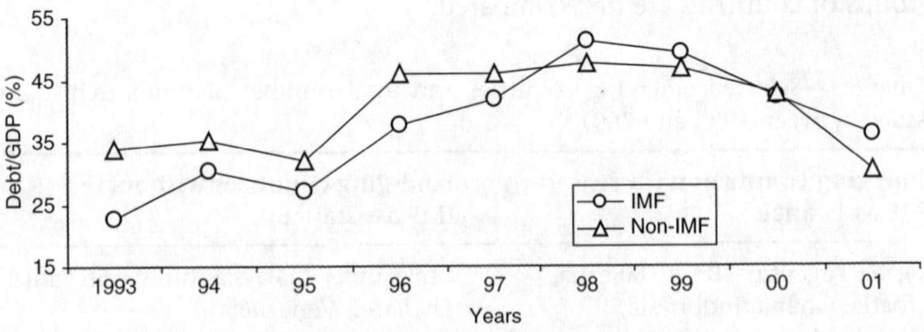

Figure 8.1 Debt/GDP ratios of emerging countries with and without IMF assistance between 1993 and 2001, per cent
Source: authors' calculations.

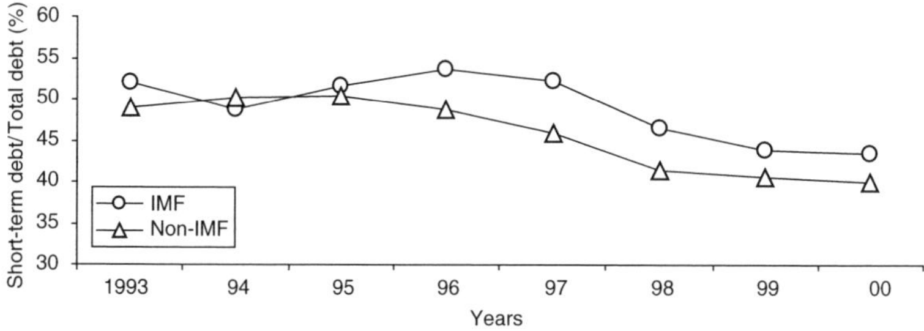

Figure 8.2 Short-term debt/total debt ratios of emerging countries with and without IMF assistance between 1993 and 2001
Source: authors' calculations.

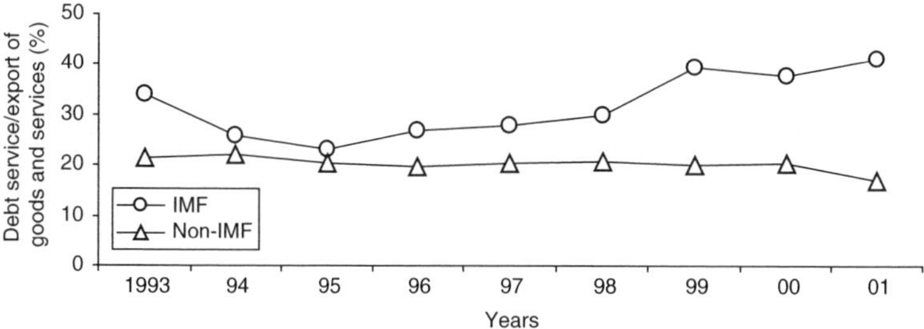

Figure 8.3 Debt service/exports of good and services ratios of emerging countries with and without IMF assistance between 1993 and 2001
Source: authors' calculations.

in 2001, although both groups had been successful in reducing the ratio, the countries that had been assisted by the IMF had been less successful in reducing it.

These patterns are repeated when the ratio of debt service payment/export income is examined in Figure 8.3. The gap between non-IMF and IMF countries was around 15 per cent at the beginning of the period and then increased to around 25 per cent at the end of it. A country's export performance, and the ensuing income from the outside world, can be related to its servicing effort on its foreign debt. As mentioned above, the countries that had not been assisted by the IMF managed to decrease their debt relative to their GDP[2] and to increase their export income, while countries assisted by the IMF failed to do so and decreased their solvency measures.

Features of syndicated loans issued to debt-distressed emerging markets

It was possible to analyse the micro-characteristics of a total of 2,665 individual loan contracts obtained by these two groups of countries, conditioning on their macroeconomic circumstances. Information (extracted from the Dealogic Loanware database) was available on the purpose of each loan (project finance, infrastructure funding, etc.), its size, maturity, pricing[3] and the borrower's sector.

The characteristics of the loan contracts are presented in Table 8.3. The average drawn return (spreads and fees) for the first subsample of emerging countries, those with IMF assistance, is 226 basis points, some 101 basis points above the corresponding figure for the second sample comprising countries that are not seeking IMF assistance. The loan size is higher by $22 m on average for countries with IMF assistance, but the maturity of an average non-IMF country syndicated loan is 1 year longer. At first glance, IMF-assisted countries seem to pay a higher price for the loans even though they are borrowing shorter term. On the other hand, countries assisted by the IMF appear, on average, to have obtained larger loans.

Business sector and loan-purpose composition

The analysis can be refined one step further by examining the micro-economic characteristics of the loans at the microeconomic level, in order compare the two groups of countries according to the borrower's business sector and the purpose of each loan commitment.[4] Figure 8.4 shows the sectoral composition of loans. Altunbaş, Chakravarty and Kara (2004) note that around 25 per cent of syndicated loans in IMF-assisted countries are granted to borrowers from the banking sector,

Table 8.3 Descriptive statistics on loan characteristics for emerging countries in financial distress in and outside the IMF umbrella, 1993–2001

Variable	No. of observations	Mean	Standard dev.	Min	Max
Countries with IMF assistance					
Drawn return (basis points)	1,580	226	151	2.38	1,275
Maturity (year)	1,580	3.98	3.69	0.1	30
Loan size (m $)	1,580	126	211	0	6,100
Countries without IMF assistance					
Drawn return (basis points)	1,085	125	98	7	1,000
Maturity (year)	1,085	4.97	3.11	0.1	25
Loan size (m $)	1,085	104	168	0.02	3,500

Source: authors' calculations.

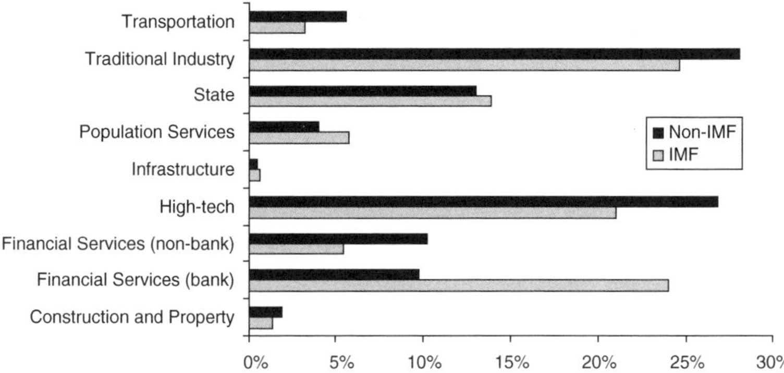

Figure 8.4 Sectoral composition of loans granted to countries with and without IMF assistance

Source: authors' calculations.

while in the second group, that ratio is only 10 per cent. Another point worth noting is that, in countries working with the IMF, banks appear to be amongst the major customers in the syndicated loan market – in several cases, governments guarantee the foreign liabilities of the banking sector.[5] The picture is different in countries outside the ambit of the IMF, where more syndicated loans are directed at the non-bank financial services sector.

Table 8.4 describes the loan characteristics for borrowers of various business sectors located in the two subgroups of countries. Bank borrowers located in countries that have worked with the IMF seem to have obtained loans of shorter maturities than banks located in the second sample of countries. Moreover, the pricing of loans granted to banks located in countries assisted by the IMF was more than twice as high as that of loans granted to banks in non-assisted countries. This difference in the average cost of loans can also be observed for borrowing by the non-bank financial services sector. The data reveals that 15 per cent of loans granted to the bank sector in IMF-assisted countries are channelled to export industries. With more expensive and shorter maturity funding, the economies of emerging market countries assisted by the IMF may become even more vulnerable to financial crises. The higher funding costs might put the goods and services of the assisted countries at a competitive disadvantage in export markets with respect to the non-assisted countries.

Another important observation is that loans obtained by the state sector in IMF-assisted countries are, on average, larger, but also up to

Table 8.4 Descriptive statistics on loan characteristics for emerging countries with and without IMF assistance between 1993 and 2001, according to borrower's business

		With IMF					Without IMF				
Business sector	**Variable**	**No. of obs.**	**Mean**	**Std dev.**	**Min**	**Max**	**No. of obs.**	**Mean**	**Std dev.**	**Min**	**Max**
Construction and Property	Drawn return	34	246	99	63	475	28	128	67	43	387
	Maturity		4.1	2.6	0.1	15.0		3.3	1.9	0.5	15.0
	Loan size		56	46	0	512		47	54	1	451
Financial Services (bank)	Drawn return	361	206	155	38	700	105	103	71	15	388
	Maturity		1.6	1.4	0.2	13.0		4.3	2.4	0.1	25.0
	Loan size		94	144	1	2,022		66	47	1	2,300
Financial Services (non-bank)	Drawn return	90	237	162	25	700	104	101	49	30	300
	Maturity		3.6	3.2	0.3	18.0		3.5	1.8	0.5	16.0
	Loan size		86	94	2	560		70	79	3	1,050
High-tech	Drawn return	237	216	162	2	1,275	210	149	122	7	1,000
	Maturity		4.2	2.8	0.3	13.5		4.7	2.6	0.2	13.5
	Loan size		126	169	0	1,750		91	95	0	1,900
Infrastructure	Drawn return	8	305	196	80	600	2	125	0	37	134
	Maturity		5.0	2.5	1.0	20.0		12.0	1.4	1.0	13.0
	Loan size		115	71	15	400		169	16	8	884
Population Services	Drawn return	72	345	183	25	750	42	88	64	45	571
	Maturity		3.0	2.0	0.3	10.0		5.0	2.4	0.9	12.0
	Loan size		114	163	0	1,100		209	293	5	287
State	Drawn return	77	202	128	20	580	44	88	64	24	356
	Maturity		4.7	4.3	0.3	17.8		5.0	2.4	0.5	21.0
	Loan size		257	487	1	6,100		209	293	2	1,350
Traditional Industry	Drawn return	309	242	143	3	700	250	139	102	15	550
	Maturity		3.9	2.8	0.2	16.0		5.0	2.5	0.3	15.0
	Loan size		113	148	0	1,152		80	110	0	2,416
Transportation	Drawn return	49	200	158	3	700	50	97	65	15	550
	Maturity		6.9	4.0	0.2	16.0		8.7	3.4	0.3	15.0
	Loan size		94	98	0	1,152		80	82	0	2,416

Note: Drawn returns are expressed in basis points; loan sizes are in m US$; maturities in years.

twice as expensive. In both sets of countries, a significant fraction (34 per cent and 55 per cent, respectively) of the funds raised on the syndicated loan markets is used for export industry financing. Again, these exports may not be competitive on international markets if the higher funding costs are reflected in higher prices. With the exception of the high-tech industry, borrowers from IMF-supported countries pay on average at least 100 basis more over LIBOR than their peers. The maximum difference is 256 basis points, in the population services sector.[6] Lending to countries under the IMF umbrella is of a shorter maturity than lending to countries that have not benefited from IMF programmes. In particular, the maturities of loans granted to the banking sector differ significantly. Thus the IMF's *imprimatur* appears to be associated with larger loans, but granted for shorter durations and at a higher cost. If this is supply-driven, then it suggests a remarkably cautious approach by international bankers, perhaps signalling disbelief in the efficacy of IMF programmes and economic policy advice.

A comparison of funding costs by loan purpose[7] between IMF-assisted countries and non-assisted ones is provided in Table 8.5. Project finance loans obtained by supported countries are 50 basis points more expensive than those granted to their non-supported peers. The largest cost difference between the two groups of countries arises in the case of loans granted for capital structure purposes. Entities from assisted countries have, on average, paid 137 basis points more to obtain funds, which is a drawback for companies seeking to compete with their peers from non-assisted countries.

The descriptive statistics presented above suggest a significant difference in the cost of funds raised on syndicated loan markets by the two groups of countries. Further analysis is undertaken below to investigate how the macroeconomic indicators of these emerging economies result in differing loan prices.

Loan pricing and debt-distressed developing country macroeconomic indicators

The macroeconomic conditions prevailing in borrower's countries influence to a great extent the pricing of the loans that they obtain. There are only a few studies in the literature that focus on the effect of the macroeconomic indicators of a country on the pricing of loans and bonds raised by entities resident in the country. Eichengreen and Mody (2000) is an important contribution to this literature. Their loan pricing logic is modified here and re-estimated on a larger loan sample.

Table 8.5 Descriptive statistics on loan characteristics for emerging countries with and without IMF assistance between 1993 and 2001, according to loan purpose

		With IMF					Without IMF				
Business sector	**Variable**	**No. of obs.**	**Mean**	**Std dev.**	**Min**	**Max**	**No. of obs.**	**Mean**	**Std Dev.**	**Min**	**Max**
Corporate Control	Drawn return	62	306	146	35	650	46	214	137	36	622
	Maturity		2.8	2.0	0.2	15.0		3.9	2.5	0.3	12.0
	Loan size		171	231	0	1,100		193	154	2	1,050
Capital Structure	Drawn return	213	257	178	2	1,275	223	120	94	15	583
	Maturity		3.2	2.3	0.3	15.0		4.4	2.2	0.2	10.8
	Loan size		185	361	3	6,100		129	255	3	3,500
General	Drawn return	428	205	138	15	900	189	119	97	10	538
	Maturity		2.2	2.0	0.1	30.0		3.6	2.8	0.2	18.0
	Loan size		93	122	0	1,750		96	133	1	2,416
Other	Drawn return	356	226	161	3	870	368	100	77	11	1,000
	Maturity		3.1	2.3	0.1	16.0		4.1	1.9	0.1	20.0
	Loan size		101	170	0	2,022		60	81	0	997
Project Finance	Drawn return	306	210	126	7	650	168	154	86	7	432
	Maturity		8.5	4.5	0.5	20.0		8.7	3.2	0.3	25.0
	Loan size		141	220	0	2,500		150	186	1	2,300
Multi-purpose	Drawn return	186	249	153	20	925	62	185	145	24	571
	Maturity		3.3	2.7	0.3	14.7		4.9	3.0	0.3	12.1
	Loan size		148	184	5	1,615		146	191	5	1,250
Transport	Drawn return	22	155	132	10	650	28	80	53	13	283
	Maturity		8.5	3.9	1.0	12.0		9.8	3.1	0.5	12.0
	Loan size		120	127	13	531		77	44	28	203

Note: Drawn returns are expressed in basis points; loan size are m US$; maturities in years.

Source: authors' calculations.

Edwards (1986) studies the effects of certain macroeconomic variables on spreads for developing country foreign borrowing,[8] using a dataset consisting of 900 Eurocurrency bank loans granted to developing countries between 1976 and 1980. He finds that countries with higher debt/GNP ratios pay higher prices for their loans. This conclusion is strengthened when the service cost of *external* debt is taken into account. A higher debt service/exports ratio is significantly associated with higher loan prices, while the economic growth rate of the country does not seem to have a significant effect on loan prices. The ratio of gross investment/GNP is found to be negatively associated with debt pricing, indicating that the level of the country risk premium is affected by the way in which the borrowed funds are spent.[9] In Edwards (1986), international liquidity (measured by the ratio of reserves/GNP) held by a country plays no significant role in the determination of the country risk premium. Finally, Edwards (1986) reports a negative relationship between maturity as well as loan size and loan spreads in emerging market borrowing.[10]

Ozler (1993) investigates the impact of borrowers' debt repayment history on credit market access and loan pricing. She analyses 1,525 commercial bank loan facilities granted to 26 emerging countries from Eurocurrency credit markets during the 1968–81 period. Unlike Edwards, she finds that a higher real GNP growth rate pushes up the cost of borrowing, perhaps because creditors are concerned that growth rates are unsustainable above a certain threshold. Another difference from Edwards (1986) is that Ozler finds that longer-term loans are more costly. Like Edwards (1986), Ozler also employs a dummy variable for IMF presence in the borrowing emerging country and finds a positive relationship with loan spreads with an estimated impact of 30 basis points. She also examines the cost of foreign borrowing when the ratio of reserves/GNP is increased. There is an inverse relationship.

Ozler and Edwards report a contradictory effect of growth rates and maturity of loans on the cost of borrowing. Using a larger sample of just over 5,000 syndicated loans containing richer information about the individual contracts, Eichengreen and Mody (2000) clarify the results. Countries with rapid growth and high levels of bank credit pay a higher price for their borrowing.[11] But a country with high growth rates that also has the ability to repay, as measured by their exports/debt service ratio, can reduce spreads. They also report that the loan spread declines with the amount borrowed and rises with loan maturity. Entities located in countries which have high debt levels (measured by the total debt/GNP ratio), a history of debt rescheduling, and a higher debt service obligation in relation to earnings from exports, pay higher spreads than comparable entities in other countries. Low values of the ratio of international reserves/short-term debt significantly raise spreads. A large share of short-term debt in the country's total outstanding bank debt has a strong, significant, positive impact on spreads. Eichengreen and Mody (2000) comes down on the side of Edwards (1986) and reports a negative relationship between maturity and loan spreads.

Altunbaş and Gadanecz (2003) build on Eichengreen and Mody (2000) by analysing an even larger data set comprising 5,010 syndicated loans granted to both public and private sector entities in developing countries between 1993 and 2001. Their findings are similar to those reported in Eichengreen and Mody (2000). Altunbaş and Gadanecz (2003), like Ozler (1993) before them, also control for IMF presence, and report that this is associated with an increased cost of borrowing. None of these studies controls for IMF presence by comparing the outcome of IMF presence with the absence of the IMF umbrella for two otherwise similar groups of countries. This is done in the present chapter.

To investigate the determinants of loan prices and to test the effect of the market's perception of the potential value of an IMF *imprimatur*, the following equation is estimated;

$$\begin{aligned}\text{Ln } drawn = {} & \beta_0 Intercept + \beta_1 maturity + \beta_2 debtgdp + \beta_3 tdstoxgs \\ & + \beta_4 restogdp + \beta_5 st\_tdebt + \beta_6 invgdp + \beta_7 credgdp \\ & + \beta_8 growth + \beta_9 cpi + \beta_{10} impexGDP\end{aligned}$$

The independent variables are selected from the literature reviewed above, and attention is paid to ensuring that the explanatory variables capture the measures of solvency, liquidity, economic growth and trade openness of the countries under investigation.

Debt/GDP (*debtgdp*) and *debt service/export of goods and services* (*tdstoxgs*) are the two solvency parameters, which are expected to have a negative relation with price of the loans. The ratio of *international reserves/GDP* (*restogd*) is expected to have a negative impact on the price of the loans. The ratio of *short-term external debt/total external debt* (*st_tdebt*) is generally used to measure countries' liquidity. It can be an advance indicator of an impending liquidity where a debtor country is unable to roll over existing debt. A high level of short-term debt relative to total debt is expected to decrease the creditworthiness of the borrower and increase the cost of borrowing. The ratio of total *imports and exports/GDP* (*impexpGDP*) is included in the equation to detect the effect of borrowing countries' economic openness on the price of loans. A more integrated economy is expected to attract lower prices, arguably because it generates more economic wealth through trade. The ratio of *investment/GDP* (*invgdp*) is controlled for to gauge if lenders take into account, albeit by discounting, future macroeconomic improvements in the borrower's country. *Higher investment/GDP* and *bank credit/GDP* ratios should indicate a distressed country's willingness to improve its economic environment. Potential creditors may respond by charging lower loan spreads from LIBOR. *Growth and inflation* (*cpi*) are included to measure the country's economic potential and ability to repay loans. A higher (unsustainable) growth rate is expected to have a damping effect on loan costs. Finally, as a microeconomic characteristic of each single loan deal, *maturity* was introduced into the equation to see the effects of long- and short-term borrowing on the price of the loan. The literature is divided on the relation between maturity and loan price, as discussed earlier. A correlation matrix for selected variables is provided in Appendix 8.1 (p. 182).

Signs of creditor moral hazard

The results for the above model are presented in Table 8.6. Maturity is significant in both groups of countries. It is negatively related to the price of loans in the sample of countries in receipt of IMF assistance and positively related to the price of loans in the other sample. This result suggests that IMF-assisted countries may have difficulty obtaining long-term loans, an observation that is in line with the descriptive statistics presented above. Another possibility is that in countries working with the IMF only firms with global reputation and high credit ratings can obtain longer-term loans with low interest rates.

The first of the two solvency measures, *debt/GDP*, is significant and negatively related with spread in both groups. This result was not picked up in earlier literature, where the data were not partitioned to identify distressed countries not under the IMF umbrella (Eichengreen and Mody, 2000; Altunbaş and Gadanecz, 2003). The second solvency measure, *debt service/exports*, is positive and significant, but only for countries in the second sample, those that are not under the IMF umbrella. Previous studies (e.g. Eichengreen and Mody, 2000; Altunbaş and Gadanecz, 2003) also appear to indicate that lenders take into consideration the ability to service debts by earning money from exports. It appears, however, that export performance in relation to a debt-service obligation is considered less important for countries under IMF supervision.

The *reserves/GDP* ratio is insignificant in both groups. Past literature (Edwards, 1986; Altunbaş and Gadanecz, 2003) findings suggest that the

Table 8.6 Regression results for emerging countries with and without IMF assistance

	Dependent variable: Natural log of drawn return					
	Emerging countries with IMF assistance			Emerging countries without IMF assistance		
Variable	**Coefficient**	**Standard error**	**P-value**	**Coefficient**	**Standard error**	**P-value**
maturity	−0.02	0.00	0.000	0.02	0.01	0.001
debtgdp	−0.01	0.00	0.000	−0.01	0.00	0.000
tdstoxgs	0.00	0.00	0.121	0.01	0.00	0.004
restogdp	0.01	0.01	0.127	0.00	0.00	0.365
st_tdebt	−0.01	0.00	0.018	0.01	0.00	0.006
invgdp	−0.01	0.01	0.018	0.00	0.01	0.476
credgdp	0.00	0.00	0.577	0.00	0.00	0.551
growth	−0.04	0.01	0.000	−0.06	0.01	0.000
impexpGDP	−0.01	0.00	0.000	−0.01	0.00	0.002
cpi	−0.00	0.00	0.024	0.01	0.00	0.067
_cons	6.80	0.17	0.000	4.77	0.23	0.000

Note: Number of observations in drawn spread regression for countries with IMF assistance is 1,438; for countries without IMF assistance is 1,038. *F*-tests are significant at the 1 per cent level.
Source: authors' calculations.

relation between this ratio and price of loans is negative, therefore although the national reserves are taken into account when pricing emerging countries loans it is not the case in when these countries are in debt distress. IMF policies on strengthening foreign exchange reserves seem not to have any effect in lenders' eyes when crediting these countries.

The coefficient of *the short-term external debt/total external debt ratio* is significant and has a positive sign when the regression is run for developing countries without IMF assistance. In contrast, it is significant but negatively related in countries with IMF assistance. Although the market includes this liquidity factor while pricing countries with IMF assistance, demanding more when short-term debt is excessive, it is taken into account adversely in the IMF-assisted countries. This might signal the issue of creditor moral hazard where a financial crisis is expected in such countries and therefore creditors charge less with an expectation of bailouts. Alternatively because the governments of such emerging countries guarantee their external debt, creditors expect that one way or the other they will get their money back.

The *investment/GDP ratio* is significant and negatively related to the cost of funds only in IMF-assisted countries. This finding matches the literature (Edwards, 1986), which suggests that a potential future economic development is credited by the lenders and decreases the cost of the loans. Inflation in countries without IMF assistance has a positive relation with the price of loans; therefore, lenders have concerns about rising inflation which may indicate an unhealthy economy.[12] Conversely, Consumer Price Index (CPI) inflation has a significant but negative relation in pricing the syndicated loans of emerging countries with IMF assistance, which does not seem rational in credit and risk evaluation. Naturally, emerging countries with macroeconomic problems face high inflation rates; however, this is also the case for the non-IMF group and loans are priced rationally in their case. This controversial result for inflation measure may again be a signal of creditor moral hazard in which in any case the funds provided are expected to be repaid by an IMF bailout. Real *GDP growth* has a significant and negative coefficient in both of the selected groups in accordance with past literature (Eichengreen and Mody, 2000; Altunbaş and Gadanecz, 2003). In lenders' eyes a vigorous (not rapid) growing country is likely to repay its debt and therefore be less risky for funds. On the other hand, a higher level of economic openness, measured by the volume of import and exports/GDP, ameliorates debt-distressed countries' cost of funding whether they follow IMF prescriptions or not.

Conclusion

The IMF has come under increasing criticism in recent years for internal contradictions in policy and questions raised about market belief on IMF prescriptions. Altunbaş, Chakravarty and Kara (2004) attempt to tackle this question by examining the effect of the IMF *imprimatur* on the cost of borrowing in the international capital markets by client states using a sample of 2,665 single syndicated loan contracts granted to public and private sector borrowers in debt-distressed emerging markets between 1993 and 2001. Two groups of countries, having the same intensity of balance of payments deficit, are analysed separately: one which has availed itself of IMF assistance by operating the GRA and one which has not.

Overall, the evidence found by Altunbaş, Chakravarty and Kara (2004) suggests that creditors may have a disbelief in the efficacy of IMF programmes and economic policy advice, and financial markets take a rather pessimistic view of the efficacy of IMF prescriptions. The data reveal that the IMF-assisted countries tend to pay higher spreads over LIBOR for short-term loans and obtained fewer long-term loan contracts compared to their non-IMF peers for the financing of similar-purpose projects. Specifically, loans channelled to export-producing sectors are more costly in IMF-assisted countries, which places their goods and services sectors at a disadvantage in the export markets in comparison to non-assisted countries. Perhaps one plausible explanation for the arguments of Prezeworski and Vreeland (2000) about lower growth rates displayed by countries under an IMF programme is the higher cost of funds faced in the financial markets. Furthermore, Altunbaş, Chakravarty and Kara (2004) find that creditors expect to take advantage of crises in IMF countries and do not behave rationally in pricing of loans, which hints at a case of creditor moral hazard. First, an increase in short-term debt levels and in inflation rates in such countries irrationally leads to a cheaper cost of funds. Secondly, their ability to repay debt is less likely to be considered by creditors. Moreover, a common policy imposed by the IMF, holding high levels of foreign exchange reserves in central banks, is ignored by financial markets when pricing debt-distressed emerging market loans.

Appendix 8.1

See Table 8A.1 overleaf.

Table 8A.1 Correlation matrixes between macroeconomic indicators of countries with and without IMF assistance

	lndrawn	*maturity*	*debtgdp*	*tdstoxgs*	*restogdp*	*st_tdebt*	*invgdp*	*credgdp*	*growth*	*cpi*	*impexp*
Countries with IMF assistance											
lndrawn	1										
maturity	−0.12	1									
debtgdp	−0.02	0.18	1								
tdstoxgs	0.11	0.00	0.07	1							
restogdp	−0.13	0.14	0.33	−0.18	1						
st_tdebt	−0.14	0.03	0.08	0.27	0.07	1					
invgdp	−0.18	0.13	−0.05	−0.10	0.19	0.09	1				
credgdp	−0.07	0.19	0.51	0.20	0.24	0.29	0.19	1			
growth	−0.30	0.06	−0.10	−0.08	−0.03	0.26	0.45	0.06	1		
cpi	−0.03	−0.06	−0.22	−0.14	−0.03	−0.05	−0.10	−0.14	−0.06	1	
impexp	−0.26	−0.07	−0.38	−0.23	0.24	0.11	−0.05	−0.19	0.15	0.13	1
Countries without IMF assistance											
lndrawn	1										
maturity	0.03	1									
debtgdp	0.02	−0.02	1								
tdstoxgs	0.15	−0.03	0.24	1							
restogdp	−0.03	0.01	0.38	−0.23	1						
st_tdebt	−0.04	−0.13	0.12	−0.17	0.38	1					
invgdp	−0.12	−0.04	−0.28	−0.76	0.28	0.53	1				
credgdp	−0.07	−0.01	−0.07	−0.77	0.35	0.24	0.77	1			
growth	−0.19	0.02	−0.65	−0.54	−0.17	0.20	0.67	0.44	1		
cpi	0.12	0.05	−0.07	0.19	−0.37	−0.16	−0.20	−0.37	0.06	1	
impexp	−0.06	−0.03	0.22	0.33	−0.07	0.41	−0.07	−0.42	−0.13	−0.08	1

Source: authors' calculations.

9
Facts and Figures, 1993–2004

Introduction

This chapter contains an extensive set of facts and figures on the trends that have prevailed on the international market for syndicated loans between 1993 and 2004. The analysis saliently focuses on micro-features of loans and borrowers, such as borrower nationality, business sector, maturity, loan amounts and spreads over time. Trends in industrialized countries – the US, UK, Japan and the Euro Area – and emerging markets are compared.

Global trends

Signings of syndicated loan facilities increased from $300 m in 1993 to $2.3 trn in 2004. Industrialized countries obtained the majority (92 per cent) of total loans, (Figure 9.1),[1] while only 8 per cent of loans were granted to emerging economies, and only 1 per cent to low-income countries.

Signings of syndicated loans totalled $2.26 trn in 2004, their highest yearly volume since they were introduced on the financial markets and almost four times the volume of 1993 (Figure 9.2). Between 1993 and 1997, volumes increased steadily and subsequently fell in 1998 at the time of the South-East Asian and Russian crises.

Emerging economies obtained an average of 8 per cent of syndicated loans between 1993 and 2003. Both the increase in average facility size and the rising number of facilities contributed to the growth of the market. In 1993, the average syndicated loan size was $100 m and rose to $250 m in 2004 (Figure 9.3). The highest number of facilities was granted in 1997, when over 9,300 loans were arranged. In 2004 over 9,100 loans were signed.

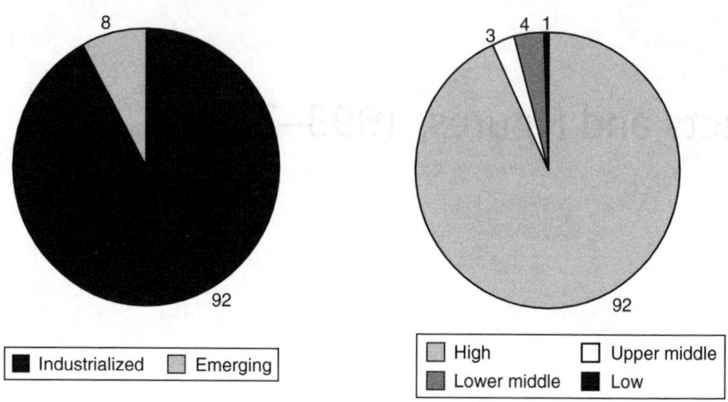

Figure 9.1 Breakdown of borrower countries, by income level, 1993–2004 per cent
Source: Dealogic.

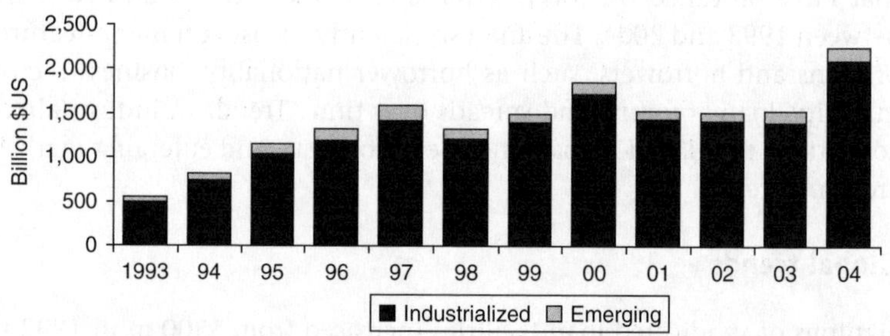

Figure 9.2 Signings of syndicated loans, 1993–2004
Source: Dealogic.

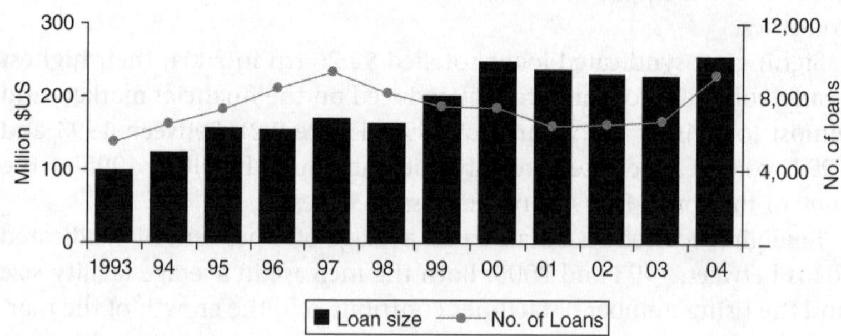

Figure 9.3 Average syndicated loan size[a] and total number of loans, 1993–2004
Note: [a] Left-hand axis.
Source: Dealogic.

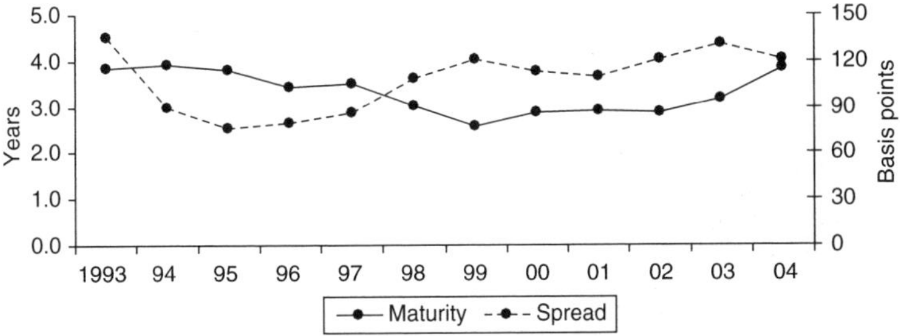

Figure 9.4 Average maturity[a] and spread over LIBOR, 1993–2004

Note: [a] Left-hand axis.

Source: Dealogic.

Average loan maturity (weighted by facility amounts[2]) showed a downward trend in the first period of the analysis and bottomed out at 2.6 years in 1999, rising afterwards to 3.6 years in 2004 (Figure 9.4). The price of funds, on the other hand, has followed a more volatile pattern. Starting with a peak of 135 basis points over LIBOR in 1993, it first followed a downturn trend and from 1999 onwards it stabilized at an average (weighted by facility amounts) of 120 basis points over LIBOR (Figure 9.4).

Borrower business

The sectoral composition of syndicated lending is analysed using a set of broad groups.[3] The traditional industrial borrowers accounted for 20 per cent of all loan issues between 1993 and 2004 (Figure 9.5). The high-tech industry, population-related services, non-bank financial services and utilities sectors obtained a total of 60 per cent of the syndicated loans borrowed in this period, while the infrastructure sector received only 1 per cent of total loans.

Of these 10 industry groups, the construction and property sector paid the highest average spread of 152 basis points between 1993 and 2004, while the state – admittedly recognized as the least risky by the fund providers – and banking sectors accessed funds at the lowest spreads, around 60 basis points on average. Average spreads on the non-bank financial services sector amounted to 70 basis points, while those on firms from the high-tech, utilities, transport and infrastructure sectors, as well as traditional industries, were higher, at approximately 110 basis points.

Infrastructure loans had the highest average maturity – 6.4 years, not surprising given that infrastructure projects often take a long time to

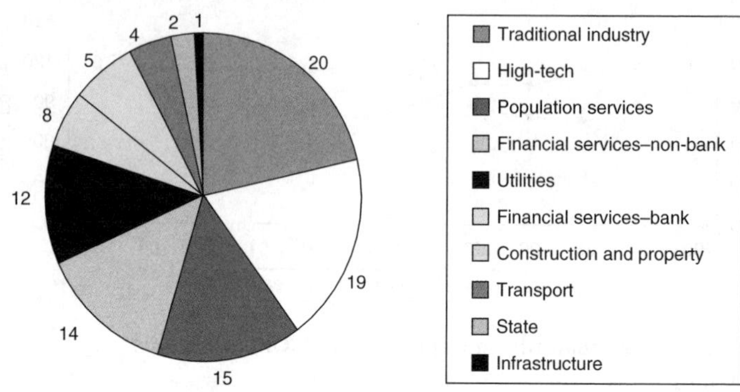

Figure 9.5 Composition of loans by, borrowers' business sector, based on US$ amounts, 1993–2004 per cent

Source: Dealogic.

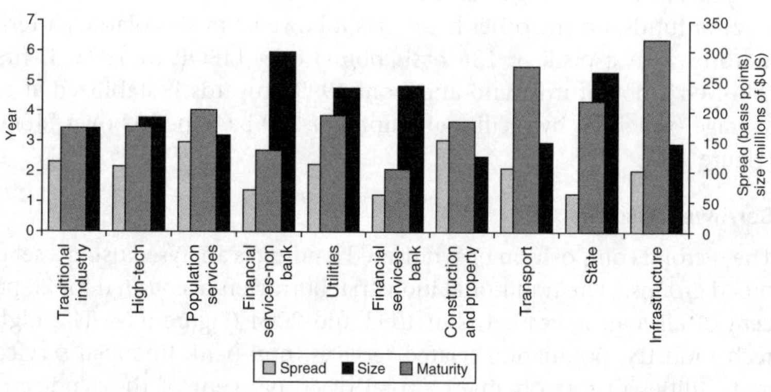

Figure 9.6 Average size, maturity and spread of syndicated loans, by borrower sector,[a] 1993–2004

Note: [a] Maturity is shown on the left-hand axis, while spread (basis points over LIBOR) and size (million US dollars) are both shown on the right-hand axis.

Source: Dealogic.

complete – followed by the transport and state sectors (5.5 and 4.3 years, respectively) (Figure 9.6). Financial sector borrowers (banks and non-banks) availed themselves of the shortest maturity loans (2.1 and 2.7 years respectively). The state sector and the financial industry (banks and non-banks) obtained the largest loans (in excess of $240 m on average). The construction and property, infrastructure and transport industries were granted much smaller facilities (not exceeding $150 m in average size).

Loan purpose

The highest amount (39 per cent of the total) of syndicated loans granted during the period under study was for capital structure purposes (Figure 9.7).[4] General corporate purpose facilities were the second most-used category, constituting 29 per cent of all loans. Corporate takeover financing was the third major motivation for loan syndications, followed by project financing, with 19 per cent and 8 per cent, respectively.

The purpose of syndicated credits can influence several of their micro-characteristics such as pricing and maturity. Average spreads and loan maturities are presented in Figure 9.8 and Figure 9.9, by loan-purpose

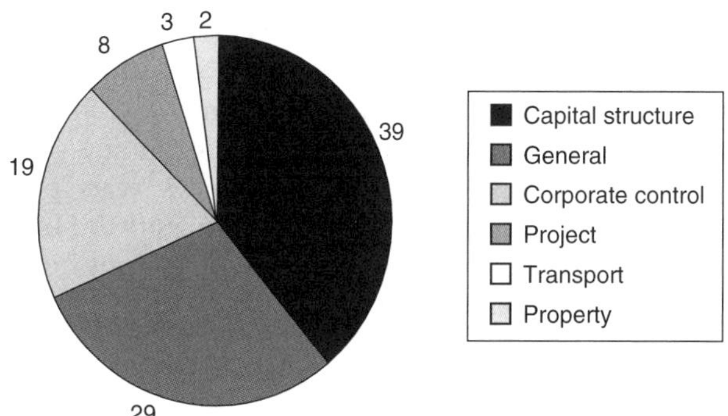

Figure 9.7 Composition of loans, by purpose, 1993–2004, based on US$ amounts, per cent

Source: Dealogic.

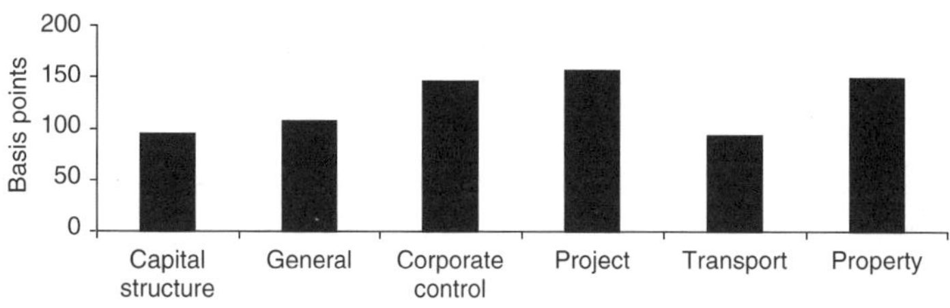

Figure 9.8 Average loan spread over LIBOR, by purpose, 1993–2004

Source: Dealogic.

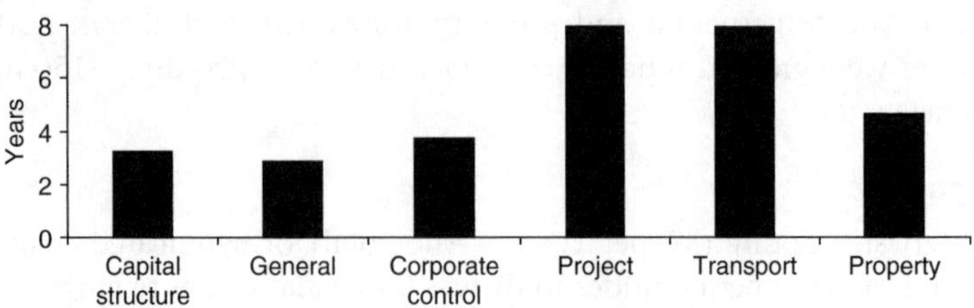

Figure 9.9 Average loan maturity, by purpose, 1993–2004
Source: Dealogic.

classification. Loans arranged for transport appear to have been perceived as the least risky: they carried the lowest spreads and the longest maturities. Project finance requires longer-term loans, with an average of approximately 8 years; however, firms borrowing for this purpose are charged a higher price of 157 basis points over LIBOR.

Capital structure and general-purpose loans cost firms around 100 basis points over LIBOR, with a maturity around 3 years on average. Firms tapping syndicated loan markets for the purpose of takeover financing arranged loans with maturities of 3.7 years on average, though they paid a higher price of 145 basis points over LIBOR. Loans for property-related purposes on average had a maturity of 4.6 years with a cost of 150 basis points over LIBOR.[5]

Industrialized countries

Developed country borrowers have been the recipients of approximately 90 per cent of syndicated credits during the period under study. A majority of loans (58 per cent of the total) went to US borrowers, with the rest divided among Euro area countries and the UK (19 per cent and 11 per cent, respectively). The liquidity and depth of US financial markets, not least in the area of credit risk transfer, is likely to have contributed to the size of the primary market for syndicated loans there. However, between 1993 and 2004, the share of US borrowers decreased from 73 per cent to 63 per cent of total loan issuance (Figure 9.10), while the share of Euro area borrowers correspondingly increased.

Although the Euro area as a geographical grouping has been the second largest recipient of syndicated credits after the US, UK borrowers follow US ones immediately when countries are ranked individually (11 per cent of total loans). Lending to Japanese borrowers represents a rather modest

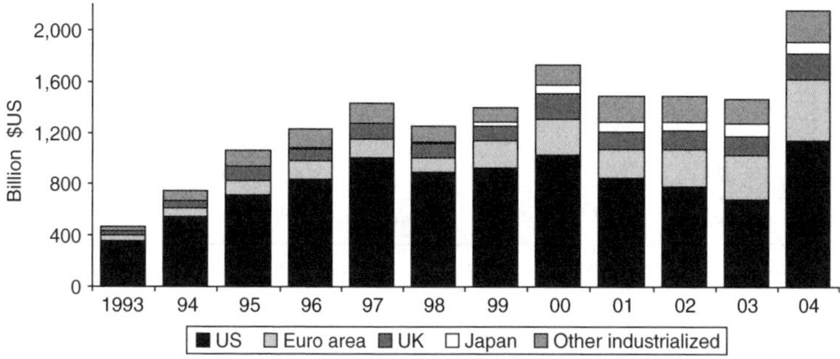

Figure 9.10 Syndicated loans granted to borrowers from industrialized countries, 1993–2004

Source: Dealogic.

6 per cent of the worldwide total, due to the dominance of bilateral corporate lending in that country.

US

Syndicated lending to US borrowers paused for a while after the South-East Asian and Russian financial crises, which resulted in a flight to quality on the major financial markets of the world. However, US volumes accounted for two thirds of global activity, reaching a peak of $1.14 trn in 2004. The growth in volumes was driven by an increase in the number of facilities signed during the first years of the period under study, and from 1997 onwards by an increase in average facility sizes, which accompanied an actual decrease in the number of facilities (Figures 9.11, 9.12). Possibly associated with the economic recession, total signings of US syndicated loans shrank by 35 per cent between 2000 and 2003, but rebounded in 2004.

The average maturity of US syndicated loans fell from 4 years in 1996 to 2 years in 1999 but has recently increased again (Figure 9.13). US borrowers, on average, have obtained the lowest maturity loans among all the industrialized countries. The average LIBOR spreads on their loans have also been the highest, averaging around 115 basis points during the period under study.

UK

British borrowers were granted 11 per cent of total funds raised on the syndicated loan market between 1993 and 2004. Their share showed a steadily increasing trend throughout the period, ranging from 8 per cent

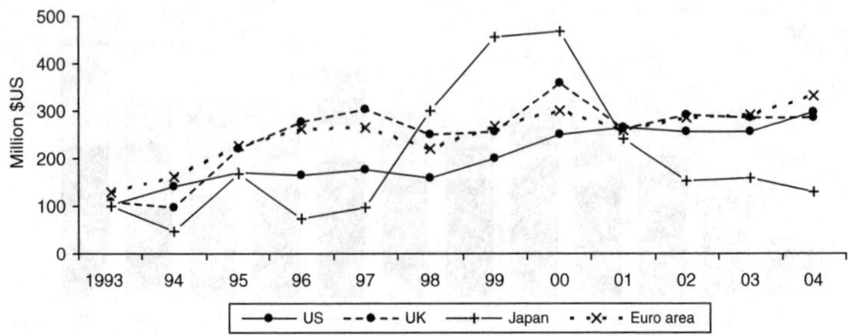

Figure 9.11 Average syndicated loan size for industrialized country syndicated loans, 1993–2004

Source: Dealogic.

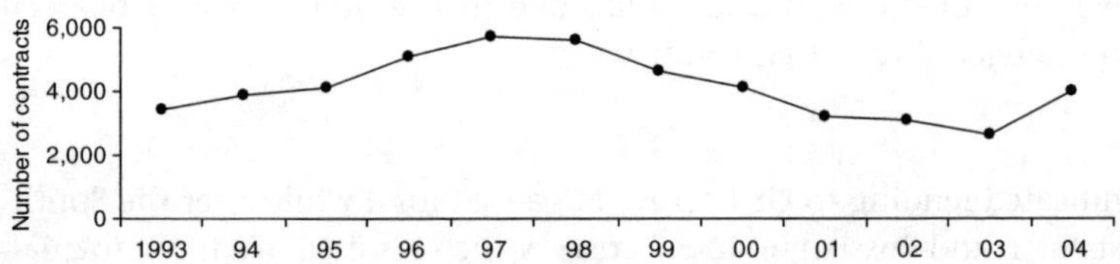

Figure 9.12 Total number of syndicated loans granted to US borrowers, 1993–2004

Source: Dealogic.

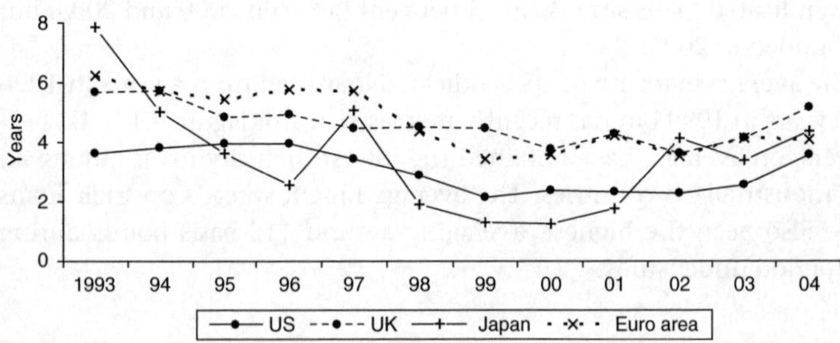

Figure 9.13 Average loan maturity for selected industrialized countries, 1993–2004

Source: Dealogic.

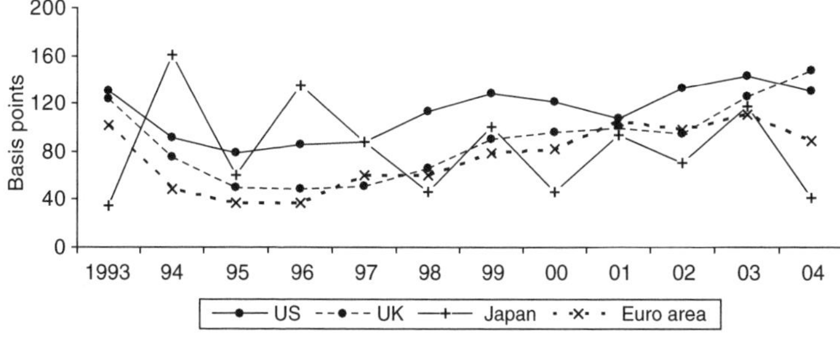

Figure 9.14 Average loan spreads over LIBOR for selected industrialized countries, 1993–2004

Source: Dealogic.

to 14 per cent (Figure 9.10). The average size of UK loans has been consistently above those of US loans, growing from \$100 m in 1993 to \$300 m in 2004. An exceptionally high average size of \$350 m was observed in 2000, in which Unilever Plc raised \$22 bn with a view to acquiring Bestfoods. The average maturity of UK loans (4.6 years) has been higher than that of US ones, while average spreads on UK loans have been consistently lower, although the gap between US and UK average spreads has been closing (Figure 9.14).

Japan

Before 2000, Japanese borrowers had limited presence on the international syndicated loan market. By the end of 2004, they had signed a total of over 1,400 loans. Syndicated lending in Japan reportedly makes up just a small – albeit growing – fraction of total domestic bank lending, not least because of the traditional importance of 'main banks' for corporations.

Euro area

A total of 1,647 loans were issued to Euro area borrowers in 2004, compared to 358 in 1993 (Figure 9.15), causing the share of Euro area borrowers in the world market and among industrial country borrowers to soar, from 10 per cent in 1993 to over 25 per cent in 2004.

German and French firms were granted 42 per cent of all Euro area syndicated loans during the period under study, growing in importance particularly after 1998, followed by Dutch and Italian borrowers (Figure 9.16).

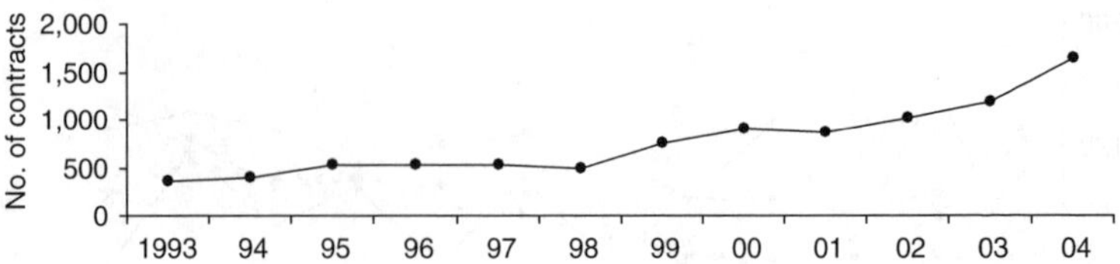

Figure 9.15 Total number of syndicated loans granted to Euro area borrowers, 1993–2004

Source: Dealogic.

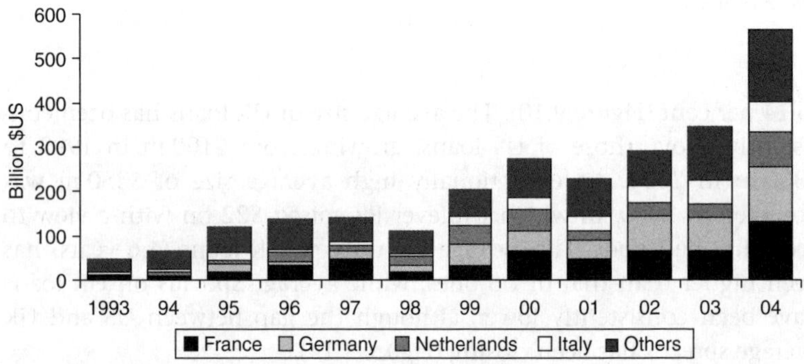

Figure 9.16 Signings of syndicated loans by Euro area borrowers, 1993–2004

Source: Dealogic.

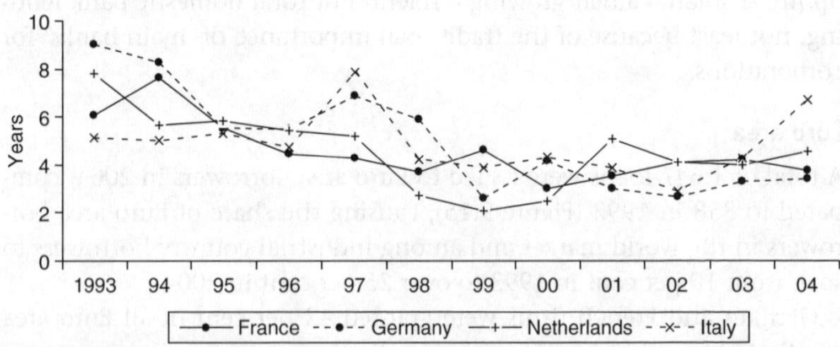

Figure 9.17 Average loan maturity for selected Euro area countries, 1993–2004

Source: Dealogic.

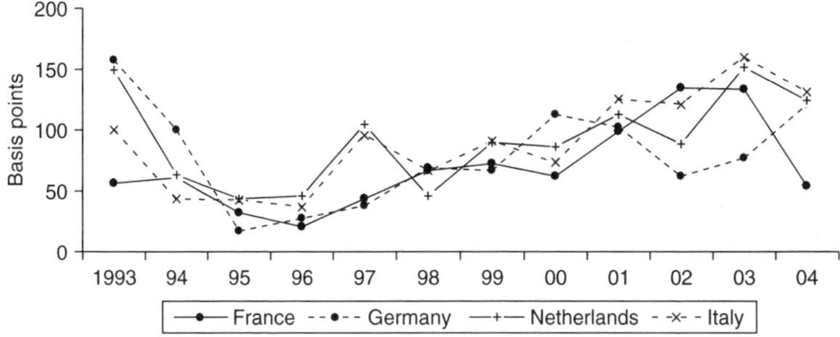

Figure 9.18 Average loan spreads over LIBOR for selected industrialized countries, 1993–2004

Source: Dealogic.

Average yearly maturities for selected Euro area countries are presented in Figure 9.17. Until 1998, the maturities of Euro area loans tended to fluctuate through time and across countries. However, the introduction of the euro seems to have been accompanied by a convergence in maturities to an average of 4 years. Average spreads on syndicated loans granted to Euro area borrowers rose by more than 70 basis points between 1995 and 2004 (Figure 9.18), particularly for Italian and Dutch entities, while French borrowers were charged the lowest spreads. In contrast to maturities, the introduction of the euro has not been accompanied by a convergence in loan spreads.

Emerging markets

Syndicated lending to emerging country borrowers has accounted for about 8 per cent of the global market between 1993 and 2004 (Figure 9.1). While over the years, lending has been increasing in absolute terms, its share of the world total has been declining.[6]

Between 1993 and 2004, Latin America and Caribbean entities attracted more than one-third of the total syndicated loans granted to emerging market borrowers (36 per cent; see Figure 9.19), followed by Asia and the Pacific (29 per cent), emerging Europe (13 per cent) and the Middle East (9 per cent) Emerging Asia and Pacific received 29 per cent of the loans followed by Emerging Europe and Middle East, with 13 per cent and 9 per cent, respectively. North Africa, on the other hand, is the emerging region with lowest share of syndicated loans for the analysed period. Middle Eastern borrowers secured the largest facility sizes and the longest maturities ($250 m and 8.4 years on average, respectively,

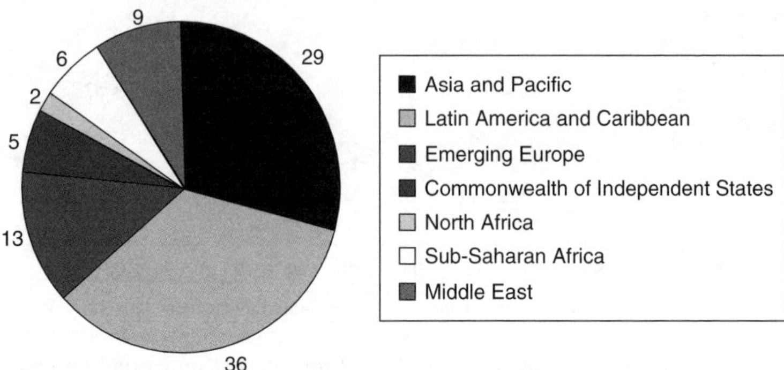

Figure 9.19 Lending to emerging countries, 1993–2004, nationality breakdown based on US$ amounts, per cent

Source: Dealogic.

possibly related to the large long-term funding requirements of the oil industry), while lending to the Asia/Pacific region was characterized by the smallest average loan sizes ($76 m) (Figures 9.19–9.21).

Possibly because lenders regard the oil industry as generating a stable source of income, Middle Eastern entities were charged the lowest average LIBOR spreads (98 basis points). Borrowers by the Commonwealth of Independent States (CIS) have paid the highest average LIBOR spreads (283 basis points, Figure 9.22), followed by Latin American entities.

Selected emerging markets

Russia, Turkey, Brazil, China and India were the main emerging market borrowers on the international loan markets during the 1990s. Lending to these countries peaked in 1997 at $49 bn, levelling off after the South-East Asian and Russian financial crises in 1999 and in 2001 (Figure 9.22). China obtained the largest amounts, the longest maturities and at a relatively low cost (Figures 9.23–9.26). Conversely, Brazilian borrowers have paid a high price for the lowest maturity loans, and attracted 25 per cent of total loans issued.

Industrialized versus emerging countries

The pricing of syndicated loans differs between facilities granted to emerging and industrialized country borrowers. On average, emerging market borrowers paid 40 basis points more than industrialized country

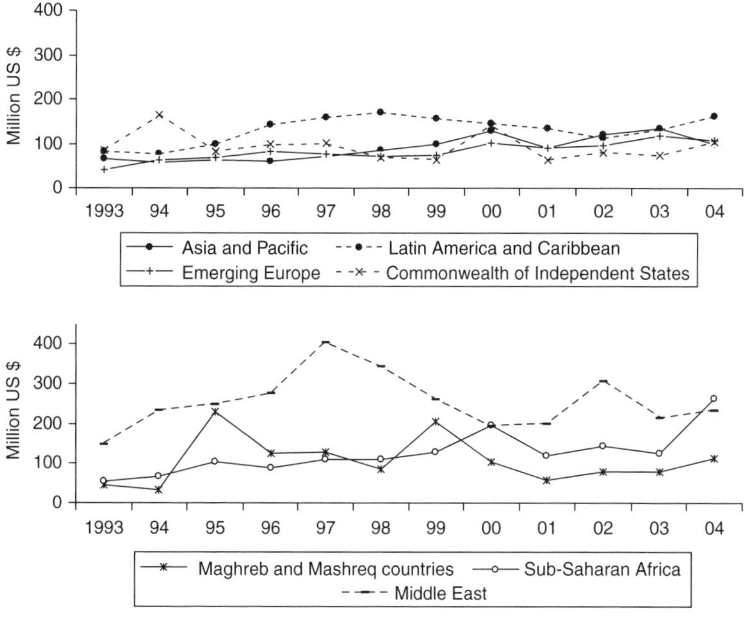

Figure 9.20 Average syndicated loan size for emerging country borrowers, 1993–2004

Source: Dealogic.

borrowers in LIBOR spreads (Figure 9.27); this gap widens to 55 basis points when the US is excluded from industrialized countries, although it has diminished in recent years. At the time of the South-East Asian and Russian crises, in 1998–9, the gap between LIBOR spreads for emerging and industrialized country borrowers widened to 100 basis points.

Average maturities on industrialized country loans (and especially on non-US facilities) are, on the other hand closer to maturities on emerging country facilities (4.6 years versus 5.0 years, respectively, Figure 9.28). There are significant differences in the sectoral composition of syndicated lending to emerging and industrialized countries. In the former group of countries, borrowing is dominated by utilities, as well as the state and bank sectors, while in the latter, high-tech and traditional industries as well as population-related services have tended to dominate. Particularly in emerging countries, the utilities sector collects 23 per cent of loans, 10 per cent higher than industrialized countries

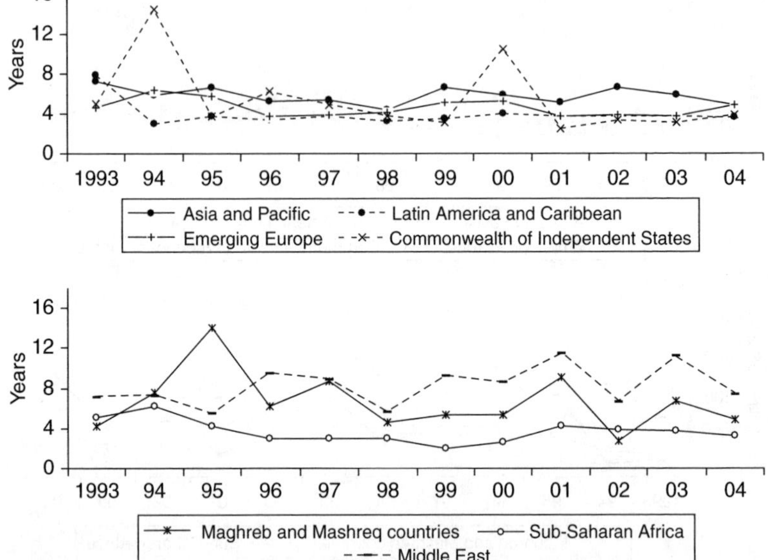

Figure 9.21 Average loan maturity for emerging country borrowers, 1993–2004
Source: Dealogic.

(Figure 9.29). Sovereign borrowing is also much more prevalent for emerging countries than for industrialized ones.

Loan purposes differ between the two groups of countries: the main loan purpose has been capital structure financing for industrialized country borrowers, and project finance for their emerging country peers (Figure 9.30).

Average spreads for various loan purposes paid by industrial and emerging market borrowers are represented in Figure 9.27. Overall, as mentioned earlier, emerging market borrowers have been paying higher spreads in almost all categories with the exception of transport-related loans, where spreads are similar to those paid by the industrialized countries (Figure 9.31). The largest difference appears to be in capital structure loans, where emerging markets are paying 55 per cent more than the industrialized countries.

There appears to be less discrepancy between the two groups of countries as far as maturities are concerned (Figure 9.32), except perhaps for corporate control, where industrialized country borrowers have obtained longer tenors.

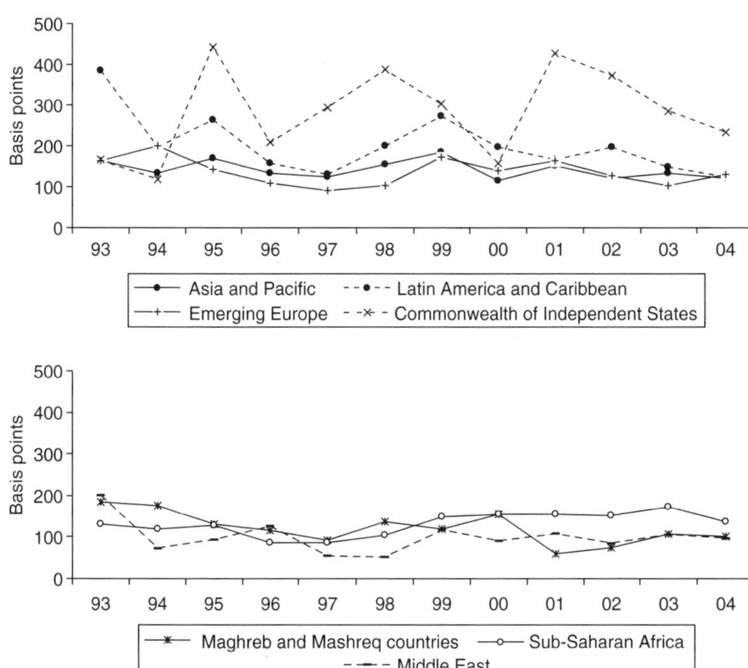

Figure 9.22 Average loan spread over LIBOR for emerging country borrowers, 1993–2004

Source: Dealogic.

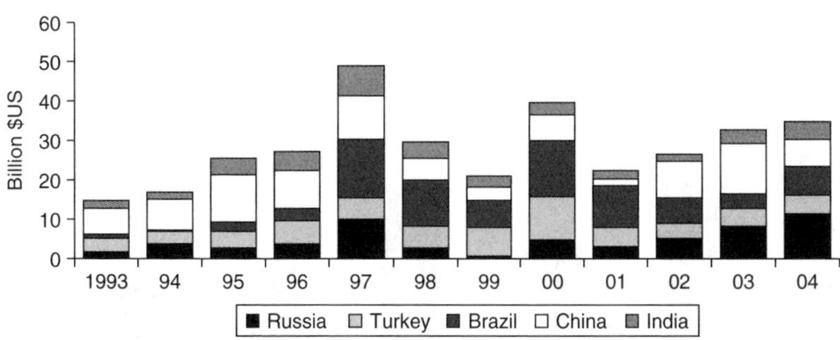

Figure 9.23 Signings of syndicated loans by borrowers in selected emerging countries, 1993–2004

Source: Dealogic.

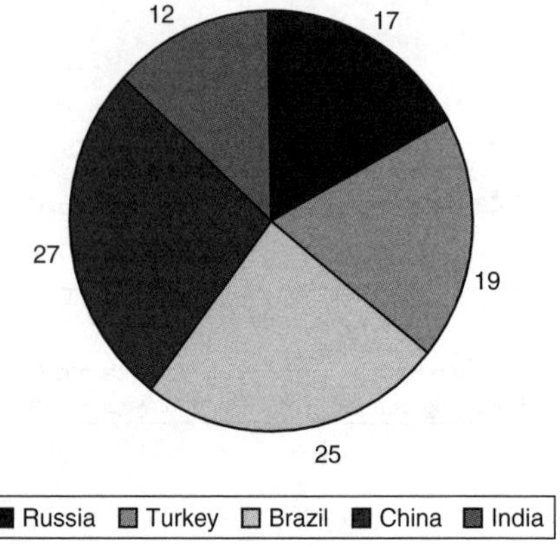

Figure 9.24 Share of selected emerging countries, per cent
Source: Dealogic.

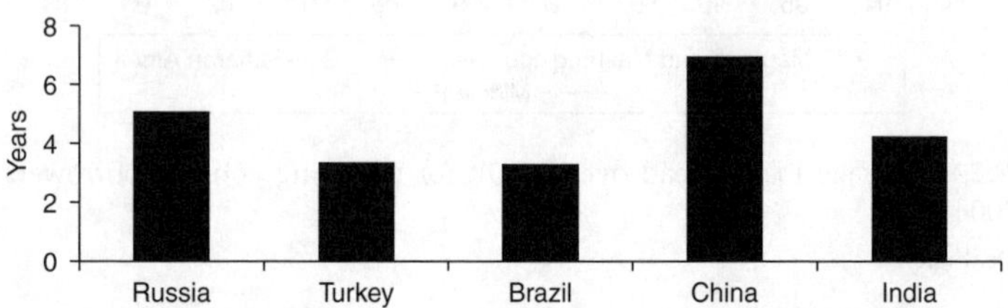

Figure 9.25 Average loan maturity in selected emerging countries
Source: Dealogic.

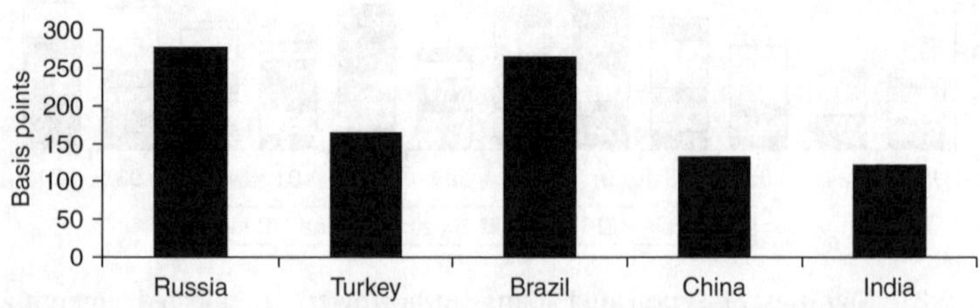

Figure 9.26 Average spread over LIBOR for selected emerging countries
Source: Dealogic.

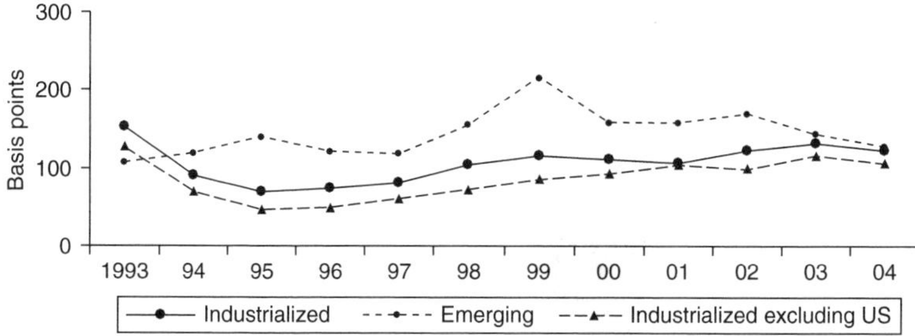

Figure 9.27 Average spread over LIBOR for emerging and industrialized country borrowers, 1993–2004

Source: Dealogic.

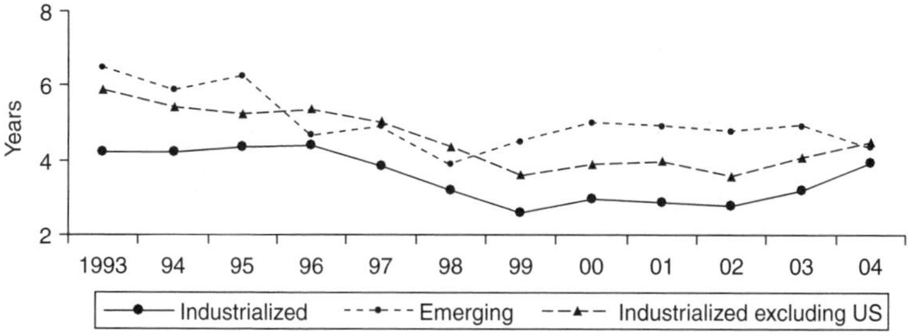

Figure 9.28 Average maturity for emerging and industrialized country borrowers, 1993–2004

Source: Dealogic.

Income level

Lower-middle-income economies have had a larger share of total lending (3.8 per cent) than the upper-middle-income economies (2.9 per cent), while low-income economies have attracted only 0.6 per cent of all funds. Lower-middle-level economies have obtained the longest maturity loans (on average, 4.9 years) but also paid the highest price (on average, 165 basis points). Conversely, loans granted to high-income economies had the lowest price of 100 basis points and the shortest maturity (3.2 years). See Figures 9.34 and 9.35 for the statistics on spreads and maturity by income level of the borrowing country.

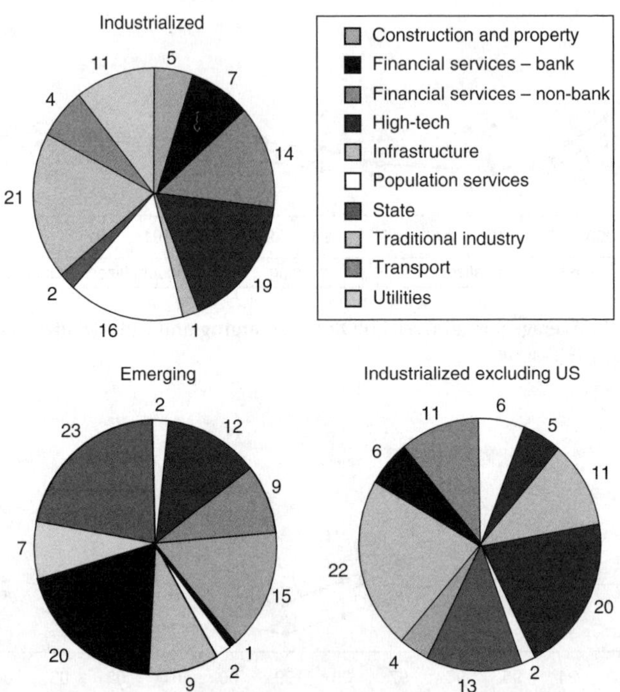

Figure 9.29 Emerging and industrialized country borrowing, by sector, 1993–2004, per cent

Source: Dealogic.

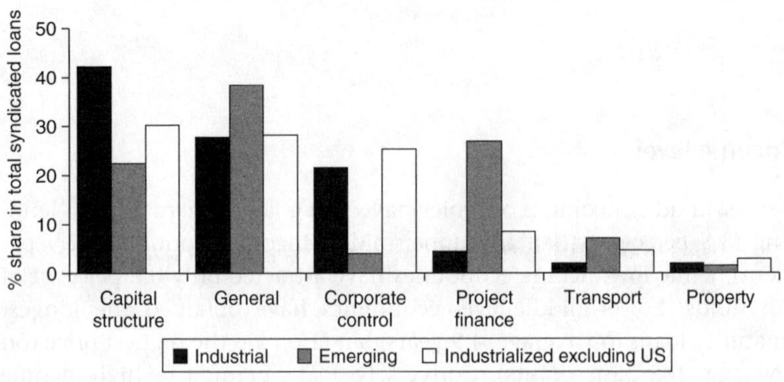

Figure 9.30 Composition of total amount of loans issued, classified by loan purpose and borrower country, 1993–2004

Source: Dealogic.

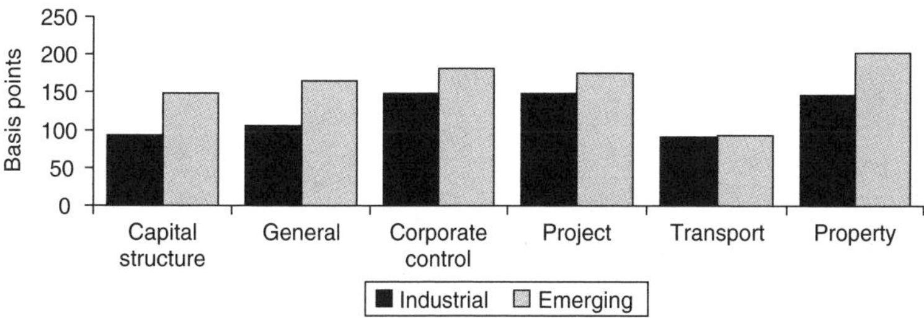

Figure 9.31 Average spread over LIBOR, by loan purpose in emerging and industrialized countries, 1993–2004

Source: Dealogic.

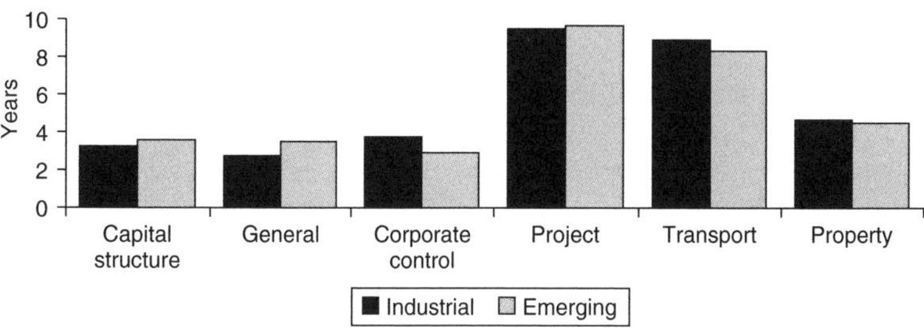

Figure 9.32 Average maturity, by loan purpose, in emerging and industrialized countries, 1993–2004

Source: Dealogic.

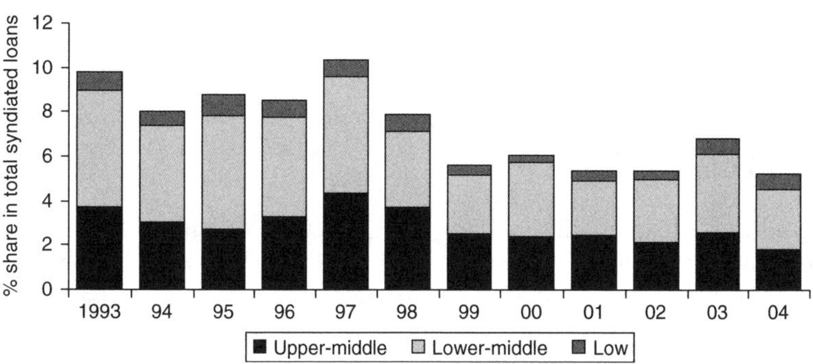

Figure 9.33 Composition of total amount of loans issued, classified by country income level, 1993–2004

Source: Dealogic.

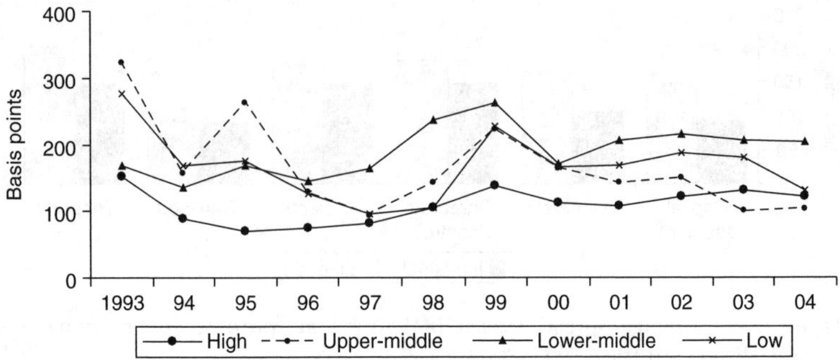

Figure 9.34 Average spread over LIBOR, by borrower country income, 1993–2004

Source: Dealogic.

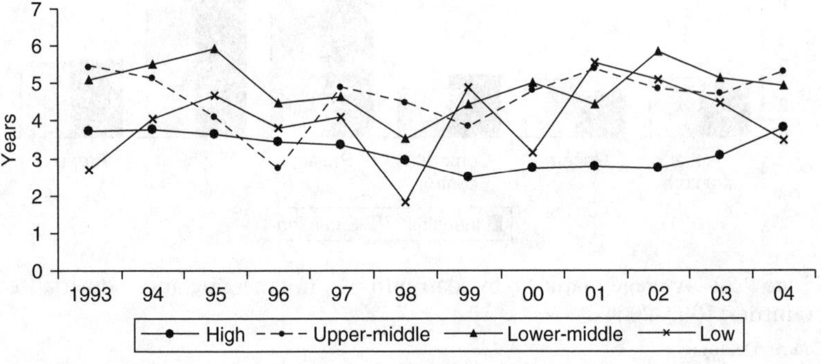

Figure 9.35 Average maturity, by borrower country income, 1993–2004

Source: Dealogic.

Conclusion

Syndicated loan market activity has increased considerably between 1993 and 2004, rising to a record high of $2.3 trn in 2004. The majority of loans have been granted to industrialized country – and in particular US – borrowers, while their counterparts from emerging markets have obtained only 9 per cent of funds during the period under study. The traditional and high-tech industries have been the main recipients of funds (obtaining 40 per cent of total lending); a significant share of loans were signed for capital structure purposes.

Appendixes

Appendix 9.1 List of industrialized countries

Andorra
Australia
Austria
Belgium
Canada
Cyprus
Denmark
Finland
France
Germany
Greece
Hong Kong
Iceland
Ireland
Israel
Italy
Japan
Korea, Rep. of
Luxembourg
Netherlands
New Zealand
Norway
Portugal
Singapore
Spain
Sweden
Switzerland
Taiwan
UK
US

Appendix 9.2 Classification of countries, by income

Low-income economies

Afghanistan
Angola
Bangladesh
Benin
Bhutan
Burkina Faso
Burundi
Cambodia
Cameroon
Central African Rep.
Chad
Comoros
Congo, Dem. Rep.
Congo, Rep.
Côte d'Ivoire
Equatorial Guinea
Eritrea
Ethiopia
Gambia, The
Ghana
Guinea
Guinea–Bissau
Haiti
India
Kenya
Korea, Dem. Rep. Of
Kyrgyz Rep.
Lao PDR
Lesotho
Liberia
Madagascar
Malawi
Mali
Mauritania
Moldova
Mongolia
Mozambique
Myanmar
Nepal
Nicaragua
Niger
Nigeria
Pakistan
Papua New Guinea
Rwanda
São Tomé and Príncipe
Senegal
Sierra Leone
Solomon Islands
Somalia
Sudan
Tajikistan
Tanzania
Timor–Leste
Togo
Uganda
Uzbekistan
Vietnam
Yemen, Rep.
Zambia
Zimbabwe

Lower-middle-income economies

Albania
Algeria
Armenia
Azerbaijan
Belarus
Bolivia
Bosnia and Herzegovina
Brazil
Bulgaria
Cape Verde
China
Colombia
Cuba
Djibouti
Dominican Rep.
Ecuador
Egypt, Arab Rep.
El Salvador
Fiji
Georgia
Guatemala
Guyana
Honduras
Indonesia
Iran, Islamic Rep.
Iraq
Jamaica
Jordan
Kazakhstan
Kiribati
Macedonia, FYR
Maldives
Marshall Islands
Micronesia, Fed. Sts
Morocco
Namibia
Paraguay
Peru
Philippines
Romania
Russian Federation
Samoa
Serbia and Montenegro
South Africa
Sri Lanka
Suriname
Swaziland
Syrian Arab Republic
Thailand
Tonga
Tunisia
Turkey
Turkmenistan
Ukraine
Vanuatu
West Bank and Gaza

Upper-middle-income economies

American Samoa
Antigua and Barbuda
Argentina
Barbados
Belize
Botswana
Chile
Costa Rica
Croatia
Czech Rep.
Dominica
Estonia
Gabon
Grenada
Hungary
Latvia
Lebanon
Libya
Lithuania
Malaysia
Mauritius
Mayotte
Mexico
Northern Mariana Islands
Oman
Palau
Panama
Poland
Saudi Arabia
Seychelles
Slovak Rep.
St Kitts and Nevis
St Lucia
St Vincent and Grenadines
Trinidad and Tobago
Uruguay
Venezuela

High-income economies

Andorra
Aruba
Australia
Austria
Bahamas, The
Bahrain
Belgium
Bermuda
Brunei
Canada
Cayman Islands
Channel Islands
Cyprus
Denmark
Faeroe Islands
Finland
France
French Polynesia
Germany
Greece
Greenland
Guam
Hong Kong, China
Iceland
Ireland
Isle of Man
Israel
Italy
Japan
Korea, Rep.
Kuwait
Liechtenstein
Luxembourg
Macao, China
Malta
Monaco
Netherlands
Netherlands Antilles
New Caledonia
New Zealand
Norway
Portugal
Puerto Rico
Qatar
San Marino
Singapore
Slovenia
Spain
Sweden
Switzerland
United Arab Emirates
UK
US
Virgin Islands (US)

10
Concluding Remarks

The unifying aim of this book has been to present an overview of the history and development of the international market for syndicated loans and to study the microstructure of this market in industrial and developing countries, with specific attention to investigating the determinants of loan pricing. Overall, this book makes several contributions to the knowledge on bond and loan pricing and bank market structure.

The developing country external finance literature was extended in several respects. The relative importance of macroeconomic and microeconomic determinants of the pricing of syndicated loans granted to developing country borrowers was investigated (Chapter 4); it was found that macroeconomic factors dominated microeconomic ones. Borrower market share and market structure variables were explicitly introduced into the analysis and conclusions were derived from this pertaining to banks' market power and the effects of perceived risk concentration on loan pricing. It was established that borrowers from developing countries that were more heavily dependent on syndicated loans were charged more to access funds; this was seen as a possible reflection of banks' market power being exploited. All this poses a particular challenge for economic development in those countries whose new loan facilities are sufficient only to roll over existing lines of credit (i.e. provide no net new funding). These countries cannot seem to obtain funding at competitive rates for improving the quality of state-provided services such as health and education, for participating in world trade, or for supporting high-tech or innovative sectors. This inhibits these countries' growth potential and convergence prospects along the lines suggested by Balassa (1986), Barro and Sala-i-Martin (1992) and Barro (1997, 1999). Not even developing countries benefiting from the *imprimatur* of an IMF programme seem able systematically to obtain syndicated loan financing at better conditions, as shown in Chapter 8.

As an innovation over earlier studies which focus on industrialized or developing countries separately, industrialized and developing country borrowers' access to bond and loan markets was analysed together (Chapter 7), with a view to comparing pricing, market structure and spillover effects from one market segment to another in times of financial turbulence. Empirically, differences were established in the way bonds and loans were priced, although theory suggests that there are also similarities. Differences were also detected in pricing mechanisms between developing and industrialized countries. The existence of the 'pecking-order theory' developed by Myers (1984) was verified for industrialized country borrowers, since loans granted to these borrowers were riskier during the 1993–2001 period than bonds issued over the same period. On the other hand, in the case of developing country borrowers, the pecking-order theory was found to be reversed, with bonds being riskier than loans. Regarding spillover effects, it was found that market access conditions faced by developing country borrowers can influence those faced by industrialized country borrowers. For the first time, the effects of the corruption index on loan and bond pricing for developing and industrialized country borrowers were studied. Differences were found in the way that corruption and political risk influence market access conditions for developing country borrowers on the one hand and industrialized country borrowers on the other.

The results offer various avenues that could be explored to help alleviate shortcomings in the availability of foreign funds to developing country borrowers.

First, the local establishment of financial institutions acting as senior loan arrangers with local knowledge about the most informationally opaque borrowers and their countries appears to be important if those borrowers are to access international syndicated credit markets (see Chapter 5). Efforts to improve the local establishment of senior banks must come with safeguards attached, though. Interbank and capital market competition can either leave banks to act like capital market underwriters and originators of transaction loans or make them return to their roots as relationship lending experts. On the other hand, the greater, and more timely, availability of borrower credit records, as well as the greater ease of processing them, makes it easier for banks to originate transaction loans even when they are at a great distance from the borrower. The book provides evidence for this interpretation. Banks appear to perform a unique service especially when lending locally to the most opaque borrowers (i.e. non-rated borrowers in developing countries). A foreign bank presence may increase the stability of available lending, by diversifying the capital and funding bases supporting the supply of domestic credit, especially in small and/or volatile economies. Foreign banks improve the quality, pricing and availability of financial services, besides enhancing infrastructure, transparency and regulation.

Secondly, the book's findings suggest that developing countries' access to bond markets could be enhanced, especially for the elements denominated in euro, which appear to be potentially less liquid than others (Chapters 4 and 8). Nowadays, the majority of emerging country bond issuers are sovereign and enhancing corporate access to emerging country bond markets could be a vital step in the right direction. Multilateral institutions that guarantee specific tranches of syndicated loans against political risk (e.g. suspension of transfers in foreign currency) also have a role to play as catalysts for marketing the non-guaranteed tranches of such loans to commercial banks. A history of successful loan contracting and repayment this initiated could then serve as a catalyst for issuing bonds.

Lastly, the evidence regarding the significance of the corruption index as a determinant of the pricing of foreign funds to developing country borrowers – but not for industrialized country borrowers – underscores the influence of a legal/political environment that is permissive to financial deepening in developing countries, as illustrated in seminal work on financial liberalization. This suggests strong incentives for developing countries to improve their legal and political environments so as to promote access to cheaper international borrowing and therefore greater financial deepening.

The contribution to the literature on the supply side of syndicated lending consists in an investigation for the first time of the relationship between lender characteristics and loan specifications at an international level. Most studies so far have used US data, mainly from regulatory (i.e. national) returns. But non-US banks appear to have arranged 54 per cent of loans for US borrowers in 2001 and funded 51 per cent of them, so the book makes an important contribution to the extant literature by extending the analysis to encompass the global syndication market.

Furthermore, a distinction was made between banks of different seniorities within syndicates when analysing the relationship between lender characteristics and loan specifications. Senior banks were found to have more pricing power in syndicates while junior banks tended to act more as price-takers. Junior banks appeared to rely more on the reputation of the senior banks when participating in syndications where information about the borrower was more opaque. Contrary to the previous literature, senior banks were found to behave in a potentially opportunistic way *vis-à-vis* junior banks by passing on relatively larger shares of riskier loans to junior participants after they had syndicated them. Transfer of risk in the economy to outsiders with possibly limited knowledge of the borrowers – banks or even non-banks such as insurance companies, pension funds, Collateralized debt obligation (CDO) arbitrage funds or non-financial corporations – should be a concern for policy-makers, especially if senior banks tend to pass on larger portions of riskier loans to junior banks. Likewise, caution should be exercised by policy-makers if the pricing of risk is influenced by the characteristics of the originators (the senior banks) at least to the same extent as it compensates for the true riskiness of the borrower. This should especially be the case if, as demonstrated in Chapter 6, poorly performing banks tend, on average, to be more involved in syndications. Policy-makers should perhaps monitor more closely the concentration of credit risk associated with syndicated loans held on the books of underperforming banks.

Notes

1 Introduction

1. See, for instance, Smith and Warner (1979), Smith (1980), Bester (1985), Besanko and Thakor (1987), Berger and Udell (1990), Eichengreen and Mody (2000) and Kleimeier and Megginson (2000).
2. See for instance, Sachs and Cohen (1982), Berlin and Loeys (1988), Berlin and Mester (1992) Eichengreen and Mody (1998), Bolton and Freixas (2000).
3. Removal of the claims from the bank's balance sheet and purchase by a special-purpose vehicle (SPV) which issues securities that are subsequently serviced by the cash flow from the loans, allowing some tranching of the risk in the process.
4. Treasurers of large corporations often use loans and bonds as complementary means of financing.

2 A Global Overview of the Syndicated Loans Market

1. These bank roles, enumerated here in decreasing order of seniority, involve an active role in determining the syndicate composition, negotiating the pricing and administering the facility.
2. In practice, though, these rewards fail to materialise in a systematic manner. Indeed, anecdotal evidence for the US suggests that, for this reason, smaller players have withdrawn from the market lately and have stopped extending syndicated loans as a loss-leader.
3. For this discussion, it has to be recalled that the same bank can act in various capacities in a syndicate. For instance, the arranger bank can also act as an underwriter and/or allocate a small portion of the loan to itself and therefore also be a junior participant.
4. One should note that the fees shown in Figures 2.2 and 2.3 are not directly comparable. In Figure 2.2, for the purposes of comparability with spreads, annual and front-end fees are added together by annualizing the latter over the whole maturity of the facility, assuming full and immediate drawdown. Figure 2.3, on the other hand, shows annual and front-end fees separately without annualizing the latter.
5. For instance, it is very common nowadays for a medium-term loan provided by a syndicate to be refinanced by a bond at, or before, the loan's stated maturity. Similarly, US commercial paper programmes are frequently backed by a syndicated letter of credit.
6. This provides an opportunity for risk-sharing between public and private sector investors. It usually takes the form of syndicated loans granted by multilateral agencies with tranches reserved for private sector bank lenders.

7. Transferability is determined by consent of the borrower, as stated in the original loan agreement. Some borrowers do not allow loans to be traded on the secondary market as they want to preserve their banking relationships.
8. The seller banks often enhance their fee income by arranging new loans to roll over the facilities they had previously granted to borrowers. They may sell old facilities on the secondary market to manage capacity on their balance sheet, which is required to hold some of the new loans.
9. For example, minimum participation amounts on the primary market may exceed the bank's credit limits.
10. Banks tend to trade blocks of loans when they restructure whole portfolios. In normal times, loan-by-loan trading is more common.
11. Nonetheless, Japanese banks have recently been very active in transferring loans on the Japanese secondary market. According to a quarterly survey conducted by the Bank of Japan, for the financial year April 2003–March 2004, such transfers totalled ¥11 trn, 38 per cent of which were non-performing loans. This was followed in the second quarter of 2004 by unusually weak secondary market activity by historical standards.
12. According to practitioners, major international banks with an Asian presence are among the main sellers of loans, while demand comes from Taiwanese and Chinese banks.

4 Borrowers-Country Economic Structure and the Pricing of Syndicated Loans

1. Guarantees, collateral, covenants can be thought of as risk mitigants.
2. In the case of loan facilities already funded by the lenders but not yet signed, the funding date was taken as a reference.
3. This sample size is considerably larger than in several other studies analysing the determinants of developing country credit spreads; Edwards (1986) and Kamin and von Kleist (1999) use 113 and 358 loan spread observations, respectively.
4. This includes both private and public debt.
5. Nevertheless, Balassa (1986) also demonstrates that while outward-oriented countries accepted a temporary decline in economic growth in the immediate aftermath of external economic shocks in order to limit reliance on foreign borrowing, their economic growth accelerated subsequently, owing to the output-increasing policies applied.
6. Although this may not be an indispensable condition if credit derivatives are used.
7. A club deal is reserved for a limited number of insider banks instead of being widely sold down on the market; in a bilateral deal, there is only one participant bank.
8. The comprehensive sample is approximately equal to the population.
9. Linneman (1980) estimates property values and rental payments for the urban housing market that are hedonic functions of neighbourhood (non-structural) and structural traits associated with each site. The partial derivative of these hedonic functions with respect to any trait describes the marginal change in the total site valuation associated with a change in that

trait when all other trait levels are held constant. These partial derivatives reveal the same marginal information as do prices in standard market analyses; for this reason, partial derivatives are often referred to as the 'shadow prices' of the underlying locational traits.

10. Surely the effects of this variable are not limited to the year of signature of the loan. The results reported in this chapter use an IMF-assistance dummy equal to 1 if Fund assistance was received during the year of signature of the loan. An alternative model specification (not shown) with a dummy for Fund assistance *preceding* the year of signature of the loan gives very similar results.
11. See n. 12.
12. The estimation results on this variable as well as on the ratio of reserves to GDP could be influenced by endogeneity issues; caution should therefore be exercised in their interpretation.
13. This interpretation is also known as 'survival bias'.
14. In fact, the dummy for large syndicate sizes is significant and positive when macroeconomic conditions are also controlled for – see the right-hand column of Table 4.9.
15. See Appendix 4.2 for the full list of sectors included.
16. In addition, a fourth model specification was run using a partial forward-stepwise estimation technique. An *F*-test was first performed, which found the four sovereign ratings dummies corresponding to the whole S&P ratings spectrum described in Appendix 4.1 – less the 'default, not rated or not disclosed' rating class – to be jointly significant determinants of the drawn return at the 1 per cent level. These sovereign ratings dummies were subsequently forced into the model together with microeconomic variables. Meanwhile, progressing from the specific to the general, the macroeconomic variables were chosen by means of forward-stepwise selection, using an entry criterion of 10 per cent significance and a removal criterion of 11 per cent. The results (available from the authors upon request) are very similar to the combined macro–micro model presented in Table 4.9 without sovereign ratings that uses OLS. Macroeconomic variables (with the exception of the inflation rate and the ratio of imports to exports), as well as sovereign ratings, are significant with the correct sign (favourable sovereign ratings dummies are negative and significant and vice versa). This confirms that there is information contained in macroeconomic variables that is not captured in sovereign ratings.

5 Lender Behaviour and the Structure and Pricing of Syndicated Loans

1. See n. 3 in chapter 7 for a definition of leveraged lending.
2. Insurance companies, pension funds and CDO arbitrage funds have become buyers of syndicated loans, especially on the leveraged and highly leveraged segments.
3. For example, loan size and maturity; borrower rating; bank size and business mix.
4. This is so despite the existence of information sources (such as credit reports and real estate appraisals) which national and local lenders can access with equal ease. But local institutions may have – among other information – credit repayment histories of the mortgagor, information on local default

rates, as well as specific legal knowledge allowing for lower servicing and origination costs.

5. See the paper by Degryse and Ongena (2002) for a comprehensive review of the distance literature.
6. Most previous studies have relied on regulatory and hence national databases.
7. Consider a syndicated credit facility granted by a syndicate consisting of Société Générale and Crédit Lyonnais. Two observations are entered for that facility into the regression. One will comprise Société Générale's balance sheet and profit and loss statement indicators, the other one will feature the same characteristics for Crédit Lyonnais. Both observations will carry the same loan transaction characteristics.
8. Tier 2 capital is not examined separately. This also follows the approach used in seminal work on the bank lending channel by Kishan and Opiela (2000).
9. A zero share was entered in case the senior bank had sold down all the loan to junior participants.
10. Collateral has a cost (Bester, 1985) so it may also be the case that the cost of arranging or warehousing the collateral is charged for in the price of the loan (Freixas and Rochet, 1997). Otherwise, financing constraints facing the borrower may be such that he accepts both collateral and a higher spread. Smith and Warner (1979) argue that collateralization is costly and that the benefits to securing the loan must exceed the cost for a particular loan to be secured. In a cross-section of loans, this means that riskier loans will be collateralized. Examination of the data sample also confirms that borrowers with poorer ratings are more likely to require collateralization. Berger and Udell (1990) also show that collateral is typically associated with riskier loans. If collateral's is main purpose to solve moral hazard problems, then riskier borrowers or those who need more monitoring will post more collateral.
11. This negative relationship between the logarithm of total assets and loan pricing may reflect scale economies for junior banks.
12. Such as US dollar, euro, Japanese yen, Swiss franc and sterling.
13. *bremu98* and *bremu99* can also be interpreted as controlling for changes in institutional structure or regulatory environment.

6 Banks' and Financial Institutions' Decision to Participate in Loan Syndications

1. The chapter restricts the analysis to institutions from industrialized countries for the sake of homogeneity and also because participation in loan syndications by banks from emerging countries represents a very small share of the total sample.
2. The original number of banks that participated in loan syndications is 1,368. However in Bankscope only 1,258 of these banks have available balance sheet and profit and loss statement information. Figure 6.2 includes all 1,368 banks' participations.
3. A correlation matrix showing the association of the bank characteristics with the syndication participation dummy is presented in Appendix 6.2.

7 Comparison of Syndicated Loan Markets with Bond Markets

1. Indeed, in order to bid for the third-generation mobile phone licenses in 2000 auctioned off by various European countries' governments, many European telecommunications firms tapped the syndicated credits market for large amounts in the first instance, subsequently aiming to refinance the initial short-term debt by later issuing medium- or long-term securities.
2. This can, for instance, be a guarantee written by an insurance company.
3. Angbazo, Mei and Saunders (1998) define as highly leveraged transaction (HLT) loans all loan financings:

   - which are used for buyouts, acquisitions and recapitalizations
   - which (1) double the borrower's liabilities and result in a leverage ratio (total liabilities/total assets) higher than 50 per cent or (2) increase the leverage ratio higher than 75 per cent
   - which are designated as HLT by the syndication agent
   - which are granted to subsidiaries of HLT companies, even when the subsidiary does not meet the HLT definitions above.

   Dealogic Loanware applies the term 'leveraged' to lending to non-investment grade companies where the ratio of debt to net worth is often high. Typically in the US and Canadian markets, HLT corresponds to a LIBOR pricing of 250bp or above. For European borrowers, the notion of leveraged loans applies to a LIBOR pricing of 150bp or above.
4. Indonesia, Malaysia, South Korea, Thailand.
5. For example, Media and Publishing, Hotels and Leisure, Retailing.
6. The data sources for the macroeconomic variables were the BIS–IMF–OECD–World Bank Joint Statistics on external debt, the IMF's *International Financial Statistics* and *World Economic Outlook* databases, the International Institute of Finance's developing country database, the OECD's *World Economic Outlook* and national statistical offices. The macroeconomic and microeconomic variables contained in the loans and bonds databases were linked on the country and the date, considering both the year the loan was signed or the bond was issued, and the previous year. Distinction is thus made between long-term and short-term effects. In fact investors and banks are expected to have incorporated some kind of macroeconomic forecasting into their pricing models. For instance, for a loan granted to an Argentine borrower in 1995, the real GDP growth variables represent Argentina's real economic growth for 1995 (noted as growth) and for 1994 (noted as growth_{-1}).
7. Transparency International (TI) assigns a score of 0–10 to most countries of the world, standardizing a number of corruption surveys conducted by public and private institutions and consisting of questions about issues such as bribing of public officials, kickbacks in public procurement, or embezzlement of public funds. For a description of the methodology, and the full dataset, please refer to www.transparency.org.
8. Examination of the data sample confirms that borrowers with poorer ratings are more likely to require collateralization.

9. For the purposes of comparability with bond pricing, only the LIBOR spread is considered in the case of loans, not fees. When including fees, Eichengreen and Mody (2000) do find a significant relationship.
10. Berger and Udell (1990) also show that collateral is typically associated with riskier loans.
11. According to the Dealogic database, developing country bond issuance in euro represented less than half of developing country bond issuance in US dollars during the 1993–2001 period.
12. Korea, Malaysia, Thailand.

8 Syndicated Loans and the Financing of Distressed Emerging Markets

1. The macroeconomic data of the borrower countries prevailing when the loans were granted were extracted from the IMF's *International Financial Statistics* and *World Economic Outlook* databases, as well as from the BIS–IMF–OECD–World Bank Joint Statistics on external debt.
2. Either by boosting their GDP or by reducing their debt.
3. For the purposes of the present analysis, the drawn return was used rather than the LIBOR or EURIBOR spread used by several authors (Cantor and Packer 1996, Kamin and von Kleist 1999, Kleimeier and Megginson 2000), since it represents the full economic cost of borrowing. It is the annual return that will accrue to a senior fund provider if the facility is drawn for the entire period of its existence. It includes the spread as above, but it also counts the fees payable for utilization, participation, provision of facility and underwriting (Altunbaş and Gadanecz 2003).
4. The 250+ base-level business sectors available are grouped into 10 main categories. The detailed list is given in Appendix 4.2.
5. Such as the Turkish (IMF, 2001), Indonesian and Thai (IMF, 1999) cases. It may also be the case that domestic banks raise loans in the international syndicated loan markets for domestic enterprises which are too small to access international capital markets on their own.
6. This sector consists of firms mostly with the main business related to health, legal and leisure services. A more detailed subdivision is given in Appendix 4.2.
7. See Appendix 4.3 for a description of how the base-level loan purposes were grouped into broad categories.
8. The data are not differentiated between state and private sector borrowing.
9. Under the provision that it is the funds borrowed abroad that are used for these investments.
10. Kleimeier and Megginson (2000) analyse syndicated loans between 1980 and 1999 and find evidence that loan size is negatively related to pricing, while loan maturity is significantly and positively related to the price. See Chapter 4 for a more in-depth discussion of these two variables. With regards to the external debt/export ratio effect on bond spreads Cantor and Packer (1996) finds a positive relationship between the two by analysing 35 Eurodollar bonds of debtor countries. Neither of these studies makes a distinction between developed and developing nations.

11. The authors explain that unsustainable growth rates fuelled by the expansion of domestic credit were viewed by the market with a concern.
12. Altunbaş and Gadanecz (2003) also find a positive relationship between loan pricing and CPI.

9 Facts and Figures, 1993–2004

1. A list of industrialized countries used in this analysis is given in Appendix 9.1. The IMF classifications of 2004 are taken as a benchmark.
2. The data on all figures showing average maturity and spreads in this chapter has been weighted by facility amounts.
3. A detailed list is provided in Appendix 4.2.
4. Defined in Appendix 4.3 as including refinancing, debtor-in-possession financing, recapitalization, receivable backed financing, debt repayment, securitization and standby/CP support.
5. Loans issued for transport and property purposes are not necessarily borrowed by the construction, property and transport sectors.
6. A list of all countries in each category is given in Appendix 9.2.
7. See Appendix 9.2 for a list of countries in each income bracket (IMF classification, 2004).

References

Allen, T. (1990) Developments in the international syndicated loan market in the 1980s, *Bank of England Quarterly Bulletin*, February.

Altman, E.I. and H.J. Suggitt (2000) Default rates in the syndicated bank loan market: a mortality analysis, *Journal of Banking and Finance*, 24, 229–53.

Altunbaş, Y., S. P. Chakravarty and A. Kara (2004) Do credit markets have faith in the IMF imprimatur? University of Wales, Bangor, mimeo.

Altunbaş, Y. and B. Gadanecz (2003) Developing country economic structure and the pricing of syndicated credits, *Journal of Development Studies*, 40, 143–73, for more information, visit http://www.tandf.co.uk.

Altunbaş, Y., B. Gadanecz and A. Kara (2005) Key factors affecting internationally active banks' decisions to participate in loan syndications, *Applied Economics Letters*, 12, 249–53.

Angbazo, L.A., J. Mei and A. Saunders (1998) Credit spreads in the market for highly leveraged transaction loans, *Journal of Banking and Finance*, 22(10–11), 1249–82.

Armstrong, J. (2003) The syndicated loan market: developments in the North American context, Bank of Canada Working Paper, 2003–15.

Balassa, B. (1986) Policy responses to exogenous shocks in developing countries, *American Economic Review*, 76(2), Papers and Proceedings of the Ninety-Eighth Annual Meeting of the American Economic Association, May.

Baltagi, B.H., J.M. Griffin and W. Xiong (2000) To pool or not to pool: homogeneous versus heterogeneous estimators applied to cigarette demand, *Review of Economics and Statistics*, 82(1), 117–26.

Banerjee S. and O. Cadot (1996) Syndicated lending under asymmetric creditor information, *Journal of Development Economics*, 49(2), 289–306.

Bank for International Settlements (BIS) (2004) 74th Annual Report, Chapter VII: The Financial Sector.

Bank for International Settlement (BIS) (various years) *Quarterly Review.*

Barnish, K., Miller, S. and Rushmore, M. (1997) The new leveraged syndication loan market, *Journal of Applied Corporate Finance*, 10(1), 79–88.

Barro, R.J. (1997) Determinants of economic growth: a cross-country empirical study, Development Discussion Paper, 579, Harvard Institute for International Development, April.

Barro, R.J. (1999) Inequality and growth in a panel of countries, Harvard University.

Barro, R.J. and X. Sala-í-Martin (1992) Convergence, *Journal of Political Economy*, 100(2), 223–51.

Berger, A. (1995) The relationship between capital and earnings in banking, *Journal of Money, Credit and Banking*, 27, 432–56.

Berger, A. and D.B. Humphrey (1997) Efficiency of financial institutions: international survey and directions for future research, *European Journal of Operational Research*, 98, 175–212.

Berger, A. and G. Udell (1990) 'Collateral, loan quality and bank risk', *Journal of Monetary Economics*, 25(1), 21–42.

Berlin, M. and J. Loeys (1988) Bond covenants and delegated monitoring, *Journal of Finance* 43, 397–412.

Berlin, M. and L. Mester (1992) Debt covenants and renegotiation, *Journal of Financial Intermediation*, 2, 19–133.

Besanko, D. and A. Thakor (1987) Collateral and rationing: sorting equilibrium in monopolistic and competitive credit markets, *International Economic Review*, 28(3), 671–89.

Bester, H. (1985) Screening vs. rationing in credit markets with imperfect information, *American Economic Review*, 75, 850–5.

Bilson, C.M., J. Brailsford and V.C. Hooper (2002) The explanatory power of political risk in emerging markets, *International Review of Financial Analysis*, 11, 1–27.

Bird, G. and D. Rowlands (1997) The catalytic effect of lending by the international financial institution, *World Economy*, 20(7), 967–91.

Boehmer, E. and W.L. Megginson (1990) Determinants of secondary market prices for developing country syndicated loans, *Journal of Finance*, 45(5), 1517–40.

Bolton, P. and X. Freixas (2000) Equity, bonds and bank debt: capital structure and financial market equilibrium under asymmetric information, *Journal of Political Economy*, 108(2), 324–51.

Boot, A.W.A and A.V. Thakor (2000) Can relationship banking survive competition? *Journal of Finance*, 51(2), 679–713.

Borio, C.E.V. (1990) Leverage and financing of nonfinancial companies: an international perspective, *BIS Economic Papers*, 27.

Borio, C.E.V. (2003) Towards a macroprudential framework for financial supervision and regulation, BIS Working Paper, 128.

Burnham, J.B. (1984) World debt and monetary order: learning from the past, *Cato Journal*, 4(1), 71–80.

Cantor, R. and F. Packer (1996) Determinants and impact of sovereign credit ratings, *Federal Reserve Bank of New York Economic Policy Review*, September, 37–54.

Carey, M., S. Prowse, J. Rea and G. Udell (1993) The economics of private placements: a new look, *Financial Markets Institutions Instruments*, 2, 1–67.

Chand, S.K. (2003) Stabilizing poverty: or how to humanize the IMF's monetary model, European Public Choice Meeting, Aarhus, 25–28 April.

Chen, A.H., S.C. Mazumdar and Y. Yan (2000) Monitoring and bank loan pricing, *Pacific-Basin Finance Journal*, 8, 1–24.

Chowdhry, B. and A. Goyal (2000) Understanding the financial crisis in Asia, *Pacific-Basin Finance Journal*, 8, 135–52.

Cline, W.R. and K.J.S. Barnes (1997) Spreads and risk in emerging markets lending, Institute of International Finance, IIF Research Papers, 97–1.

Coffey, M. (2000) The US leveraged loan market: from relationship to return, in T. Rhodes (ed.), *Syndicated Lending, Practice and Documentation*, London, London: Euromoney Books.

Degryse, H. and S. Ongena (2002) Distance, lending relationships and competition, Centre for Studies in Economics and Finance Working Paper, 80, Dipartimento di Scienze Economiche – Università degli Studi di Salerno.

Dell'Arriccia, G., I. Schnabel and J. Zettelmeyer (2002) Moral hazard and international crises lending, Paper presented at 1st annual IMF research conference.

Dennis, S. and D. Mullineaux (2000) Syndicated loans, *Journal of Financial Intermediation*, 9, 404–26.

Diamond, D. (1984) Financial intermediation and delegated monitoring, *Review of Economic Studies*, 51, 393–414.

Diamond, D. (1991) Monitoring and reputation: the choice between bank loans and directly placed debt, *Journal of Political Economy*, 99(4), 689–721.

Dooley, P.M. (1994) A retrospective on the debt crisis, NBER Working Paper, 4963.

Dreher, A. (2004) Does the IMF cause moral hazard? A critical view of the evidence, unpublished discussion paper, http://www.axel-dreher.de/.

Easterly, W. (2003) IMF and World Bank structural adjustment programs and poverty, in M. Dooley and J.A. Frankel (eds), *Managing Currency Crises in Emerging Markets*, Chicago: University of Chicago Press, 361–82.

Eaton, J. and M. Gersovitz (1981) Debt with potential repudiation: theoretical and empirical analysis, *Review of Economic Studies*, 48, 208–309.

Edwards, M. (2000) Re-evaluating the catalytic effect of IMF programs, Rutgers University, mimeo.

Edwards, S. (1983) LDC foreign borrowing and default risk: an empirical investigation, NBER Working Paper 1172.

Edwards, S. (1986) The pricing of bonds and bank loans in international markets, *European Economic Review*, 30, 565–89.

Edwards, S. (1998) Abolish the IMF, *Financial Times*, 13 November.

Eichengreen, B. and A. Mody (1997) What explains changing spreads on emerging-market debt: fundamentals or market sentiment?, International Monetary Fund, mimeo.

Eichengreen, B. and A. Mody (1998) Interest rates in the north and capital flows to the south: is there a missing link?, *Journal of International Finance*, 1 (1).

Eichengreen, B. and A. Mody (2000) Lending booms, reserves and the sustainability of short-term debt: inferences from the pricing of syndicated bank loans, *Journal of Development Economics*, 63(1), 5–44.

Ergin, E. (1999) Determinants and consequences of International Monetary Fund Programs, PhD Dissertation, Stanford University.

Evrensel, A. (2002) Effectiveness of IMF-supported stabilization programs in developing countries, *Journal of International Money and Finance*, 21, 565–87.

Ewert, K.S. (1988) The international debt crises, in *The Freeman*, a Foundation for Economic Education, Inc., 38(9).

Feder, G. and R.E. Just (1977) An analysis of credit terms in the Eurodollar market, *European Economic Review*, 9, 221–43.

Federal Deposit Insurance Corporation (FDIC) 1998: *History of the Eighties – Lessons for the future. I: An Examination of the Banking Crises of the 1980s and Early 1990s*, www.fdic.gov.

Flannery, M. (1989) Capital regulation and insured banks' choice of individual loan default risks, *Journal of Monetary Economics*, 24, 235–58.

Folkerts-Landau, D.F.I. (1985) The changing role of international bank lending in development finance, IMF Staff Papers, June.

Fons, J.S (1994) Using default rates to model the term structure of credit risk, *Financial Analysts Journal*, 50, 25–32.

Forbes, K.J. and R. Rigobon (2002) No contagion, only interdependence: measuring stock market comovements, *Journal of Finance*, 57(5), 2223–61.

Freixas, X. and J.C. Rochet (1997) *The Microeconomics of Banking*, Cambridge, MA: MIT Press.

Frenkel, J. (1983) International liquidity and monetary control, in G. von Furstenberg (ed), *International Money and Credit: The Policy Roles,* Washington, DC: IMF.

Gadanecz, B. (2004) The syndicated loan market: structure, development and implications, *BIS Quarterly Review*, December, 75–89, available at http://www.bis.org/publ/qtrpdf/r_qt0412g.pdf.

Gaughan, R.A. (2000) Mergers and acquisitions in the 1990s: a record breaking decade, *Journal of Corporate Accounting and Finance*, 11(2), 3–5

Gersovitz, M. (1985) Banks' international lending decisions: what we know and implications for future research, in G.W. Smith and J.T. Cuddington (eds) *International Debt and the Developing Countries*, Washington, DC: World Bank.

Goldberg, L.S. (2001) When is US bank lending to emerging markets volatile?, NBER Working Papers, 8209.

Goldberg, L.S., B.G. Dages and D. Kinney (2000) 'Foreign and domestic bank participation in emerging markets: lessons from Mexico and Argentina', NBER Working Papers, 7714.

Goldberg, L.S. and R. Grosse (1996) The boom and bust of Latin American lending, 1970–1992, *Journal of Economics and Business*, 48: 285–98.

Goldsbrough, D., K. Barnes, Y. Meteos, I. Lago, and T. Tsikata (2002) Prolonged use of IMF loans, *Finance and Development*, 39(4), 34–7.

Gooptu, S. and R. Brun (1992) The role and cost of short-term trade credit, in *Beyond Syndicated Credits*, World Bank Technical Papers Series, 163, 1–42.

Gould, E.E. (2003) Money talks: supplementary financiers and International Monetary Fund conditionality, *International Organization*, 57, 551–86.

Grauda, G. (2000) The distributional effects of IMF programs: a cross-country analysis, *World Development*, 28(6), 1031–51.

Grinols, E. and J. Bhagwati (1976) Foreign capital, savings and dependence, *Review of Economics and Statistics*, 58(4), 416–25.

Hale, G. (2005) Bonds or loans? The effect macroeconomic fundamentals, Yale ITC Wording paper no. 03–02, Cowles Foundation Discussion Paper Vol. 1403.

Hanson, J.A. (1974) Optimal international borrowing and lending, *American Economic Review*, 64, 616–30.

Harberger, A.C. (1980) Vignettes on the world capital market, *American Economic Review, Papers and Proceedings*, 70, 331–7.

Hernandez, L. and H. Rudolph (1995) Sustainability of private capital flows to developing countries – is a generalised reversal likely?, World Bank Policy Research Working Paper, 1518.

Holmstrom, B. and S.N. Kaplan (2001) Corporate governance and merger activity in the US: making sense of the 1980's and 1990's, MIT Department of Economics, Working Paper, 01–11.

Howcroft, B. and C. Solomon (1985) Syndicated lending by banks, in J. Revell (ed.), *Bangor Occasional Papers in Economics*, 22, Bangor: University of Wales Press.

IMF (1998) Policy responses to the current crisis, *World Economic Outlook*, Chapter I, October.

IMF (1999) IMF-supported programs in Indonesia, Korea and Thailand, Occasional Paper, 178.

IMF (2000) *International Capital Markets Report,* Chapter 5, *Developments and Trends in Mature Capital Markets.*

IMF (2001) *Capital Markets Report,* Chapter 3, *Emerging Market Financing,* 22 August.

IMF (2002) *Independent Evaluation Office Report, Evaluation of Prolonged Use of IMF Resources,* 25 September.

James, C. (1987) Some evidence on the uniqueness of bank loans, *Journal of Financial Economics,* 19, 217–35.

Jones, J., W. Lang and P. Nigro (2000) Recent trends in bank loan syndications: evidence for 1995 to 1999, Economic and Policy Analysis Working Paper, 2000–10, Comptroller of the Currency Administrator of National Banks.

Jordan, J.L. (1984) Restoring credibility to international lending, *Cato Journal,* 4(1), 131–46.

Joyce, J.P. (2002) Through a glass darkly: new questions (and answers) about IMF programs, Wellesley College Working Paper, 2002–04.

Kamin, S.B. (2002) Identifying the role of moral hazard in international financial markets, International Finance Discussion Papers, 736, Board of Governors of the Federal Reserve System.

Kamin, S.B. and K. von Kleist (1999) The evolution and determinants of emerging market credit spreads in the 1990's, BIS Working Papers, 68.

Kaminsky, L.G. and C.M. Reinhart (1999). The twin crises: the causes of banking and balance-of-payments problems, *American Economic Review,* 89(3), 473–500.

Kishan, R.P. and T.P. Opiela (2000) Bank size, bank capital, and the bank lending channel, *Journal of Money, Credit and Banking* 32(1), 121–141.

Kleimeier, S. and W. Megginson (2000) Are project finance loans different from other syndicated credits?, *Journal of Applied Corporate Finance,* 13(1), 75–87.

Kohler, H. (2003) Towards a better globalization, Inaugural Lecture on the Occasion of the Honorary Professorship Award at the Eberhard Karls University in Tübingen, 16 October.

Kruger, A. (2001) Address to the National Economists' Club, American Enterprise Institute, Washington, DC, November.

Linneman, P. (1980) Some empirical results on the nature of the hedonic price function for the urban housing market, *Journal of Urban Economics,* 8(1), 47–68.

Lipworth, G. and J. Nystedt (2001) Crisis resolution and private sector adaptation, *Finance & Development,* 38(2).

Madan, R., R. Sobhani and K. Horowitz (1999) The biggest secret of Wall Street, Paine Webber Equity Research.

Marchesi, M. and P.J. Thomas (2000) IMF conditionality as a screening device, *Economic Journal,* 109(454), 111–25.

Martinez Peria, M.S. and S.L. Schmukler (2001) Do depositors punish banks for bad behaviour? Market discipline, deposit insurance and banking crises, *Journal of Finance,* 56(3), 1029–51.

Mauro, P., N. Sussman and Y. Yafeh (2002) Emerging market spreads: then versus now, *Quarterly Journal of Economics,* 117(2), 695–733.

McKinnon, R.I. (1984) The international capital market and economic liberalisation in LDCs, *The Developing Economies,* 22, 476–81.

Melnik, A.L. and S.E. Plaut (1991) The short-term Eurocredit market, Monograph Series in Finance and Economics, Monograph 1991–1, Stern School of Business, New York University.

Mitchell, M.L. and J.H. Mulherin (1996) The impact of industry shocks on takeover and restructuring activity, *Journal of Financial Economics*, 41, 193–229.

Myers, S.C. (1984) The capital structure puzzle, *Journal of Finance*, 39, 575–92.

Myers, S.C. and N. Majluf (1984) Corporate financing and investment decisions when firms have information investors do not have, *Journal of Financial Economics*, 13, 187–221.

O'Driscoll, G.P., Jr. and E.D. Short (1984) Safety-net mechanisms: the case of international lending, *Cato Journal*, 4(1), 185–204.

Oram, J. (2003) Standing up to the competition? The future of european mergers, New Economics Foundation, Corporate Breakdown, 5.

Ozler, S. (1993) Have commercial banks ignored history?, *American Economic Review*, 83(3), 608–20.

Pavel, C. and D. Phillis (1987) Why banks sell loans: an empirical analysis, *Economic Perspectives*, Federal Reserve Bank of Chicago, 3–14.

Pennacchi, G. (1988) Loan sales and the cost of bank capital, *Journal of Finance*, 43, 375–96.

Pennacchi, G. (2003) Who needs a bank, anyway?, *Wall Street Journal*, 17 December.

Petersen, M.A. and R.G. Rajan (2000) Does distance still matter? The information revolution in small business lending, Kellogg Graduate School of Management Northwestern University and Graduate School of Business University of Chicago, unpublished manuscript.

Prezeworski, A. and R.J. Vreeland (2000) The effect of IMF programs on economic growth, *Journal of Development Economics*, 62, 385–421.

Rajan, R. and A. Winton (1995) Covenants and collateral as incentives to monitor, *Journal of Finance*, 50, 1113–46.

Rhodes, T. (1996). *Syndicated Lending, Practice and Documentation*, 2nd edn, London: Euromoney Books.

Rhodes, T. (2000) *Syndicated Lending, Practice and Documentation*, 3rd edn, London: Euromoney Books.

Rhodes, W.R. (1989) A negotiator's view, in C. Bogdonowicz-Bindert (ed.), *Solving the Global Debt Crisis: Strategies and Controversies by Key Stakeholders*, New York: Harper & Row, 19–28.

Roberts, R. (2001) *Take your Partners*, London: Palgrave Macmillan.

Robinson, M. (1996) Syndicated lending: a stabilizing element in the Latin markets, *Corporate Finance Guide to Latin American Treasury & Finance*.

Rodrik, D. (1998) Who needs capital-account convertibility? *Essays in International Finance*, 207, International Finance Section, Department of Economics, Princeton University, 55–6.

Rowlands, D. (2001) The response of other lenders to the IMF, *Review of International Economics*, 9(3), 531–46.

Sachs, J.D. (1984) Theoretical issues in international borrowing, *Princeton Studies in International Finance*, 54, July.

Sachs, J.D. and D. Cohen (1982) LDC borrowing with default risk, National Bureau of Economic Research Working Paper 925.

Simons, K. (1993) Why do banks syndicate loans?, *New England Economic Review*, Federal Reserve Bank Boston, 45–52, Jan/Feb.

Sirmans, C.F. and J.D. Benjamin (1990) Pricing fixed rate mortgages: some empirical evidence, *Journal of Financial Services Research*, 4, 191–202.

Smith, C.W. (1980) On the theory of financial contracting: the personal loan market, *Journal of Monetary Economics*, 6, 333–57.

Smith, C.W. and J. Warner (1979) On financial contracting: an analysis of bond covenants, *Journal of Financial Economics*, 7, 111–61.

Sommerville, C.T. (2001) A booming market is where the heart is: local vs national lenders and real estate development financing, University of British Columbia, unpublished manuscript.

Stiglitz, J.E. (2000) Capital market liberalization, economic growth and instability, *World Development*, 28(6), 1075–86.

Stiglitz, J.E. (2002a) *Globalization and its discontents*, New York. W.W. Norton.

Stiglitz, J.E. (2002b) Development policies in a world of globalization, Paper presented at the seminar, New International Trends for Economic Development, Brazilian Economic and Social Development Bank, Rio Janeiro, 12–13 September.

Stiglitz, J.E. (2003) Globalization and growth in emerging markets and the New Economy, *Journal of Policy Modelling*, 25, 505–24.

Thakor, A. (1996) Capital requirements, monetary policy and aggregate bank lending: theory and empirical evidence, *Journal of Finance*, 51(1), 279–324.

Tillmann, P. (2001) Switching risk-perception on bond markets: does IMF lending induce moral hazard?, University of Cologne, mimeo.

Tucker, A., J. Madura and T. Chiang (1991) *International Financial Markets*, St Paul, Minnesota: West Publishing Company.

Van Rijckeghem, C. and B. Weder (2001) Sources of contagion: is it finance or trade?, *Journal of International Economics*, 54(2), 293–308.

Vine, A. (2001) High-yield analysis of emerging markets debt, in F. Fabozzi (ed.), *The Handbook of Fixed Income Securities*, 6th edn, New York: McGraw-Hill.

Vreeland, R.J. (2002) The effect of IMF programs on labor, *World Development*, 30(1), 121–39.

Weintraup, R.E. (1984) International debt: crises and challenge, *Cato Journal*, 4(1), 21–61.

Zhang, X.A. (1999) Testing for 'Moral Hazard' in emerging markets lending, Institute of International Finance Research, Paper 99–1.

Index

Notes: f = figure; n = note; t = table; **bold** = extended discussion or heading emphasized in main text.